Between Field and Cooking Pot

Texas Press Sourcebooks in Anthropology, No. 15

BETWEEN FIELD AND COOKING POT

The Political Economy of Marketwomen in Peru

By Florence E. Babb

University of Texas Press, Austin

First Edition, 1989

Requests for permission to reproduce material from this work
should be sent to Permissions, University of Texas Press, Box 7819,
Austin, Texas 78713-7819.

LIBRARY OF CONGRESS CATALOGING-IN-PUBLICATION DATA

Babb, Florence E.
  Between field and cooking pot : the political economy of
marketwomen in Peru / Florence E. Babb. — 1st ed.
    p.   cm. — (Texas Press sourcebooks in anthropology ; no. 15)
  Bibliography: p.
  Includes index.
    ISBN 0-292-70775-4 (alk. paper). — ISBN 0-292-70776-2 (pbk. :
alk. paper)
    1. Women merchants—Peru.   2. Peddlers and peddling—
Peru.   3. Women—Employment—Peru.   4. Informal sector
(Economics)—Peru.   I. Title.   II. Title: Marketwomen in
Peru.   III. Series.
HD6072.6.P4B23   1989
331.4'8138118'0985—DC19   89-4800
                                                           CIP

*To the memory of my mother,
Marjorie Knapp Babb*

Contents

Preface

ON OCTOBER *19, 1987, the workers and sellers
of Mercado Central in Huaraz were dislodged from their market
with promises from their union and the mayor that within eight
months they would have a new model market. The sellers were
relocated in various places . . . Mamá is next to the San Antonio
convent, rather far away, where there is little business. Her compañeras, on the other hand, are closer in, perhaps for having offered
bribes to those in charge. On the 20th, that is, the next day [after
the dislocation], the market was demolished, left as though there
had been another earthquake. All this was very sad and it wasn't
easy to overcome; the marketwomen shed many tears and there
were many days of sorrow. They organized a procession and brought
out the Virgin [of Fatima], patron of the market. The mayor was
not seen again and when the sellers went to his office he refused
to come out, acting almost cowardly, pretending ignorance. Now
neither the union nor the mayor is doing anything to begin [con-
struction of] a new market.*

FROM A LETTER WRITTEN BY MY SIXTEEN-YEAR-OLD *AHIJADA*
(GODDAUGHTER), JUNE 15, 1988, HUARAZ, PERU
(MY TRANSLATION FROM THE SPANISH)

Thus I learned how the market in Huaraz, which had nearly mirac-
ulously withstood the impact of a major earthquake in 1970 and that
had been at the center of my research in Peru from 1977 to 1987, was
recently torn down and the marketers directed to sell in distant
streets. I had interviewed the mayor and a number of local planners,
as well as many marketers, just two months before, but no one had
hinted that such an action would be taken. Indeed, great concern
was expressed about the large number of "informal" street vendors,
but the marketwomen selling at "permanent" stalls in Mercado

Central were expected to remain in their market until a new one was built.

Such dramatic measures are being taken in Peru, most notably in Lima but in smaller cities, too, in the name of urban renewal and of controlling petty commerce. In the process, the lives and work of many marketers and street vendors are irrevocably changed. When I return to visit my friends in Huaraz, I will expect to find many in economic decline and experiencing more difficult working conditions. Moreover, the community of women who sold together for as long as thirty years will be gone, and with it the basis for support and solidarity that these marketers had established.

In the chapters that follow, Mercado Central is described as it was during the years of my research in Huaraz, Peru. I also examine some of the developments that led to the forced removal of urban marketers to peripheral areas and the consequences for these marketers.

Acknowledgments

FOR OVER TEN years I have lived with this book. Since my original fieldwork in 1977, my summers have included either visits to Peru or analysis and writing based on my research there. Over the last decade I have also undergone the transformation from graduate student to new faculty member to tenured professor. Along the way I have incurred debts to many people in the United States and Peru who have assisted me.

As a doctoral student in anthropology at the State University of New York at Buffalo, I had the exceptional support of my advisor, William W. Stein, who made it possible for me to conduct my first period of research in Peru under a grant from the SUNY Research Foundation. Also at Buffalo, Elizabeth Kennedy lent her encouragement and her feminist insights to my study. Both of these individuals served as my mentors in the fullest sense of the word.

At Colgate University and the University of Iowa, my colleagues in anthropology and women's studies have offered invaluable support. Most of all, I am grateful to Margery Wolf, who has been the major force behind me these last two years, urging me on to finish my writing. She has been a fine critic and an inspiration through her own work. My students have also been a source of encouragement and several research assistants have provided much-needed services. Christine Deaval, Sharon Wood, Kendall Thu, Kathleen Jackson, and Catherine Lundoff all helped at various stages of my work. María Elena Mujica has had a special relationship to later phases of my research, accompanying me on my most recent trip to Peru and contributing data she collected for my study. At the University of Iowa I have received institutional support through Old Gold Summer Scholarships, a grant from the Center for International and Comparative Studies, and scholarly facilities at University House.

Other scholars in the United States, especially Andeanists, have offered critical support. I wish to acknowledge my intellectual debt to Elsa Chaney, June Nash, Carmen Diana Deere, Margo Smith, Judith-Maria Buechler, William Roseberry, and many others, including the reviewers of my manuscript, Jane Collins and Kay Warren, whose thoughtful remarks have proved very useful in the final writing of this book. It has been a pleasure to work with the staff at the University of Texas Press whose encouragement and close attention to my manuscript have kept the project on course. The editors of the journals *Ethnology* and *Review of Radical Political Economics* kindly gave me permission to use material published earlier, here in revised form.

My most hearty thanks go to the people of Huaraz, Peru, who welcomed me into their homes, allowed me to raise seemingly endless questions about their lives and work, and shared with me their knowledge. My *compadres,* Socorro Sánchez and Vicente Camino, drew me into their family and gave me their warmth and assistance throughout all my visits to Peru. Their oldest son, Tomás Camino, was an excellent field assistant during the early period of my research, and the three younger children all helped in various ways to educate me regarding families and marketing in the region. Throughout my study, the names of marketers and their families have been changed to protect the privacy of individuals. Though their names do not appear, I hope that those who participated in the research will accept my most sincere appreciation.

My special thanks are due to several others in Huaraz, including Blanca Tarazona, feminist schoolteacher, and José Sotelo, local scholar and recent mayor, for their interest and cooperation as well as their friendship. Personnel in the Ministries of Food, Agriculture, Transportation, and Commerce, and in the Huaraz Public Library and the library of the CORDEANCASH (an agency for regional development) aided me in gathering needed materials. Faculty at the Universidad Nacional de Ancash and members of the Instituto Nacional de la Cultura offered me opportunities to exchange ideas with persons knowledgeable about the situation in Huaraz.

In Lima, point of entry and departure for my trips to Peru, I have long benefited from my association with the organization Perú Mujer, and particularly with Blanca Figueroa and Jeanine Anderson, feminist social scientists whose concerns like mine include urban women and development issues. On my first trip to Peru, Blanca opened her home to me and Jeanine shared unpublished research data from a study of marketwomen in Lima. My return to Peru in 1982 was due in large part to an invitation and financial support from Perú Mujer to participate in a congress on Andean women, after which I spent several months doing research in Huaraz. Other Peruvians, including Carlos Wendorff and Jorge Osterling, whose work has concerned the informal sector in Lima, have offered valuable suggestions.

Back home, my family has given me enduring support through the long process of writing this book. Stanley Ziewacz made one trip with me to Peru and lent his keen observations to my work. Our four-year-old son, Daniel, has waited patiently for me to finish this project, and he will share with me the pleasure of a summer ahead without a book to write.

The Virgin of Fatima, patron saint of Mercado Central, the central market.

One　　***Introduction***

THE STRAINS OF traditional Andean music poured out of the large double doors leading into Mercado Central, the central market. Native flutes and drums mixed freely with brass instruments in a familiar dance tune, or *huayno*, popular in towns of the region. Once I was inside the market, the source of these sounds became apparent as I saw a dozen men parading between rows of women selling vegetables, fruits, and assorted cooked foods. The men's festive dress was enhanced by embroidered sashes worn across their shoulders, a marked contrast to the plain white aprons and simple blouses and skirts of the marketwomen.

The musicians were followed by a group of younger men and boys dressed in white tunics and pants, with bundles of seeds tied to their lower legs. As they danced, the seeds provided a rhythmic percussion for the musicians. These *shaqsha* dancers, as they are called in Quechua, are a frequent presence at Andean fiestas, and the marketwomen nodded with pleasure as the young men passed by.

Mass had just been celebrated at a small chapel located at the center of the market. A flower-strewn litter carried the Virgin of Fatima, patron saint of the market, from her usual place in the chapel on a tour of the market. The procession of musicians, dancers, and the Virgin wound through the aisles of fresh produce and then out into the streets, accompanied by a hoard of children running along behind.

The central market had an air of gaiety on this weekday morning as sellers paused in their work and customers leaned on market stalls to enjoy the music and admire the Virgin in all her finery. The color and festivity of the scene were enhanced by the melange of smells emanating from the stalls of fresh produce, meats, poultry, fish, and the regional specialties prepared for on-the-spot consumption. For the moment, however, even these culinary temptations could not compete with the excitement of the procession.

These were the sights, sounds, and smells that greeted me the first time I ventured into Mercado Central in Huaraz, Peru. My mind was on becoming acquainted with some marketwomen, but I was distracted by the array of stimuli to my senses. What I saw surprised me because it so closely fit the folkloric view of Latin American markets as colorful places of recreation to which women come to gossip as much as to sell.

In fact what I saw was not at all typical. Although I was assisted on that day by a young woman knowledgeable about the markets, neither she nor any of the sellers I spoke to thought to tell me that they were having a once-a-year celebration of their market's patron saint. To them it was obvious. Surely one only sees processions and *shaqsha* dancers and garlands of flowers on holidays of one sort or another. And while marketwomen were once required to wear white aprons every day, the aprons are now worn only on special occasions. Moreover, only on such occasions do marketers slow their pace to any degree. Any child in Huaraz would have known this. Yet it was several days before my questions and observations made clear to me the circumstances surrounding my first day in the market.

Perhaps it was fortuitous that I should arrive in the market on a day so unlike other days. Just as I had learned to question appearances in the wider Peruvian society, I now began to question appearances in the Huaraz marketplace. I already appreciated the paradox of a country so rich in natural splendor and cultural diversity yet so marked by desperate poverty. In Huaraz, I began to observe the difficult conditions and hard work of marketing beneath the appearance of persistent cultural tradition. The contradictions experienced by marketwomen—picture-postcard figures with full skirts, broad-rimmed hats, and long braids who in fact underwrite the Peruvian national economy—became a major focus of my research in Huaraz.

For the half year I remained in Huaraz in 1977 and during the summers of 1982, 1984, and 1987 when I returned to that provincial city, I considered the work and social lives of marketwomen within the broad framework of economic underdevelopment in Peru. Only in that context could the most vexing questions of the Huaraz marketplace be understood. For example, what attracts so many women to petty commerce, probably the leading occupation for women in Huaraz and second only to domestic service as a source of female employment throughout Peru? What kind of work do marketers perform and what role do they play in the economy? Are marketers independent entrepreneurs or are there economic forces that constrain and subordinate sellers? What underlies the recent campaigns to portray small-scale marketers as inessential and even pernicious to the society, and to curtail retail trade at a time when few alternatives await displaced marketers and street vendors?

Nearly 80 percent of sellers in the Huaraz market are women, and elsewhere in Peru a large majority of sellers are likewise women. Women predominate in the marketplace because they have fewer options than men for contributing to family support and because selling offers a unique opportunity to integrate income-generating activity outside the home with domestic responsibilities. In general, marketwomen have some control over their hours of work and over the products they sell. To a lesser degree, they may control other aspects of their work. Many are able to bring market work home and household work to the market, taking advantage of flexible conditions in order to carry out all the work in their busy days. To understand the work lives of marketwomen, then, we must consider both their productive, market-related activities and their reproductive, household-related ones.

Marketers are rarely regarded as productive workers, yet it is precisely their productive contribution that I have found most striking in the Huaraz markets. Close attention to marketers at work reveals that traders go well beyond the distribution of goods to add value to the goods they sell. In addition to the work of locating, transporting, sorting, and safeguarding items for sale, sellers often process their goods. This ranges from peeling and chopping fresh vegetables to the preparation of entire meals, the raising of guinea pigs, and the sewing of garments for sale to buyers.

As for their reproductive activity, marketwomen frequently meet their own family needs as they work, caring for their children, beginning preparations for dinner, and so on. However, marketing itself has a reproductive aspect in providing basic needs to society. If marketing is an extension of women's household roles, as some maintain, this commercialized "housework" keeps the national house in order.

Far from being successful entrepreneurs, most Huaraz marketwomen barely manage to get by, earning little from their long hours of hard work. Rarely do sellers expand their business, and contraction is more often the order of the day. Furthermore, although on-the-job autonomy is generally considered an advantage of marketing, some marketwomen do not have that privilege. An increasing number of sellers are subordinated to larger commercial interests and to manufacturing concerns located in Peru's major cities. Among marketwomen in Huaraz, many work as commission sellers for local interests, and some hold contracts with coastal firms. Others are simple wageworkers, hired as occasional pieceworkers by other marketers, or as full-time employees in market restaurants and shops. With the economic downturn of recent years, it is not surprising to find some workers in the marketplace earning no more from their employers than free meals and tips.

Useful as marketwomen may be, they have served for more than a decade as scapegoats for economic woes in Peru. Campaigns have been launched to bring goods directly from producers and wholesalers to consumers and to eliminate the small retailers. Known by the slogan "From the field to the cooking pot," these efforts have generally failed and continue to fail. Under present economic conditions, retail marketing and street trade are not actually being eliminated but rather are being restricted and made the focus of media criticism. Attacks on marketers have the political objective of satisfying urban middle-class consumers during a period of national crisis.

National and regional developments between 1968 and 1970 were particularly critical at the local level in Huaraz. A bloodless coup in 1968 brought a reformist military government to power. Among the first acts carried out under the new regime was a major agrarian reform in 1969 aimed at dismantling the *hacienda* system of large landed estates in the Peruvian Andes. The political change of this period was substantial in the Huaraz area, affecting a number of large landowners and peasant workers. An even more fundamental change came when Huaraz and its surrounding valley suffered a devastating earthquake in 1970. The loss of human life and the severe destruction in the city and the towns of the region touched nearly every family in Huaraz. The urban population in the valley bottom was most affected by the earthquake, while peasant communities in the uplands escaped injury. The loss of class privileges by townspeople whose homes and property were ruined led to a deep resentment, which is still expressed today.

The early 1970s were years of reconstruction and reorganization in the Huaraz area. Gradually, the city was rebuilt and landholdings in the region were restructured under new terms of ownership and use. The ways in which these changes were brought about were still a topic of debate in 1977 when I first went to Huaraz. Townspeople were unhappy with the social service agencies that delivered assistance to disaster victims, with the broad new city streets and modern downtown plaza, as well as with the food supply problems, which they attributed to the inexperience of peasant farmers who benefited from land reform.

By the mid-1970s, Peru had entered a period of grave economic crisis. Harsh austerity measures were mandated in 1977 by the International Monetary Fund (IMF) as a condition for future loans. The Peruvian sol (S/.) began devaluing at a dramatic rate, dropping from approximately S/.75 to the U.S. dollar in 1977, to S/.750 in 1982, S/.3,400 in 1984, and S/.30,000 during my most recent trip to Peru in 1987. In Huaraz, as throughout the country, poor and working people felt austerity most.

My field research in Huaraz spanned a time of transition in Peru, from military rule in the seventies to civilian government in the eighties. The return to an elected leadership has been accompanied by more economic hardship and political conflict of serious proportion, as the rebel group Sendero Luminoso (Shining Path) and the government stand off in brutal confrontation. The increasing militarization of the country has led to flagrant human rights abuses. Although Huaraz is not located at the center of political conflict, which has tended to occur in the southern Andean region and in Lima, the tension that has gripped the nation is felt here, too.

The 1985 presidential election of Alan García Pérez meant a victory for the opposition party, APRA (Popular American Revolutionary Alliance). Yet, despite the broad dissatisfaction with government leadership that García's election signaled, it is still uncertain how significant a change he ushered in. While the new administration made promises to such impoverished groups as marketers and street vendors, more attention has focused recently on state-level matters, including nationalization of private banks and management of the political crisis.

Nevertheless, it is very clear to anyone who has spent time in Peru during the last few years that the "informal sector" of the economy, in which small-scale sellers are located, is regarded as an urgent social and economic problem. A number of Peruvian researchers have traced the phenomenal growth of the informal sector to the massive rural-to-urban migration in recent decades and, ultimately, to the economic crisis of the state (e.g., Matos Mar 1984). Others are less interested in the underlying causes and more concerned with national action. While the middle class has long demanded more forceful control of the expanding population of retailers swelling city streets, a new and influential voice has called for the deregulation of "informals." The Institute for Freedom and Democracy, headed by the economist Hernando de Soto, views petty manufacturers, traders, and transport agents as a seriously undervalued group that may be the hope of Peru's economic future. The main obstacle to the entrepreneurial success of those in small-scale commerce is bureaucratic red tape, which forces many to work underground, or illegally. This message, whether or not it is heeded, has been widely discussed, following the phenomenal sales of de Soto's 1986 book, *El otro sendero* (The other path), often sold on street corners by vendors themselves.

Despite widespread interest in this more sympathetic analysis of the contribution of the urban poor, de Soto's position is flawed by his reluctance to examine the broader structural problems that drive so many into the informal sector in the first place. At best, some short-term improvements (e.g., fewer restrictions on informal workers, greater access to lines of credit, etc.) may grow out of this policy orientation, but little in the way of sustained economic development appears likely in the near future.

I began this chapter by describing a rather unusual day in the Huaraz marketplace known as Mercado Central. Let me follow now with the description of an ordinary day in the life of a seller in the same marketplace.

Of the marketwomen I knew in Huaraz, Elena is the one with whom I came to have the closest relationship. She is married, has four children, and lives in the outskirts of the city. While the peripheral location of the home of Elena and her family allowed them to escape injury in the earthquake, that location also means they lack the urban amenities of running water and paved streets. Like most Huaraz townspeople, who are *mestizos*, Elena is bilingual in Quechua and Spanish, and although she wears the traditional Andean *pollera* (full skirt), she covers it with a more modern, slimmer skirt. Her husband, a tailor, makes her clothes when his health, which is failing, permits him to work.

I never spent a full day with Elena—I would have slowed her down—but I accompanied her often enough as she carried out her normal routines to be able to describe her "typical" day. Of course, every day is different, and some tasks, like washing clothes, are only done once or twice a week, but most housework and market work is done daily.

Elena's day begins early. She rises before the rest of the family, at 4:30 A.M., leaving the bed she shares with her husband, Renato (and sometimes her young daughter, Pilar). It is still hours before daybreak, and the cold night air requires bundling up in a couple of sweaters. She is ready within minutes to make the first of her two

The expanding informal sector in Huaraz.

daily trips to the bakery where she buys bread. Sometimes Renato gets up and goes with her; but on this morning, like many others, Elena ties her huge bread basket to her back and makes the trip alone.

She leaves the house without taking time for tea or coffee and makes her way through the dark streets and over the Quillcay River to the Soledad barrio, where the bakery is located. When she arrives at the bakery, ten or fifteen minutes later, a dozen other women are already waiting for the fresh-baked bread to be piled into their baskets. The women, who like Elena buy for their housefront stores, chat as they wait. When the bread is ready, Elena buys one hundred rolls at the full price and receives twenty extra as her "commission" (the extra rolls will be mainly for her family). After the women have received their bread, they do not linger but hurry off to their homes.

When Elena returns home around 5:30, Renato is up and ready to be on hand to sell bread to the neighbors. Renato puts a kettle of water on the kerosene stove, where it will stay hot for the children, who rise around 6:30. He makes himself some tea and eats a few rolls, interrupted now and then by a neighbor calling out for bread. After a while he will go to his work area where he sews garments for clients. He and his older daughter, Teresa, stay within hearing of calls for bread. In the past, the family store had many more items for sale, but the expense of keeping it up and Renato's failing health have made it impossible to manage selling anything more than bread.

Elena, once she has unloaded her bread, is soon off for the market. She knows Pilar is safe in Teresa's care, so she takes her market basket and *lliklla* (shawl) and heads down the river and across the bridge to La Parada, a sprawling open-air market to which many wholesalers come. Arriving around 6:00 A.M., she is later than many other marketers and she must work faster to find produce to buy. She moves about quickly, sizing up the situation and checking the places where she customarily buys from wholesalers. Unsatisfied with what she finds to buy in La Parada, she heads for the area between Mercado Central and the Frigorífico Pesquero, a fish distribution center, where a few trucks often stop. Having marketed since she married twenty-five years ago at the age of twenty-three, Elena knows the marketplace well and has many acquaintances with whom she does business. She buys occasionally from the large wholesalers but more often purchases from women who work on a smaller scale and from *campesinas* (rural women) who come to Huaraz with produce from their own fields.

Today, Elena's purchases include fifty kilos of *zapallo* (calabash), which she bought for S/.10 per kilo and will sell at S/.12 per kilo; ten bunches of garlic, bought at S/.5 per bunch, to be sold at S/.7 per bunch; and five portions of small onions for which she paid S/.10 per portion and will divide into smaller portions to sell for S/.5 each.[1] (Elena will divide the portions of onions into two parts and then take a little out of each part, her "profit," to be taken home for the family.)

It is nearly 8:00 A.M. when Elena arrives at her market stall. This is already close to the peak hour of market activity, so she wastes no time getting ready. She takes her chair down from the table where she had placed it when closing the day before and, pushing back yesterday's goods, arranges her new produce on the table space. For the next forty-five minutes, Elena prepares her vegetables for sale, interrupted once in a while by customers, whom she greets as she works. She peels the outer skins of the onions slightly, and then arranges portions for sale, putting aside the remainder to be taken home. Then she examines the quality of some tomatoes she bought a few days ago and picks out a few bad ones; these she passes over to her friend Blanca as a gift for her pigs.

By 9:15, Elena is weighing the quantities of potatoes, carrots, and onions that she peels every day to sell to her neighbor who operates a restaurant in the market. Before she begins the peeling, however, she takes a short break for some tea and bread, offered by her neighbor in exchange for her work. Then she sets to work peeling, assisted after a while by her sister-in-law, María, who sells at a nearby stall. They talk as they work, and when customers come they often join in the conversation, sharing news in Quechua. Elena leaves for a few minutes to make some purchases to take home for the day's meals, while María looks after her stall. When she returns, word is circulating that a PIP (Peruvian Investigative Police) official is present in the market, and the sellers keep a discreet eye on him until he leaves. Elena finishes her peeling around 10:45 and takes the vegetables to her neighbor's restaurant.

By this time, Elena begins to clean her stall in order to be ready to leave around 11:00. She again makes sure her stock is well arranged, then goes to wash her knife and dump the pail of water she used for the peeled vegetables. Finally, she covers her table space with some old burlap bags, places her chair on top, and ties up both the food she bought for the family and the vegetable peels she will give to her animals. She leaves the market a bit earlier than most marketers in order to have the noon meal ready before Teresa and her brother Manuel go to school.

When Elena reaches home, Teresa has the meal underway. Elena unloads the fresh goods she has brought and begins preparing the fish that will be served with today's meal of wheat soup, onions, and potatoes. It is ready just in time for Teresa and Manuel to eat quickly before they leave for school at 12:30. Elena's older son, Guillermo, arrives home as his sister and brother are leaving, and he and the others sit down to eat somewhat more leisurely. During the meal, Renato and Guillermo lead the conversation. Though Elena is listened to with respect when she speaks, she is often quiet during mealtime discussion. In part, this may be because Elena has not been to school and cannot read or write (though she says Guillermo is going to teach her). Renato, who is ten years her senior, completed two years of secondary school and keeps well informed by reading the newspapers and listening to the radio. Their son Guillermo is considered the family intellectual; in their family, as in most Huaraz families, education is highly respected. Elena defers to the men even on issues she knows more about, such as marketing, child care, and the Quechua language. She contributes only occasionally to the conversation and directs her attention instead to keeping an eye on Pilar.

After the meal, Guillermo leaves for his studies at the normal school (teachers' college) and Renato returns to his work area to sew, while Elena washes the dishes. Around 2:00 P.M., she prepares for her second trip to the bakery. Pilar sometimes goes with her or sometimes stays at home with her father while he sews at his machine. The afternoon trip is much like the morning trip, with the benefit of light and warmth. Elena again buys one hundred rolls and receives twenty extra.

Some days, when there is work to be done on the family's small plots of land, Elena goes to work there after her second trip for bread. Renato's health makes it difficult for him to do heavy work, leaving to Elena the tasks that men customarily perform. Today, Elena takes Pilar and goes to a woodland area to gather eucalyptus branches for firewood. They each take along a shawl to carry wood back home and head up a path to the woods. Elena gathers a large bundle of wood while Pilar gathers a small bundle, and before long they are ready to return home. There is still some time before Elena must begin cooking the evening meal, and once home she quickly collects a plastic tub full of dirty clothes to launder and then encourages Pilar to hasten her steps as they walk down the road to the river.

Elena soaks the clothes in the river water and then places them on some rocks in the stream, where she rubs them with a large bar of soap and "beats out the dirt" with a wooden paddle. After the clothes are rinsed clean and wrung out, Pilar assists her mother in spreading the clothes over bushes and rocks where they have a few minutes of sun to speed their drying. Since time is short today, they will be gathered together and taken home to finish drying on a line stretched across the household corral.

Home again, it is 5:00 P.M. and Guillermo, Teresa, and Manuel return from their schools. They have some tea and bread as a before-meal snack, or *lonche*. Meanwhile, Elena has hung the laundry and is getting ready to prepare dinner. This will be another hearty meal, though a little lighter than the noon meal. She begins by crushing some garlic and *ají* (chili pepper) between a small round stone and a large curved one, her *mano* and *metate*. She puts the crushed garlic and *ají* into a pot along with chopped onions and tomatoes, shredded carrots, and a little water. This makes a sauce for flat noodles, which she cooks next, resulting in a dish called *tallerín*. When meat or poultry is available, it completes the dish, but tonight Elena just puts grated cheese on top.

It is no wonder that Elena is tired by the time she sits down to eat, just after 6:00 P.M. The hot food tastes good as the night's chill sets in, but it also makes her sleepy. The family talks about the day and

Morning activity in Mercado Central.

enjoys the meal. After they have finished, Teresa and Manuel are encouraged to do their schoolwork, but they beg to put it off until morning and go watch television at their cousins' house in the barrio instead. Guillermo goes his own way, and Pilar is soon put to bed. Elena quickly washes the dishes and sits relaxing with some knitting for a short while. By 8:30, however, she can no longer stay awake, and she retires to bed.

This was the shape of Elena's day in 1977, and it was still the shape of her day ten years later. She works approximately sixteen hours each day, seven days a week, at home and in the marketplace. There is little variation and little time for rest. Indeed, by the early eighties Elena's workday was intensifying as a result of worsening economic conditions in Peru. As rising food prices and increased competition in the market caused Elena's business in Mercado Central to decline, she began preparing packets of chopped vegetables to sell for use in soups. To do this, she often started peeling vegetables at home the night before, completing the task the next day in the marketplace. In addition, she found it necessary to add a third trip to the bakery to her already full day. She has needed to sell bread more aggressively, too, seeking out customers on her way back home.

When times are especially hard, she sells wood from the family's modest eucalyptus groves. In spite of Elena's best efforts, her family's standard of living has fallen off sharply in the last few years.

Located in the north-central Andes of Peru, Huaraz is the commercial and administrative capital of the department of Ancash, roughly equivalent to a United States state capital. This highland city is estimated to have doubled in population, from some 45,000 people in the mid-1970s to around 100,000 by the second half of the 1980s. Such rapid growth is attributed in part to the vast expansion of the tourist industry in the area and to the entry of many into petty commerce in recent years. By my own count, Huaraz marketers increased in number from approximately 1,200 to almost 2,000 over the research period. The vast majority of women in marketing are concentrated, like Elena, in the retail sale of fruits and vegetables, though some sell cooked food, meat, fish, clothing, and other manufactured goods, and a few participate in wholesale trade.

In my original fieldwork as well as during follow-up visits, I collected data through a combination of participant observation and open-ended interviewing. In most cases I worked alone using Spanish, but I occasionally worked with local assistants to interview Quechua monolinguals or to perform other research tasks. Considerable time was spent in Mercado Central, one of the four daily markets in Huaraz, to acquire an in-depth understanding of the nature of market work. Many informal interviews were carried out in the other three Huaraz markets, especially in the open-air marketplace, La Parada. A more formal approach was taken midway through the first period of fieldwork, when I designed a question schedule of open-ended items that were intended primarily for couples, marketwomen and their husbands. In 1977, I interviewed a total of some three hundred people, many of whom I reinterviewed during later visits.

During all four periods in Huaraz, my schedule generally followed that of the marketers I studied. I rose early in the morning to go to the market, often in time to observe the transactions of wholesalers and retailers, which take place from around 4:00 A.M. to 8:00 A.M., and I usually stayed until most of the sellers had left, around 1:00 or 2:00 P.M. In the late afternoon I frequently visited the homes of marketers who were too busy to talk during their hours of business. Other times I attended meetings of the market union, worked on my maps of the markets, or interviewed shopkeepers for a census of three blocks of stores in Huaraz. Occasionally, I traveled outside Huaraz to nearby communities and towns to interview producers and marketers in the region. In addition, I followed national events and news reports closely during my field research to provide a broader context in which to understand the local situation. More time was devoted during the follow-up research to collecting documentary support from ministries and libraries as well as to conducting many more market interviews.

A word of explanation is due concerning my use of the present tense in much of this book. I count myself among those anthropologists who are concerned to present a historically grounded analysis and who are suspicious of the indiscriminate use of the "ethnographic present." Because my research was conducted over a ten-year period, this raises the question of adequately representing both continuities and changes that have occurred over the course of my study. Bearing this in mind, I have chosen to use the present tense in instances in which conditions have not substantially changed since my research was carried out. This has the advantage of reflecting the many continuities in marketwomen's work, and it gives a more immediate sense of that work and of marketwomen's lives. Despite the dramatically changing national picture that I discuss, the nature of marketers' work and the way they describe it remain quite consistent over the decade. Where processes of change are in evidence, these are documented.

One important exception to the above considerations must be noted. Shortly after my most recent trip to Peru in 1987, I received reports of the demolition of Mercado Central and the forced relocation of sellers to peripheral areas in Huaraz. Because this book was going into press as I learned the details of these events and because it would be awkward to change all references to Mercado Central to the past tense, I still describe this market in the present tense. I will say more about these recent developments in Chapter 8.

Much of the descriptive material presented in this book was gathered during the first research period. Where the context does not indicate otherwise, the description, figures, prices, and so on reflect the situation in 1977. However, some of the interpretations I offer have been reexamined in light of my more recent visits, and I contrast my earlier observations with more recent findings in order to consider the process of change as it is occurring in Huaraz and throughout Peru.

Close examination of the conditions of women's marketing in Huaraz over a period of ten years revealed the social and economic value of their work, while at the same time making clear the increasing marginalization of these marketers at both the local and national levels. My research focuses on the experience of women engaged in petty commerce in one provincial city in Peru, but it is my intention to show that the relationship of women to men, urban poor to urban elite, and the Andean region to the nation must also be examined if we are to understand these women's experience.

The central topic addressed in this book is how we may understand the situation of these marketwomen, given the terms of economic and political change since 1968 in Peru, specifically since the economic crisis of the mid-1970s contributed to the impoverishment of the large majority of working people in the country. To approach this question, the second chapter locates Huaraz in history and then examines national-level developments that have had a significant impact on the city and the region.

The third chapter points to some new directions in research on marketing in the Third World and charts the theoretical issues to be explored in the present study. I emphasize those areas of research and theory that are the most useful in informing my own work: the relationship of marketing to the entire production process in society, the increasing marginalization of so-called informal sector workers in Third World cities, the role of marketwomen as producers and reproducers, changing modes of production and the proletarianization of marketers, and the significance of national political economy for local-level marketers.[2]

The fact that these matters would appear to concern men as well as women deserves comment. It is certainly true that, to the extent that men participate in the informal sector as marketers, they are often marginalized and impoverished and affected by the same conditions as women marketers. Accordingly, throughout this work, I will have fairly frequent occasion to mention the men who work in the Huaraz markets (the percentage of men I interviewed is roughly proportionate to their representation there). The common experience and socioeconomic condition of many male and female marketers make the inclusion of this material most appropriate.

Nevertheless, the disproportionate entry of women into petty commerce and their concentration in the lower ranks of market trade remain to be explained. I will argue that the historical tradition of women's marketing in Peru, the ideological support given to women's present activity in the informal sector, and the increasing poverty in the urban centers combine to explain the proliferation of women in petty commerce. Despite the low status of the women who work in this sector, we shall see that they are productive workers in an economy dependent on their labor.

This analysis is introduced early in the book, but it is not developed until later chapters. In between is a detailed description of the context in which Huaraz marketwomen lead their everyday lives. This rather conventional ethnography of the marketplace and its actors is perhaps unusual in its emphasis on the historical role of marketing and its productive aspect and on the contribution of women in this sphere of activity. Further consideration of the precise character of women's work as marketers is grounded in this ethnographic description and in my assessment of the as yet ambiguous social class position of marketers in contemporary Peru.

Chapter 4 focuses on the commercial history and contemporary markets in Huaraz. The social and economic organization of marketers and the division of labor in the marketplace are considered, with an emphasis on the gender division. In the fifth chapter, I examine marketing as a form of livelihood, noting especially its productive component, and I go on to suggest how we may conceptualize this work.

After examining the broad features of the work of marketing, I consider the place of marketing in women's lives as a whole and how their activities outside the home integrate with those they perform within the home. The sixth chapter situates marketwomen in the wider context of family, society, and modes of production in Huaraz and the nation.

Chapter 7 examines the social relations of marketwomen, their participation in market unions, and their identification with national-level political issues. I take on the thorny question of the class consciousness of women in the informal sector, arguing that some marketwomen are ready to mobilize in their own interest.

In chapter 8, recent developments and policy making at the national level in Peru are shown to have an unfortunate effect on marketers at the local level in Huaraz. Government actions that threaten marketers and the marketers' response were only becoming apparent by 1977, though by the early eighties these were strengthened. Peru's government has attempted to divert attention from its role in the economic crisis by scapegoating marketers and street vendors as unnecessary intermediaries, thus threatening their livelihood. Even more enlightened efforts to improve the situation of petty traders in the informal sector have had negative consequences for some of the most marginalized of marketers, and women are especially concerned in these developments.

Chapter 9 draws some final conclusions and suggests how we may conceptualize marketwomen in the economy and society. I argue that, at a time when women throughout Latin America and other areas of the Third World are entering the urban work force in large numbers and finding themselves in such impoverished sectors as that of petty commerce, it is particularly important to investigate the consequences that economic underdevelopment has for women. The marketwomen of Huaraz offer an example of resourcefulness and courage under conditions that pose a threat to the livelihood of poor people, especially women, in Peru.

Two   *The Peruvian Political Economy*

Local History

The city of Huaraz, capital of Peru's department of Ancash, lies in a valley in north-central Peru at an altitude of 3,027 meters between two Andean ranges, the snow-covered Cordillera Blanca to the east and the rugged Cordillera Negra to the west. This valley, the Callejón de Huaylas, is drained by the Santa River, which flows north through it. Huaraz is bounded to the west by the Santa, and it is divided into northern and southern halves by a tributary, the Quillcay River. The Quillcay is one of a number of rivers in the region draining the western slopes of the Cordillera Blanca and into the Santa River. It provides a source of water for crops, consumption, washing clothes, and bathing for the population in and around Huaraz. The region is characterized by a rainy season, extending from November to April, followed by a cooler dry season.

Settlement in the area of contemporary Ancash dates back some millennia. The first large-scale regional culture, Chavín, spread through the north-central highlands around 800 B.C. Other important cultures predating the Incaic period have also been investigated in the region. The rich archaeological record of the area's early period is not matched, however, by an equally rich written record of more recent times. There are few historical studies of the Ancash region, and relatively little has been written of the period before the nineteenth century.

The Ancash region was apparently a center of resistance to Inca domination in the fifteenth century (Fernandez 1962:14). However, once conquered by one outside force, the region made an easier transition to Spanish rule in the next century, as reported by *corregidores*, provincial representatives of the Crown (Gridilla 1937:xxviii). Even so, the people of Ancash evidenced both resistance and accommodation to Spanish penetration in the Callejón de Huaylas in the sixteenth and seventeenth centuries (Alvarez-Brun 1970: 113). There was an increasing synthesis of Andean and European elements during this colonial period, with the *kurakas* (Indian chiefs) acting as mediators (Varon Gabai 1980).

The rich mineral and agricultural resources of the Callejón de Huaylas attracted a growing population during the colonial period, and by the time of independence in 1821, the area was considered an important one (Fernandez 1962: 14–15). Huaraz became a strategic base of operations for the forces of Bolívar, who was so impressed by the people there that he honored the town with the title "Very Noble and Generous City." Huaraz was established by law as a political-administrative entity on July 25, 1857, a date that came to be celebrated there along with the national independence day, July 28.

The situation in Huaraz could not have been tranquil during the eighteenth century, when rebellions over the payment of Indian tribute were widespread in Ancash (Alvarez-Brun 1970: 113–125). The Republican period of the nineteenth century was also marked by episodes of social unrest. In 1854, for example, when the unpopular government of José Rufino Echenique issued orders for the recruitment of young men to military service, a group of women in Huaraz led a protest against the order that would take away their sons and husbands. They showed such strong resistance that government officials were driven out of the city by the women's physical assault (ibid.: 173–174).

The best-known uprising in Huaraz occurred during the aftermath of the War of the Pacific with Chile (1879–1883). The rebellion of Atusparia in 1885 resulted when Huaraz officials attempted to reintroduce the collection of the *contribución personal*, a head tax on the rural population that had been abolished formally in 1854. In more general terms, the uprising came as a response to the continued abuse of rural people by the dominant classes in Peru. With the support of some urban dissidents in Huaraz, the rebels successfully seized control of the city and installed an independent government, which endured two months before national troops arrived (Stein 1980).

The sociopolitical events in and around Huaraz during the twentieth century, though significant, have paled as a consequence of the natural disasters that the city has experienced in recent times. A major flood in 1941 killed more than 6,000 Huaracinos and destroyed the sector of the city north of the Quillcay River known as Centenario. This barrio, reconstructed, was later to be the only part of the urban center that did not receive serious damage when an

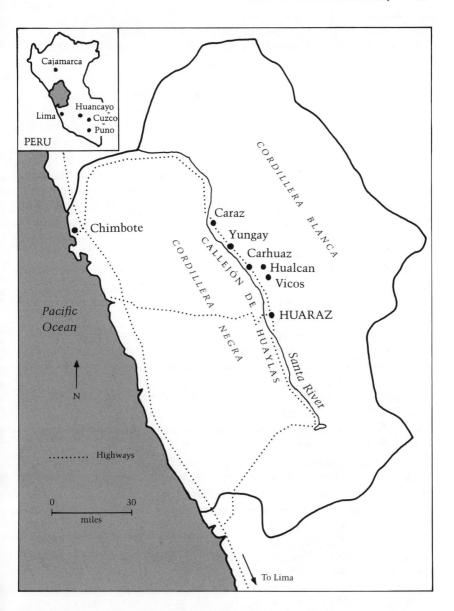

Department of Ancash, Peru. Based on Stein (1961:iv).

earthquake destroyed much of the city and its population in 1970. This second disaster was the worst recorded earthquake in the history of the Western Hemisphere, killing 70,000 people, 20,000 of whom lived in Huaraz. The four traditional barrios to the south of the Quillcay—Belén, Huarupampa, San Francisco, and Soledad—were almost totally destroyed. The narrow, crowded streets of adobe houses could not withstand the impact of the earthquake or the tremors that continued for some days afterward. The survivors of this disaster, who were in some cases the resettled survivors of the 1941 flood, were forced to relocate and move back to Centenario or to emergency camps set up in outlying barrios. The magnitude of the earthquake made it a critical experience in the lives of Huaracinos; they recall other events as happening "before" or "after."

By 1977, the reconstruction of the urban center of Huaraz was well under way. Streets had been broadened and were lined with modern-style homes built of aseismic concrete, the new civic and cultural centers were in operation, and the central plaza, the Plaza de Armas, was being restored. More buildings for departmental administration were in progress, and the construction of new homes continued as the population of postdisaster Huaraz grew rapidly. Clearly, much has changed in Huaraz since the earthquake, and the most dramatic change has been in population size and composition.

Population figures for Huaraz are difficult to locate through history and are often questionable. For the colonial period, estimates given by Spanish writers ranged from 5,000 to 8,000 (Gridilla 1933: 119–120). After independence, official census figures put the population at 4,873 in 1876 and 7,646 in 1907 (*Censo de la Ciudad de Huaraz* 1907).[1] Gridilla (1933:119–120) estimates that at the time of his writing the population was between 18,000 and 20,000. A more recent figure suggested by H. Buse (1957:49) sets the population at 15,000 at his time of writing, when the population may have been reduced as a result of the 1941 flood. The 1961 census reported a population of 20,345, and the 1972 census reported 31,382. During my second visit to Huaraz, the provisional results of the 1981 census were made available to me and put the population of Huaraz at 45,116 (*Censos Nacionales VIII de Población—Resultados Provisionales* 1981). In 1987, during my fourth trip, local planners estimated that the number had approached 100,000.

National census data as well as the estimates of local experts may be in error. Nevertheless, widespread migration to the city did rebuild the population at an extraordinary pace. What has been most significant about this phenomenon is the changing social class composition of the city that has developed since the earthquake. Middle-class highland Peruvians have dominated Huaraz, as they have dominated Andean society generally, before and since the disaster in 1970. But the traditional separation of middle-class *mestizos* and subordinate-class *campesinos,* corresponding to town and country, was to a certain extent broken down after 1970. When many townspeople and their homes along the valley floor in Huaraz were destroyed, *campesinos* began to take up residence in the city in much greater numbers than ever before.

Of course, prior to 1970 the population of Huaraz was not undifferentiated, and while most people might be called *mestizos,* there were inequalities in the distribution of wealth among them. For example, obvious differences existed between small shopkeepers and large landowners who resided in Huaraz. However, the juncture of political-economic events of 1968–69, ushered in by the government of Gen. Juan Velasco Alvarado and agrarian reform, and the natural tragedy in 1970 led to a rapid exodus of the wealthiest Huaracinos. Many among this elite who had not already departed as their landholdings were expropriated left for the coast when their homes were destroyed.

Among the *campesinos* who came to Huaraz in the 1970s, many surely came as part of the ongoing urban migration of rural Peruvians who, not benefited by land reform, were no longer able to make a living on their land. Others came, as townspeople bitterly told me, because they saw an opportunity to engage in commerce or any of a number of reconstruction activities that demanded an urban labor force. Although migrants in the city have undergone a change in social status from *campesinos* to urban dwellers, the point to be emphasized here is that, while they may lose their rural identity in this process, they generally acquire another subordinate status, that of the marginalized urban poor. In this way, the social class structure of Huaraz is changing, but class distinctions continue to be clearly marked.

The analysis of the changing class composition in Huaraz sketched here differs somewhat from that given by Barbara Bode (1974, 1977), whose work considers Huaracinos' explanation of the earthquake within the context of the city's changing social structure. Bode provides a useful investigation of the explanation that the earthquake occurred as punishment to the *mestizo* towns of the Callejón de Huaylas because of their historical mistreatment of *campesinos* in the valley uplands. She describes the earthquake as a leveler of social class differences, as rich and poor were forced to share the same humble conditions of the survivor camps. The rhetoric of the Velasco government turned the disaster into an experiment in social change in which equality was to characterize the recon-structed city. Bode (1977 : 253) discusses the progressive action of the government two years after the crisis, when the urban center of Huaraz was officially expropriated in a unique case of urban reform in Peru. Previous property owners were to be compensated in bonds for their holdings, and all Huaracinos were to be allowed to purchase equal parcels of land. As it turned out, many people were unable to afford the long-term loans necessary to buy the land parcels and concrete houses built on them, and they remained in the "tempo-rary" camps.

Bode, who carried out fieldwork in Huaraz between 1971 and 1972, describes both the willingness of townspeople to cope with their impoverished condition and their uneasiness over the rapid en-try of *campesinos* to the city. If their acceptance of the situation pre-dominated in the immediate aftermath of the earthquake, the bal-ance seems to have changed considerably by the time I went to Huaraz in 1977. At that time, many townspeople had reclaimed their former positions, whether through benefit of compensation for their former property, through the help of relatives, or through the class privileges of their education and social network. Class dis-tinctions had been reestablished, and to whatever extent the rural migrants had made any gains at all, the middle class was openly un-happy or even contemptuous. Furthermore, it had become abun-dantly clear to poor people in Huaraz that, far from promoting equal opportunity, the government agencies set up to oversee the rebuild-ing of the city were acting in their own class interests to control the proliferating urban poor.

Huaraz in 1977

When I arrived in Huaraz in 1977, the city had the appearance of an urban center undergoing rapid modernization. Actually, the reconstruction of Huaraz after the earthquake had been slow to be-gin, but seven years later the results were impressive. Approaching Huaraz by car from the southern end of the Callejón, one enters the city by way of Avenida Gamarra (now renamed Avenida Mariscal Luzuriaga), passing the Belén Hospital, the Plaza de Armas, and the civic center.[2] A major commercial boulevard, Avenida Gamarra has the unique distinction of being a divided thoroughfare, and the place where it intersects with Avenida Raimondi, another principal street, is the busiest in the city. Here, street vendors settle with their wares, Lima newspapers are spread on the sidewalk for sale, and shoeshine boys congregate. Continuing north past this intersection on Avenida

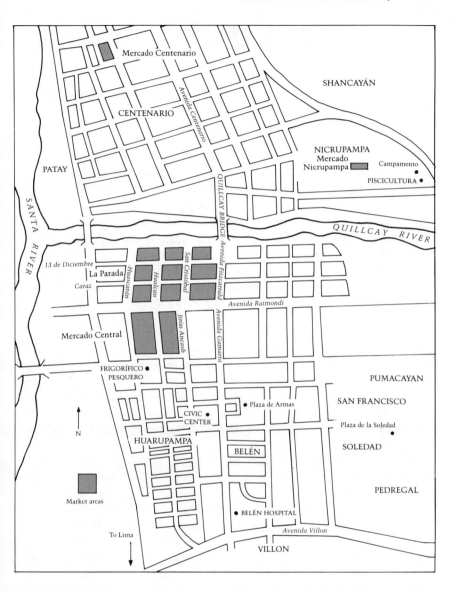

City of Huaraz.

Fitzcarrald, one crosses the Quillcay River to Avenida Centenario. Once the main commercial avenue, this street shows signs of declining business activity as the new urban center attracts more people. The Centenario district retains the appearance of the barrio before the disaster, however, its residences and business establishments having suffered relatively little damage.

The streets described here, Gamarra, Fitzcarrald, and Centenario, form a sort of backbone in the city, and they are part of the route that connects the major towns through the valley. Although most Huaracinos themselves do not own vehicles, there is a steady traffic on these streets of private cars, trucks carrying people and produce, and buses serving the city, the Callejón, or heading for the coast. Added to this traffic are men on *triciclos,* or bicycle carts, carrying goods to the Huaraz markets, and of course a regular stream of pedestrians.

The streets to either side of this route are also busy with urban activity. The Ministries of Education, Agriculture, Food, Transportation, and Industry and Tourism are located here, as are the churches, primary and secondary schools, and the normal school. Commerce extends to all parts of the city, with small shops operating on every street. The city's three movie houses and its growing number of hotels, restaurants, and bars are scattered throughout the downtown area. By the time of my first visit to Huaraz, the city was spreading out to accommodate the increased population in the city. The growth of new barrios has been primarily in the direction of the valley uplands to the east, toward the Cordillera Blanca. Like the traditional barrios, the new ones have their own small plazas, churches, and annual barrio holidays.

The changing physical structure of Huaraz corresponds to a changing social structure in the city. The middle class has been able to purchase plots of land and houses in the urban center, while the newer outlying barrios are the neighborhoods of the urban poor, newcomers and long-time residents alike. The barrio Nicrupampa, where I lived, is a good case in point. This barrio is located far enough up from the valley floor that it was not greatly affected by the earthquake. Many families still live in the adobe homes built by their relatives several generations ago and work small plots of land up in the heights (*las alturas*). Nicrupampa became the site of the largest survivor camp (*campamento*) in the aftermath of the earthquake, and stories are told of this strange new neighborhood where doctors and lawyers lived next door to *campesinos.* By 1977, the professionals seemed to have left, and others who were unable to return to the urban center felt humiliated by their living conditions in this poor barrio. Women with whom I washed clothes at the river often volunteered information to me, apologetically, about their better situation "before."

Social class in Huaraz is to some extent suggested by barrio residence, but more significant indicators exist as well. The most visible cultural markers are language and dress style. Most people in Huaraz are bilingual Quechua and Spanish speakers. Middle-class townspeople know Quechua, although they may use it only rarely. *Campesinos* who have recently come to Huaraz or who come on a casual basis (or sometimes those who live in the outskirts of town) may be monolingual in Quechua. Most of the people I knew, those involved in petty commerce, used both languages depending on the situation. For example, many women who appeared most comfortable speaking Quechua at home or with other women of their class in the marketplace were quite capable of using Spanish with wholesalers, market officials, and others in town.

Dress style follows this same pattern, reflecting social class. Middle-class men and women are easily recognized by their European-style dress and hairstyles. The most fashionable purchase their clothes on the coast. In sharp contrast is the traditional Andean dress of *campesinos* entering the city. Their homespun clothes and distinctive hats mark them as Quechua speakers and peasants. For women, this dress is particularly striking with their colorful wool skirts (*polleras*), their characteristic blouses and shawls (called in Quechua *llikllas*), and their long braided hair. On their way to town or the market, these women often carry babies or large bundles in the shawls on their backs. Many of the women of Huaraz adopt elements of each of these two styles. A great number of fully bilingual women wear braids and the characteristic hats of the region, but while they put on *polleras,* they cover them with the more somber skirts preferred in town. It was some weeks before I discovered that the woman whose home I shared wore a bright *pollera* beneath her straight black skirt; she was amused, and perhaps a little embarrassed, when I commented on it. Marketwomen as a group range from women who come in from the countryside in full *campesina* dress to women with Western-style slacks and sweaters and short hair styled in permanent waves.

Educational differences among Huaracinos are pronounced, and schooling is a fairly sensitive measure of social standing. The Ministry of Education (Ministerio de Educación 1976*a*) determined that of the 70,274 people in Huaraz province's two school districts 16,304 were illiterate. Breaking down the results by sex, we find that 11 percent of males and 35 percent of females were illiterate. A higher illiteracy rate for women than for men was found in every age group, although illiteracy is declining among young people of both sexes. Whether the level of schooling attained by young women will approach that attained by young men is not certain. Enrollment figures for 1977 (Ministerio de Educación 1977) show that males and females attend primary school in nearly equal numbers, but in secondary school males far outnumber females. By the final year of secondary school, females make up only 20 percent of the student body.

Changes are occurring in the area of education in Huaraz, despite persistent inequalities. Huaracinos express a great deal of confidence in education as a means to individual mobility and to progress for their city. This is particularly notable in view of the long struggle, dating from the late nineteenth century, they have waged for a university in Huaraz. In 1968, with the support of *mestizos* and *campesinos* in the Huaraz area, a group of students marched to Lima to make their desire for a university known to the national government, but they returned with nothing except promises. On May 16 of that year, 40,000 people from all sectors of the population in the region rallied together for what was probably the largest political demonstration in Ancash history. The next day, students clashed with police in a second demonstration, which resulted in an undetermined number of deaths and many wounded.[3] It was not until 1977 that a firm commitment was made to open a university in Huaraz—a decision that was greeted with joyous celebration in the city.[4]

The increasing aspirations of parents for their children and of young people for themselves, which I discovered in Huaraz in 1977, center on the opportunity to acquire an education. Many marketers, for example, with little or no schooling themselves, have the expectation that their children will complete secondary school and perhaps go on to have a profession. The likelihood of social mobility among marketers and their families will be discussed later, but here we may note that Huaraz offers relatively few employment options, even for the educated, at the present time.[5]

Aside from a small number of people in Huaraz who own land outside the city and hire laborers to work and take the product to market, people rarely have enough land to produce for the market. Judging from the urban poor I encountered in my neighborhood and in the markets, many have one or two small parcels of land (*chacras*), usually amounting to less than a hectare (about 2.5 acres). The food they grow and the animals they raise on these landholdings provide only a small part of what they need to subsist. Recently arrived *campesinos* sometimes have land back in their communities, but their decision to come to the city generally means having to give part of whatever income they earn to someone who will look after their fields. Nevertheless, access to small landholdings is critical at a time when many families cannot support themselves solely from other sources of livelihood. Crops frequently grown are potatoes, wheat, barley, corn, beans, and *oca* and *olluco* (tubers), and animals raised include sheep, chickens, pigs, rabbits, and guinea pigs.

Primary extractive activities in the region attract some Huaracinos, mainly men, as wage laborers. A small number work on agricultural cooperatives created as part of the agrarian reform of 1969. Others work in mines in the region where lead, zinc, sulphur, copper, silver, and gold are extracted for export. A fishing enterprise along the Quillcay River in Nicrupampa, the Piscicultura, hires around thirty employees (only the secretary is female), making it a major employer; here, several varieties of trout are produced to stock the rivers and lakes of Ancash and throughout Peru for eventual consumption. Local Huaracinos are rarely the consumers, however, and rather resent the Piscicultura. This was often expressed in Nicrupampa by residents who view the locked enclosure of the fishery with evident dislike. Another commercial enterprise in Huaraz for the distribution of fish to consumers is the Frigorífico Pesquero, located in the urban center. From here, a dozen men work to supply forty species of fish to locations throughout Ancash, and in the city itself eight species are sold in the markets by several vendors, male and female, who work on commission for the Frigorífico.

The secondary, or industrial, sector in Huaraz is the least developed in the local economy. Even if we include the fish industry, few enterprises in Huaraz employ more than a half dozen employees. The soda bottling plant, Fenix, is the single factory in the city, and it is a small company. One of the oldest factories in Peru, Fenix formerly employed around eighteen workers, but with newer machinery just four men work there now. Several grain mills along the Quillcay River employ women and men, and a number of bakeries in the city also require workers. Other industries are generally very small-scale, often based at the home of a skilled craftsperson aided by paid assistants. Such crafts as shoemaking and repair, hatmaking, tailoring, table and chair production, and adobe and brick production primarily involve men. Women are employers and workers in small dressmaking and embroidering concerns and sometimes work with their husbands as artisans in the production of ponchos, sweaters, pots, and other articles.

Some men work periodically as day laborers in construction. Since the earthquake, the skills of masons and carpenters have been in demand, but the work is sporadic and was tapering off by 1977.

Work in construction was supervised by ORDEZA, the government organization overseeing the reconstruction of the area affected by the earthquake, and by the Provincial Council (Concejo Provincial).

The tertiary sector in Huaraz is large and cuts across all social classes. Middle-class professionals in this service sector include lawyers, doctors and other medical personnel, teachers, and the administrative and office personnel associated with local government. Others include government personnel with ORDEZA, based in the city after the earthquake, and SINAMOS, an agency established for "social mobilization" (but often viewed by the poor as an instrument for social control). In addition, the petty bourgeois of Huaraz operate stores, restaurants, hotels, tourist agencies, baths, movie houses, and so on. The expansion of the tertiary sector in Huaraz, however, has less to do with the professional and petty bourgeois population than with the urban poor.

The overwhelming activity that poor people, especially women, turn to in Huaraz is petty commerce, which offers a chance to get by when other alternatives are not available. Occasionally, poor women choose to work as domestic servants or launderers, but generally they prefer marketing for the degree of control they have over their work. Men have somewhat greater flexibility in the services, working in such areas as the transportation industry driving buses or trucks, serving as porters, and acting as guides for mountain climbers and tourists.

Occupational differences are accompanied by huge income and consumption disparities between the elite and the impoverished in Huaraz. The Ministerio de Educación (1976*b*) compared income and expenses among three occupational groups in Huaraz: government functionaries with monthly salary of S/.17,500 and expenses of S/.17,700 (S/.200 deficit); manual laborers with monthly pay of S/.6,210 and expenses of S/.6,300 (S/.90 deficit); and shoemakers with monthly earnings of S/.3,000 and expenses of S/.4,200 (S/.1,200 deficit).[6] All groups had higher expenses than income from their primary source of livelihood, but obviously the self-employed shoemakers had the most difficulty. The self-employed are stratified themselves, with the unskilled earning much less than shoemakers and other artisans. The same study found fruit sellers to average only S/.900 in earnings, similar to what I found among this group in 1977.

Socioeconomic differences are linked to the relationship of various groups of Huaracinos to the work they do, that is, the degree of control they have over the work process and over the product of their labor. The precise identification of social classes is rather difficult since the present economic crisis makes it necessary for most families to participate in diverse economic activities, but class inequalities are certainly clear. The placement of Huaracinos engaging in petty commerce in the social class structure presents particular problems, which will be considered at greater length in later chapters.

Recent Political-Economic Developments in Peru

The situation of marketwomen at the local level in Huaraz must be viewed within the terms of the contemporary Peruvian political economy and the crisis now experienced at the national level. The present structure of underdevelopment in Peru affects the lives and work of small marketers like those in Huaraz and, because of the marketers' strategic position in society, takes on a significance beyond the specific areas in which they trade. Some recent developments in Peru, particularly changes in the political economy since 1968, are considered, first at the national level and then from the vantage point of Huaraz.

Peru is frequently described as a country of remarkable contrasts. Geographically, it includes desert coast, high Andean mountains, and tropical jungle. Its population of some eighteen million, except for about 10 percent living in the jungle, or *selva*, is divided between coast and sierra. The contrast of Andean and coastal dwellers is often made, accentuating differences in language, dress, and economic condition. The average annual income of $870 (U.S. dollars) in Lima may be compared to the $280 average income in five of the poorest Andean departments in Peru (Webb 1975 a : 85). While some observers unfortunately conclude that Andean underdevelopment is due to lack of integration in the national economy, many others recognize the substantial inequalities between sierra and coast as a structural consequence of Peru's political economy—which itself is conditioned by the country's position in the world capitalist system.

From the time of the Spanish conquest, the history of Peru, like that of other Latin American nations, has been one of changing forms of foreign domination. Thus, in 1968, when a military coup brought to power a junta that declared itself an anti-imperialist alternative to both capitalism and socialism, debate arose over how serious a break with the past this represented. At first, the coup in Peru drew the attention of many who considered it to be the most important "experiment" in progressive social change in Latin America since the Cuban revolution. Indeed, not long after the military was installed under General Velasco, major expropriations of foreign interests and a broad program of agrarian reform were carried out.

These and other reforms confirmed for many the commitment of the military to lead the country from its dependent position in the world capitalist system to a path of development in the interest of the various sectors of Peru's population.

Coming at the end of a decade of increasing fiscal problems and social unrest, including peasant and worker mobilization, the Velasco government responded to the need for immediate action. Nevertheless, soon there were reasons to doubt whether a decisive break with foreign domination had in fact occurred. Though the government's rhetoric emphasized autonomous national development and worker participation in and control of production, its actions demonstrated an unwillingness to lose the support of the national private sector and foreign capital. By the early 1970s, Peru's industrial development was as dependent upon foreign support through international loans as it was previously through direct foreign investment. By 1975, a series of economic crises led to a conservative turn toward further dependence on the Western nations under the leadership of Gen. Francisco Morales Bermúdez, who replaced Velasco.

As more critical discussion has advanced, Peru's "revolution" has been described as "peculiar" (Hobsbawm 1971), "ambiguous" (Lowenthal 1975), and generally full of contradictions. Marxist dependency theorists (Quijano Obregón 1971) describe the reforms brought about after 1968 as Peru's attempt to renegotiate the terms of international dependency rather than to end dependency. In this view, the coming to power of a government devoted to satisfying the interests of the national bourgeoisie, with the attendant loss of power among the traditional landed oligarchy, signaled no abrupt change. The traditional elite was already weak and the capitalist sector was long established in Peru; thus Velasco's government was following the course of history rather than making history.

Other Marxists (Dore, Weeks, and Bollinger 1977) regard the coup of 1968 as a decisive bourgeois revolution. Although they recognize the continued importance of foreign influence, they focus their attention at the national level where the changing class structure may be examined. Placing more emphasis than the dependency theorists on modes of production and class relations in Peru, supporters of this position view the military seizure of state power in 1968 as the end of the period when the landed and exporting bourgeoisie held sway and the beginning of national industrial capitalist hegemony.

Both these views have merit and both have informed the present study. Together they take into account the ascendancy of the national bourgeoisie as a political force, while recognizing the particular consequences this has for a Third World country dependent on Western nations. Even if, as the dependency theorists note, the political alliance between the Peruvian oligarchy of semifeudal landowners and the export bourgeoisie was already in decline before the coup, we may agree that 1968 marked the close of one chapter in the nation's history. Yet those Marxist analysts who emphasize progressive change at the national level need to examine as well the consequences of Peru's growing integration and dependency in the world economy. As the dependency theorists have argued, Peru's soaring international debt has played a very critical role in maintaining the nation in a position of structural dependence vis-à-vis the advanced capitalist countries. Dominated by the United States, international agencies, such as the IMF and the World Bank, and private international banks have made political as well as economic demands in order to ensure that Peru continues to act in the interests of the center capitalist countries.[7]

Economic Policy Since 1968: Dualism or Dependency

The marked contrasts and persistent inequalities between sierra and coast in Peru lead some observers to characterize the country in dualistic terms, suggesting that the poverty of the former stems from insufficient integration with the latter. However, underlying the explanations of Latin American underdevelopment that rely on the notion of dual society and economy are misguided assumptions that have served to support oppressive social structures (Frank 1969). Indeed, for Peru a more accurate description of the relationship of coast and sierra would be based on internal colonialism rather than dualism (Cotler 1970).

Although several of the most important economic studies of Peru make use of the concept of dualism (Webb 1975a, 1975b; Fitzgerald 1976; Thorp and Bertram 1978; Figueroa 1984), they also incorporate an analysis of dependency, presenting a more complex perspective. Richard Webb (1975a), for example, finds striking differences between coast and sierra incomes, but he shows that the picture is still more complicated. The primary distinction is not a simple geographic one, but rather it is between what he terms "modern" and "traditional" sectors, distinguished by high and low productivity and comprising about one-third and two-thirds of Peru's population, respectively. While the modern sector is predominantly located in coastal cities, the traditional sector is split geographically into rural and urban components. Since Peru's marketers fall within the traditional sector (more recently called the "informal sector"), it will be useful to consider some of the results of economic research.

In his research on income distribution across the modern and traditional sectors, Webb (1975a) assesses the degree of economic change brought about through reforms under Velasco's government. He finds that economic reforms have been mildly progressive throughout Peru, but that redistribution across sectors has been minor. Because the reforms have been directed mainly to the modern sector, the traditional sector has grown relatively more impoverished. The one reform of any magnitude in the traditional sector is, of course, the agrarian reform of 1969, but this has benefited a minority of small landholders, and wealth transfer has been minimized since the recipients of land are required to purchase it and former landowners, or *hacendados*, are compensated for their loss of land. Webb (ibid.: 122) concludes that under the Velasco regime dualism was reinforced because of the priority given to the highly capital-intensive heavy industries rather than the labor-intensive traditional sector.

For middle-class elites, growth in the modern sector offered a guarantee of political stability as well as economic security. But for the rest of the population, "the apparent lack of immediate benefits to the poor [led] to some strain in the political system" (Fitzgerald 1976:28). Still, the decision to revive the capital-intensive modern sector rather than to attack dualism was a conscious choice of the Velasco government. The assumption was that the traditional sector could be ignored without affecting the growth of the modern sector (Thorp and Bertram 1978:305–307). This decision appears inevitable, for as E. V. K. Fitzgerald points out, "the dominance of the modern sector is bound up with the interests of the middle class, and a determined attack on duality might well require a politically unfeasible degree of resource allocation" (1976:96).

The domestic food supply was a politically sensitive area of economic policy under the military government. Securing enough food to meet the country's needs had been a problem for some time, an unfortunate situation for a nation in which 35 percent of the work force is employed in agriculture. Farmers produce about 80 percent of the domestic food requirements, and the balance is imported. Food imports are almost a quarter of total imports and perhaps a half of the metropolitan food supply. To avoid urban shortages, the policy under Velasco was to subsidize food imports rather than to support the agricultural sector through improvements in production and marketing. The short-term politically acceptable "solution" was chosen (Fitzgerald 1976:72–73).

In 1970 the Empresa Pública de Servicios Agropecuarios (EPSA) was established to control external trade and internal markets of basic foodstuffs (especially wheat, rice, meat, and milk) and to extend support services to farmers. However, the chief function of EPSA was to secure "adequate deliveries to urban areas at politically tolerable prices. On the domestic front, it was hoped that EPSA could, by reducing wholesale and transport margins, both hold down prices to the consumer and raise these at the farmgate" (Fitzgerald 1976:51). Nevertheless, prices to consumers were kept down only through large subsidies for imported goods—and when farm prices did not rise, food output continued to stagnate.

A law passed in 1972 brought the production and marketing of all agricultural products under state control (Strasma 1976:310). By the end of 1974, the rising domestic food deficit and costs of subsidizing imports, along with temporary shortages and administration problems, led to the formation of a Ministry of Food. These problems in the domestic food supply can be attributed to the lack of a policy of investment and credit for peasant food producers and not to the marketing system (Fitzgerald 1976:52).

The issues of food policy and price controls are also significant at the local level of Huaraz marketing. Although farmers are generally said to suffer from pricing policy, the situation of petty marketers should be examined, too, since they have been no more favored by price controls than the producers.[8] Just as John Strasma (1976:310) argues that since the agrarian reform it has been convenient for price controllers in Lima to treat peasant producers as profit-making landowners who must be restrained from exploiting urban consumers, so, too, impoverished petty marketers are often the convenient scapegoats for the government's economic problems. While a relatively small number of wholesalers earn high profits and exploit both producers and consumers (Matos Mar, cited in Stein 1978: 149–150), this does not appear true of the much larger number of small marketers. Indeed, during the 1970s the Ministry of Food set prices at every level, virtually doing away with marketers' control of basic food prices, and margins of profits were kept low.

Exploitation has surely occurred, but not at the level of individual producers, marketers, or consumers. The decapitalization of the agricultural sector, the restriction of economic reforms to the modern sector and industry, and price controls all contributed to the draining of wealth from the already poor sectors in Peru into the dominant sectors. William W. Stein describes the process as "increasing exploitation with the transfer of wealth out of agriculture into industry, out of the rural sector into the urban sector, out of lower income groups into higher income groups, and out of the Peruvian nation into richer nations, principally the United States, thereby increasing inequality not only in Peru but in the capitalist world"

(1978:137). Government policy on industrial and agricultural production, aimed at maintaining political stability in the urban areas by ensuring inexpensive consumer provisions, also maintained sharp economic inequality in the country.[9]

Peru Since 1975: Another Look at Dependency

While economists have described Peru as a dual society, they generally agree that the capital-intensive modern sector and the low-income traditional sector are bound together in a relationship of dependency (Webb 1975a, 1975b; Fitzgerald 1976, 1979; Thorp and Bertram 1978). Adolfo Figueroa (1984:119–120), for example, argues against the view that Peru's problems can be traced to dual, or separate, economies; his study suggests instead that the economic sectors are well integrated, to the detriment of the traditional sector. He points to the unequal income distribution and the mechanisms that support it to account for poverty in the country.

Even so, several of these writers have expressed reservations about the conclusions drawn by dependency theorists. Citing data on income growth between 1950 and 1966, Webb (1975a:91–92) notes some positive trends in the standard of living across sectors; he takes particular exception to the application of the marginality concept to the urban traditional sector. Yet Webb himself notes that the data do not allow a comparison over time of the incomes of the poorest 10 to 20 percent of the urban population, including such occupation groups as street vendors, "and it could be maintained that their income has not risen" (ibid.: 92). The more recent trends in Peruvian political economy, especially since 1975, appear to be more consistent with the analysis of the dependency theorists. To Webb's formulation of the limits of reform, which does not include horizontal transfers from the modern to the traditional sector, we need to add an analysis of the ongoing transfer of surplus from the traditional to the modern sector. Without this contribution from the dependency or marginality analysts, who have clarified for us the mechanisms of political domination, Webb's argument loses force.

Other objections to the dependency view have been made. Fitzgerald (1976:97) argues against the position that military intervention represented a continuation of the hegemony of foreign and domestic capital. And Rosemary Thorp and Geoffrey Bertram state, "The picture in some dependency writing of 'marginalized' social groups waiting in the wings to provide political and economic backing for a new order could hardly be further from the truth" (1978: 327). However, Peru's history of peasant struggles and the recent opposition to government actions shown by participants in the traditional sector labor force make this less certain. Indeed, the current crises in Peru have resulted in more significant mobilization of the marginalized sectors of the country's periphery, as we will see.

The year 1975 was a turning point for the military regime in many respects. Writing of the crises that faced Velasco that year and forced his replacement by Morales, James Petras and A. Eugene Havens state: "The key socio-economic obstacle that emerged during the Velasco period centered around the incapacity of the state to satisfy the immediate interests of workers and, at the same time, pay for the development of productive forces within the framework of a national capitalist model. Unwilling to capture the profits and capital of the national private sector through nationalization, the regime sought foreign capital, as the only solution to the investment problem. In turning to foreign finance capital, however, the regime's commitment to national independent development began to disintegrate" (1979:30).

Velasco's inability to combine a populist base with state capitalism reached a crisis in 1975 when Peru's exporting capacity fell as a result of the overestimation of oil reserves, the disappearance of anchovies for fish meal, and the decline in copper prices. The replacement of Velasco by Morales signaled a return from reformism to a more orthodox capitalist economic program designed to overcome Peru's crisis (Pásara 1979). However, Morales's policies increased the country's international debt and deepened the economic depression, leading to mass popular opposition.

Strengthening ties with the center capitalist countries as a means to emerge from economic crisis has clearly worsened the situation. Peru's foreign debt had already increased from $1 billion to over $3 billion between 1971 and 1975. By 1976 Peru was completely in the hands of international banks, and the debt in 1977 and 1978 rose to approximately $8 billion. Moreover, servicing the debt accounted for between 35 and 50 percent of export earnings (Petras and Havens 1979:27).

Since 1977 the IMF has been the dominant lending agency in Peru, and it has imposed stringent demands for the management of Peru's economy as a condition for granting further loans to the country. Its first initiative for 1977 was to declare a Year of Austerity, calling on the government to drastically reduce public spending and decrease inflation, eliminate subsidies on gasoline and food items, and devalue the sol. In line with these measures, conditions have been made more favorable to foreign capital (Stallings 1978).

In human terms, the policies dictated by the IMF have had a serious effect. In contrast to the first phase of military government, when reforms made some absolute improvement in all sectors, after 1975 the standard of living was eroded at every level. Naturally, "austerity" hurt the working class and the traditional sector most. For wage laborers, real wages dropped 47 percent from 1973 to 1978, and as a result protein and calorie intakes fell well below the minimum set by the Food and Agriculture Organization. For the majority of the population in the traditional sector, who do not share in the benefits of stable employment, the situation was even worse (Petras and Havens 1979:34).

Food expenses to urban consumers became an explosive issue when cuts in subsidies on food imports and rising gasoline costs led to steadily rising prices. Still, prices for agricultural products were controlled while the prices of manufactured goods were allowed to increase greatly, and the unequal relationship of the modern and traditional sectors persisted.

In the late 1970s, opposition to the military's measures grew in response to the soaring cost of living and increasing political repression. On July 19, 1977, a general strike was successfully organized for the first time since 1919. Several more general strikes occurred after that one, with greater portions of the population becoming involved, including peasants as well as workers (Petras and Havens 1979:36).

With little support remaining for the military, in 1977 discussion turned to the restoration of power to a civilian government. The following year a constitutional assembly was elected, with nearly a third of the seats going to leftist parties—an overwhelming number, particularly since the 40 percent of the population that was suffering most from the economic crisis could not vote because of the literacy requirement.

However, by the time of the 1980 election, the United Left, or Izquierda Unida (IU), coalition was divided. The president who was unseated in 1968, Fernando Belaúnde Terry, was brought back to power. The return to a "free market" policy, applied to all but a few staple foods, meant little relief for the impoverished population. On the contrary, under the terms of the economic policy unveiled in January 1981 and in subsequent economic "packages," price rises and other measures were devastating.

General discontent in Peru has led to an increasing mobilization of the population since the mid-1970s. Strikes and other political protests of the late 1970s were organized by militant sectors of the working class. However, the peasants, the semiproletarianized, and even to some extent the impoverished urban petty bourgeoisie, despite their isolation and social orientation, were radicalized as well

(Quijano Obregón 1977 : 15). In Lima, support for the left has come primarily from the *barriadas,* or squatter settlements, where migrants and other marginalized city dwellers are concentrated (Petras and Havens 1979 : 37). In recent years, of course, Sendero Luminoso has mobilized an increasing number from the rural and urban sectors. Seemingly, whatever degree of satisfaction was attained by the marginal sectors as a result of Velasco's reforms has turned to growing anger over more recent policies.

Since 1975 the Peruvian government has proved itself willing to cooperate with Western nations in an effort to overcome its economic crisis. The resulting hardship endured by poor and working people, and their rising opposition, have shown that the military regime's attempts to play down class conflict and maintain political stability during that critical period failed. The civilian government of Belaúnde meant only worsening economic and political conditions as the national crisis deepened. It is still difficult to say what the civilian government of Alan García Pérez, of the APRA party, will mean for Peru's political economy. The results of the 1985 election demonstrated, at the very least, the strong dissatisfaction felt by the majority of Peruvians, who were willing to shift their support somewhat to the left. Yet halfway through García's term in office, most Peruvians have become highly critical of his inability to ameliorate conditions in the country. The views of Aníbal Quijano Obregón and other dependency writers, who stated during the early phases of the military government that the Peruvian "revolution" was a renegotiation of Peru's position in the world capitalist economy and that continued dependency would mean deeper problems for the marginalized social sectors, gain added force in light of recent developments.

The View from Huaraz

The national events of 1968–69, the military takeover by Velasco and the agrarian reform, were somewhat overshadowed in Huaraz by the 1970 earthquake, and yet all these events are intertwined in the minds of Huaracinos. As throughout Peru, the initial optimism in Huaraz over the early reforms introduced by Velasco was replaced by a growing awareness of the limits of those reforms and of the worsening conditions in most people's lives. Huaracinos are particularly critical of the way in which the government directed aid to their city after the earthquake and the slow pace of reconstruction. In the intervening years since 1970 and especially since the conservative turn in national government in 1975, the people of Huaraz have grown increasingly troubled and angry over what they see as the government's incompetence and lack of concern for Andean development. By 1977 almost no one I spoke to had kind words for the Morales regime, and many revealed a bitter assessment of the national situation.

The reform of the Velasco period that should have had the greatest effect in the Huaraz region, the agrarian reform, had direct benefits for only a small number of people now living in the area. Most Huaracinos look with favor on the dismantling of large landholdings (*latifundios*) in the Callejón de Huaylas, but only a few of the people I met in the city had worked on these landholdings or received portions of the land that was divided up. Instead, the numerous people who held small plots of land (*minifundios*) before the reform continue to work the same land.

Not far from Huaraz several agricultural cooperatives known as SAIS's (Agricultural Societies of Social Interest) were established in the 1970s to market their products in the Callejón. Members of these societies viewed themselves as the privileged recipients of reform benefits, though under the terms set by the government they must purchase their land, and this could take some years to accomplish. The president of a SAIS near Carhuaz, twenty-five miles from Huaraz, spoke to me about the advantages of production on the collectives. He compared workers' cooperation on the SAIS's to the situation of the independent *campesino* producers who received land after the reform but who have a low level of workers' consciousness and "do not work together to increase their productivity." He noted, however, that the government administrators carrying out the reform measures often made matters worse by failing to provide the technical assistance that small farmers need.

From the perspective of marketers in Huaraz, land reform ushered in new problems. Some adopt a higher-class urban sentiment and complain that, whereas *hacendados* used to produce enough to maintain the region through the marketing of their goods, the *campesino* owners now produce just to meet their own needs. Those who express this view, that "the *campesinos* don't want to produce," sometimes consider these small producers responsible for the difficult conditions encountered in the marketplace. The majority of marketers, however, trace the problem to the government, as we shall see.

In 1970 the earthquake presented a kind of testing ground for the government's commitment to the Peruvian people, especially to the poor highlanders, who were at this time experiencing extraordinary hardship.[10] When people describe the aftermath of the earthquake, they express suffering and a good deal of bitterness concerning their government's handling of the disaster. While they note with gratitude and pride the international assistance that was forthcoming as nations donated the materials and labor to build homes and health care centers, their own nation fell short of their expectations.

Relief in the form of temporary shelters, food, clothing, and medical assistance arrived in Huaraz but not in adequate supply for all the survivors of the disaster. Consequently, the distribution of aid became a highly charged issue. Many Huaracinos believe that the Red Cross, as the allocator of relief supplies, favored certain sectors, like the urban elite and those associated with the military and local government, while neglecting some of the neediest. Some marketers told me that the Red Cross itself grew rich as a result of hoarding supplies.

Huaracinos came to resent all the attention the city received when it was not accompanied by material aid. The entry of "experts" was rapid and included planners, social workers, health personnel, and missionaries. People grew accustomed to their presence and their surveys, though many found them irritating. Considerable annoyance was expressed regarding the government agencies that were established in the city to oversee the reconstruction (ORDEZA) and the social mobilization (SINAMOS) of the region.

The people of Huaraz disliked ORDEZA because they saw it as representative of the unsatisfactory way that redevelopment was proceeding; with ORDEZA in control of government spending for reconstruction, Huaracinos had little power when they protested that too much money was going into the bureaucracy of the organization and too little into the city itself. Yet SINAMOS was considered the more odious of the two agencies, for its purpose was perceived to have more to do with demobilization than with its alleged function of "mobilization." The offices of SINAMOS were viewed as a repressive arm of the national government that promoted national policy through propaganda campaigns and other efforts to weaken class consciousness and political opposition. Elena's husband, Renato, for example, was particularly vocal in his anger about the way SINAMOS acted as an instrument of control, dividing workers and weakening unions.

It was felt that ORDEZA and SINAMOS represented a drain on the Huaraz economy in several ways. First, as mentioned, it was believed that employees in the bureaucracy received the principal portion of monies destined for the city. Second, it was pointed out that these employees, who were among the small number of people with regular salaries in Huaraz, were generally recruited from the coast.

This meant that the agencies were not providing as many jobs to the local population as they might have. Furthermore, employees from outside Huaraz often returned to their families on weekends and did not contribute to the local economy by spending their earnings in the city. When we add to all this the condescending attitude of the bureaucratic elite toward the local people, it is not surprising that neither government employees nor the organizations they represented were well liked in Huaraz.

Huaracinos have much to say about the economic situation in Peru. Like most Peruvians, they have experienced serious difficulties since the nation's economic problems reached crisis proportions and the Year of Austerity was declared in 1977. The conditions that affect them affect the nation but are felt most acutely by the impoverished sectors: low wages and other earnings, rising prices and taxes, and the high level of unemployment. The views of working people and the poor in Huaraz regarding the situation in 1977 are best revealed in their own words. When asked for their opinions, and often without being asked, many offered critical assessments. A marketwoman stated:

> The cost of living is the worst. It's very bad. The rich alone have everything, while we poor people don't have anything. With the prices of rice, sugar, . . . our earnings don't stretch to pay for them. We sell little, and the prices go up more. How can we pay with the prices going up? How can we support our children? I have faith in God and God has always protected me, blessed me, aided me. If I had an education, I would go to the president to say these things as I am saying them to you. But he wouldn't receive me. He would say I'm an Indian, a *chola*, that I don't have decent clothes. But I'm not afraid, I would go. People here too [in Huaraz] treat us as Indians, *cholas*, because we don't know how to read or write. But it doesn't matter. I'm going to continue selling to support my children.

The following was offered by the husband of a marketer: "We're trapped. We work just to survive. . . . The situation is very bad. The military is taking advantage, and we're getting squeezed. It's difficult to move ahead. [What should be done?] Naturally, a structural change—it would have to be an abrupt change. The present government is just killing people. The higher classes are those that count. There is going to be a reaction from the people."

The combination of a sense of potential power and a recognition of relative powerlessness revealed in the above comments characterizes the statements of many others in Huaraz. One woman said, "The government of Pancho [Morales] is strangling us. How can things change? When we rise up, we can't defend ourselves. Like tiny birds, or chicks, we expire rapidly. We can't defend ourselves. The government would have arms but we don't have them. We must await death." Others expressed the belief that successful struggles could be waged elsewhere—in other countries or other parts of Peru—but not in Huaraz. One man (who had lived and worked in Ecuador for eight months) argued that in other places people are united but in Peru they are not, since the military represses any strike or act of resistance. A woman maintained that a struggle could be initiated in Puno (in southern Peru, where there had been reports of an uprising) but not in Huaraz.

Sometimes the elderly, especially those monolingual in Quechua, expressed particular concern about the situation. Several women described their fears as they stood in the long line of people waiting to pay the annual property taxes in Huaraz (Declaración Jurada). One, an occasional seller, explained the hardship of paying taxes when one is poor and needs to hire a bilingual assistant to fill out forms. This woman showed deep despair at not being able to do this without falling into debt. She wept as she said that she had heard the government was going to kill old people because they are worthless. Another marketwoman spoke of the poverty of her family and said that if she were a man she would turn to robbery. A poor woman, she said, cannot get along.

Most people I spoke to in Huaraz criticized the government of Morales for the country's economic problems, and many said they looked forward to the promised civilian elections. As one woman said grimly: "The government does nothing for us, the poor. If it is a 'revolutionary' government, they should treat everyone the same." She spoke hopefully of a change of leadership. Others, however, showed a sophisticated understanding that the problems go deeper than any single administration. When a rumor circulated for a few days that Morales had resigned, some people expressed optimism, but others said a new government could be the same or even worse. The need for revolutionary change was suggested often, by women as much as men. Several people traced Peru's problems to the national debt. One marketwoman noted the link between rising prices and the debt to foreign bankers. She said that the government had no choice under the circumstances and that, even with a new government, the situation would be the same as long as the country is kept in debt. Another woman commented that Peru's relationship to the

United States is one of dependency based on the national debt and that more than a change of presidents would be necessary to improve the situation.

Indeed, my return visits during Belaúnde's administration in 1982 and 1984 and García's government in 1987 revealed even deeper dissatisfaction as the cost of living rose sharply and as more people entered petty commerce to earn ever more meager incomes. Some even looked back on the period of the 1970s as a time when things were not so difficult, when families ate better and could afford health care, and when children could pursue their education in the hope of achieving more than their parents.

The views presented here are not unusual among Huaracinos. I have quoted some of the more articulate people whom I interviewed, but many others offered similar comments about the political-economic situation in Peru. Issues of current importance are discussed frequently and publicly, and the marketplace is a common arena for discussion. The uneducated as well as those with a few years of schooling quickly learn of developments through the radio and by word of mouth—the latter often the only way of learning about political unrest—and form their own opinions.

Three   **Marketwomen and Theory**

A STUDY OF marketwomen in a provincial Andean city may at first glance appear narrowly focused. Yet the lives and work of these women offer a rich source of material relating to a number of current problems in theory and research. Indeed, the difficulty of providing a theoretical framework for this book is that the research lends itself to several contending frames of reference. First, this book is an examination of Latin American women who are experiencing the human consequences of underdevelopment. But it is also a study of urban workers in what is called the informal sector, so rapidly expanding in Third World cities. Moreover, it is a study of a population constrained by national and international political economies but seeking to achieve a better living for itself.

The book is organized around several related problems. It brings together an analysis of the microlevel work and social relations of marketwomen and the macrolevel political-economic conditions that shape these women's lives. Throughout, an examination of the nature of marketwomen's work remains at the center of my investigation. Like some other writers concerned with examining the condition of working women relative to development and underdevelopment in the Third World, I find the recent theoretical discussion of production and reproduction to be useful. Feminists have suggested that across societies we find a sexual division of labor whereby men engage in production, and women, whether or not they work outside the domestic unit, carry out reproductive activities. These activities range from biological reproduction of the family to social reproduction of the labor force and of the larger society. Marketwomen are uniquely situated, with their market work and domestic activities closely integrated, and one can argue that both forms of work are fundamentally reproductive in nature.

Women's marketing does resemble work performed in the household and so is reproductive in character. This commercial activity is also productive in the Marxist sense insofar as it adds to the value of goods sold. The feminist discourse on the reproductive aspect of women's work and the Marxist discussion of what constitutes productive labor have generally remained separate. Rather than alternative theoretical frameworks, however, they may be viewed as complementary to a broader analysis. In this book, the insights of both feminism and Marxism will be brought to bear on the question of how to conceptualize marketwomen and their work in Peru.

My study departs from most research on marketing in arguing that, while marketers have an obvious role in distribution, they have a less obvious though no less significant productive role as well. Raising the question of marketwomen's position as productive workers requires that we locate these women within the context of the entire production system. Viewed in that context, marketers may be understood to extend the productive process, which is begun in other hands. That they are more usefully regarded as petty commodity producers and sellers than as petty entrepreneurs becomes clear as we examine their place in interlinking modes of production in the Andean social formation.

However, our investigation of the organization of work and the social relations of production among producers, wholesalers, and retailers raises new questions. We will see that, while some marketers may operate as independent petty commodity traders, others are subordinated to larger interests at the point of production or at the point of exchange with wholesalers. Marketers who deal in manufactured items from coastal firms have little control over the terms of trade and often work as dependent commission sellers. And those who purchase goods from large wholesalers in the region may find themselves virtual wage slaves, though the wage form is disguised as credit. This complex situation requires that we consider to what degree marketers are proletarianized workers and whether this is a growing phenomenon.

More detailed discussion of the productive and reproductive aspects of marketwomen's work and of their proletarianization will await later chapters. Here we will examine some new directions in market studies and in Peruvian studies and note the contribution of the present study.

Since anthropologists began to take an interest in Third World marketplaces a few decades ago, research has followed the currents of thought in economic anthropology. Beginning in the 1950s, the influence of the formalist school emerged, as concepts from classical economic theory were applied to peasant and small-scale marketers

(Tax 1953; Katzin 1959, 1960; Dewey 1962; Belshaw 1965; Davis 1973; Beals 1975). This work raised such issues as the rationality of marketers' decision making, the determination of prices, and the maximization of economic satisfaction. At least one early writer (Mintz 1955, 1956, 1959) was not constrained by the prevailing ideas in economic anthropology, but in general the pioneering market studies sought to demonstrate that throughout human societies the economy could be investigated with the same tools Western economists use to study advanced capitalist societies.

Nevertheless, the economic historian Karl E. Polanyi's (1957) challenge to formalist thinking led to the development of an alternative, substantivist approach to studying markets cross-culturally (Bohannan and Dalton 1962). Recognizing the qualitative differences among market and marketless economies, the substantivists devised typologies whereby classical economic theory would be applicable only to those societies in which the market principle was present. For nonmarket societies and societies with peripheral markets, where other forms of economic integration held sway, new formulations of the processes of reciprocity and redistribution needed to be advanced.

Marxist writers (e.g., Dupré and Rey 1973) have been critical of both the formalist and substantivist schools, suggesting that there is actually little difference between them. The typologies of the substantivists reveal an assumption that the intrusion of the market principle is inevitable as the highest economic stage and that this results automatically in the decline of "traditional" marketplaces. They are, therefore, unable to account for the persistence of small-scale marketing in dependent capitalist societies, and when their attention is turned to the phenomenon, they rely—as do the formalists—on classical economic analysis. Most substantivists, then, do not really challenge the underlying beliefs of the formalists but simply restrict their own use of formal theory to those societies they judge to be integrated in market economies.

New Directions in Market Studies

Today, economic anthropology and market studies may be less polemical (e.g., Plattner 1985), yet differing theoretical tendencies remain apparent. The most promising approaches are now coming from some recent work that takes a more critical view of the liberal economic analysis employed by most anthropologists and other social scientists. In this work, significant advances have been made in several areas, including research that places marketing in the context of the entire production process, work that views Third World marketers as marginalized workers in the expanding informal sector of underdeveloped economies, studies that go beyond the local level to analyze the articulation of local markets with the regional or national level economy, and, finally, research that explores women's participation in marketing, furthering our understanding of why women so often market in Third World countries and of how their marketing experience and social position are related.

Marketing and the Production Process

To the extent that marketing has received attention, its economic function generally has been viewed within the sphere of distribution. Problematic to this is the failure to see as a unified process the production of goods for exchange, their passage from producer to marketer, and the realization of the exchange value of these goods as they pass from marketer to consumer. Only by understanding this as a total process is the marketer's livelihood seen to depend fundamentally upon the production of goods and is marketing seen as the final step in the process that realizes the goods' value. Without such an analysis, most research has attributed marketers' subsistence to their ability to maximize profits, taking for granted the goods they have for sale; that is, value is mistakenly viewed as originating in the exchange process based on price determination, rather than in the labor process.

The importance of taking production as the starting point in the integrated process linking production to distribution, exchange, and consumption was set forth by Marx ([1859] 1970:193–194), who pointed to the superficiality of trying to study distribution apart from the entire process (ibid.: 201–202). Research on exchange systems, according to the Marxist view, must be placed in the context of the modes of production in which they are found (e.g., Dupré and Rey 1973; Cook and Diskin 1976b).

In the recent scholarship on marketing, Scott Cook's (1976a) work stands out in its insistence upon analyzing the whole production process. Cook shows the influence of Marx when he writes, "As an intermediate phase in the economic process, marketing depends upon production to generate and sustain it, just as it, in turn, facilitates and sustains utilization" (ibid.: 139). Cook's research on peasant artisans of Oaxaca, producers and sellers of *metates* (stones for grinding maize and other grains), necessarily examined the production of *metates* as the starting point and viewed the marketplace as a sort of way station in the flow of products. In the marketplace, however, traders played an essential role as finishers of *metates*.

Cook (ibid.: 157–160) again follows Marx in distinguishing between producers, whose objective in selling their products is to obtain needed goods and services, and marketers, whose objective is to
convert a quantity of money into a larger quantity of money through
the mediation of the goods and services they sell. This distinction,
while theoretically straightforward, is in practice complex, since the
roles of producers and sellers so often overlap. Thus, sellers add
value to *metates* by acting as finishers, extending the production
phase into the marketplace. Furthermore, Cook notes that the primary objective of marketers is to provide for their families, not to
expand their businesses—casting doubt on the image of marketers
as petty entrepreneurs.

Here we may note the importance not only of situating marketing in the production process but also of recognizing the productive component in the work of marketers. That is, while marketers
may work primarily in a distributive capacity, their role generally
contains a processing or, I would say, productive component. Sometimes this is plainly evident, as where producer-sellers are concerned
(e.g., Cook 1976a; Littlefield 1979; Chiñas 1975; Gerry 1978). Other
times, marketers are mainly involved in locating, buying, transporting, and reselling goods, and then, too, it may be argued that this is
socially necessary, or productive, work (Mandel 1970:191–192).
Most often, certainly, marketers' work is a complex combination of
activities, many of which add value to what is sold.

Several researchers have borrowed from Marx the concept of
simple commodity production and circulation to describe Third
World market economies located within dominant capitalist modes
of production (Cook and Diskin 1976b; Gerry 1978; Barker and Smith
1986). As formulated by Marx ([1867] 1967:761–762), the simple
commodity, or petty, mode of production is a transitional stage characterized by an incomplete separation of labor from the means of production. Yet, as a result of distorted development in Third World
countries today, small-scale producers and traders are not disappearing but proliferating, integrated in but subordinate to capitalist production. That they are increasing in number may be due in part not
only to their own initiative but also to the benefits they offer the
dominant capitalist mode through their self-employment and the
low-cost goods and services they provide.

While they may benefit capitalism, small-scale producers and traders themselves rarely manage to accumulate capital (e.g., Bromley
1978b; Forman and Riegelhaupt 1970; Moser 1980). Those favoring
the petty commodity production analysis have emphasized the difficulty that petty producers and sellers have in maintaining their

present conditions and the unlikelihood of their evolving into entrepreneurs, that is, of their being able "to harness the production process to and evolve relations of production commensurate with the
accumulation of capital, rather than reproducing the same amount of
capital with unchanging objective conditions of production" (Gerry
1978 : 1154−1155). Despite some potential problems in extending the
petty commodity production concept to marketers, who are traditionally regarded as nonproducers, this analysis has the decided advantage of bringing market studies out of the limited discussion of
exchange and entrepreneurship and into the broader discourse on
modes of production in society.[1]

Marginalization and the Informal Sector

While most market studies to date have focused on "peasant" societies in rural areas of the Third World, a growing number of researchers are examining the situation of urban marketers and street
vendors as an increasing population in the cities of underdeveloped
countries. In contrast to earlier work that viewed marketers as the
survivors of dying traditional cultures (e.g., Bohannan and Dalton
1962), more recent writers have noted that, rather than diminishing
with capitalist expansion, this group is swelling in size. This may be
explained by reference to the specific forms that capitalist development has taken in the Third World.

Dependency theorists (e.g., Frank 1969) have argued that to regard
changes occurring in most Third World countries as development
at all is a mistake; historically, colonialism and imperialism initiated a process of underdevelopment, or distorted development, of
the world's majority while benefiting the minority in the Western
countries. Consequently, to expect the economies of underdeveloped
countries to follow the pattern of growth of the dominant capitalist
nations is a mistake. Instead of absorbing an ever-larger number
of workers in the industrial labor force, the capital-intensive sector
is only able to accommodate a limited portion of the population.
More people who are attracted to urban areas because of the impoverishment of their rural homes or the hope of a better livelihood
in the city find their only alternative is to enter such marginal occupations as domestic service and marketing (Amin 1976; Quijano
Obregón 1974).

Since the view of marketers as participants in an expanding informal sector rests on an analysis of dependency and marginalization,
we may note that considerable debate surrounds this perspective.
Criticism has come from Marxists as well as non-Marxists. Some

Marxists have questioned whether the dependency model's emphasis on circulation in the world capitalist system can be usefully combined with an analysis of modes of production to yield a better understanding of class relations (e.g., Harding and Bray 1976; Oxaal, Barnett, and Booth 1975). These critics of dependency theory have demonstrated the limitations of any view that does not take into account the concepts of social class and mode of production. Class analysis and dependency analysis are by no means mutually exclusive, however, and the most useful approach links class analysis of production and distribution to a historical understanding of dependency relations.

A problem arises, however, when the concepts of marginality and dependency are taken out of the context in which they were formulated and applied in an ahistorical, static way. Analyses that use the concept of marginality to distinguish between the "modern" and "traditional" sectors of Third World cities may succeed only in updating the dual society theory whose shortcomings were discussed in the last chapter. Recent discussions of the formal and informal sectors have suffered from the same tendency. Those researching the informal sector of petty production and commerce (which is characterized by easy entry, high participation by the indigenous population, and low earnings) have often emphasized the divergence of this sector from the dominant capitalist sector without examining the interlinkages.

Some non-Marxist critics of the dependency and marginalization frameworks (e.g., Peattie 1975; Perlman 1976) have also pointed to the danger in viewing the poor in underdeveloped countries as a group apart from, and not integrated with, the dominant social sectors. Such a view leads to the mistaken conception of traditional, or backward, sectors existing independently of the modern society. The historical reasons for the poverty of marginal groups are thus masked, and the present exploitation that occurs as a consequence of their integration in society is ignored. Nevertheless, the degree to which some individuals achieve personal success and contribute to economic growth through participating in the informal sector in underdeveloped countries may be hidden in an analysis that views these individuals as helpless victims of the dominant capitalist system.

Non-Marxists have raised these issues in disagreement with the marginalization thesis, but the same problems are discussed by writers who are more sympathetic to such an analysis (Bromley 1978*a*, 1978*b*; Gerry 1978). Such writers oppose the concept of marginality as it is limited to a static description of "excluded" social groups.

The dynamic concept of marginalization can be far more powerful when it makes the "crucial connection between the life-situations of these urban workers and the *mechanisms* (necessarily linked to the ongoing process of capitalist accumulation) through which they are exploited, partially proletarianized, impoverished and, if you will, *marginalized*" (Gerry 1978 : 1148).

Similarly, in spite of some basic problems with the dualistic usage of the informal-formal classification of economic activities, a significant contribution has been made by those using the model to examine little-known economic activities and social groups (Bromley 1978a). Furthermore, a more precise and meaningful description of the informal sector allows for a systematic investigation of the interlinkages with the dominant economic sector. However, some critics of the dualistic approach to the informal sector, which is based on the assumption that "a reformed capitalism is capable of spreading 'development' to the contemporary underdeveloped world" (Gerry 1978 : 1147), have turned instead to the concept of petty commodity production.

Without an understanding of marginalization, we might conclude that the increasing numbers of people entering the impoverished informal sector in so many Third World cities are simply small-scale and unsuccessful entrepreneurs. However, when we recognize the unique features of dependent capitalist "growth" that result in a condition of structural inequality between the petty commodity and capitalist modes, we are not surprised to discover little capital accumulation in the expanding informal sector (Quijano Obregón 1974). The point to be made is that external, structural constraints (access to resources, exploitation by large-scale enterprises) are generally more significant than internal, individual ones (entrepreneurship) in accounting for the lack of growth of small-scale enterprises. Even so, under certain conditions individuals may seize opportunities for expansion. Within an overall picture of hardship and struggling survival experienced by the majority in the informal sector, we find economic differentiation allowing a few individuals to achieve success (Peattie 1975; Moser 1977, 1980; Schmitz 1982).

Marketing and the Regional and National Levels of Analysis

Over a decade ago, several authors remarked on a welcome development in market studies, noting "a potentially fruitful shift of emphasis from particularistic and static description to the relationships of marketplaces and internal market systems to wider economic and political fields of action" (Mott, Silin, and Mintz 1975 : 6).

In order to integrate an analysis of production systems with an analysis of expanding economic sectors, research must indeed go beyond the limits of the local marketplace. A number of market studies, though still a minority, have broadened their scope from single markets to marketing systems at the regional level.

Geographers concerned with market formation and periodicity at the regional level (e.g., Bromley 1975) have often had a leading role in this development. Anthropologists (e.g., Smith 1977; Appleby 1976*a*, 1976*b*) have borrowed some of the models of geographers, including central place theory and the dendritic model, to examine market distribution at the regional level. However, these anthropologists have found it necessary to go beyond the models to comprehend the constraints on marketing systems as economic systems. They consider such issues as rural-urban relations, the role of urban food needs in the formation of markets, and the ways marketing systems of allocation constrain the organization of production. One advocate of regional analysis has proposed to replace the dependency and modernization models with a new one, which he calls the "sectorial model" (Orlove 1977), to examine the diversified economy of production and exchange in southern Peru.

In some cases, raising the level of analysis of marketing to regional networks is of primary theoretical importance. By examining regional marketplaces at different levels of socioeconomic integration, such research has shown that, contrary to the thesis of Paul J. Bohannan and George Dalton, the maintenance of traditional markets is sometimes the result of a closer integration of peasants into the national economy (Ortiz 1967; Forman and Riegelhaupt 1970).

The need to extend from the local level to the regional and national levels is made particularly clear in the extensive studies of peasant marketing in Oaxaca, Mexico (Beals 1975; Cook and Diskin 1976*b*). The substantial effects of capitalist penetration on local-level economies can only be understood within the terms of the national economy and problems of underdevelopment. Scott Cook and Martin Diskin (1976*a*: 275) write:

> It is clear to us, in conclusion, that we must combine a macroscopic (metropolis-down) view of the Valley of Oaxaca economy with a microscopic (village-up) view if we are to avoid distorting the real nature of its evolution and present structure. Obviously this regional Mexican economy is not experiencing a smooth, normal, autochthonous transition from petty commodity production to the capitalist mode of production. Rather, its evolution and structure have been partially skewed to meet the demands of increased develop-

ment and prosperity in the metropolitan capitalist economy, and its future course is inextricably linked to the developmental fortunes of the latter.

Regional and national analyses have made a significant contribution to our understanding of the place of marketers within the broader socioeconomic setting. Sometimes, however, these analyses have tended to lose sight of the human beings at the local level whose lives are under study. A balance to the regional analysis is offered by the approach that examines the convergence of groups from different social sectors to the local-level marketplace. Three decades ago, Sidney Mintz (1959) described marketplaces as centers of social articulation, and since then others have taken up issues concerning conflicts and cooperation among sellers from different social strata (Arizpe 1975; Swetnam 1978). Ethnic and class differences have been investigated to discover how broad social-structural features are reflected in the social relations of the local marketplace. A number of studies have suggested that, despite rural-urban cultural or ethnic differences, the fundamental issue is a socioeconomic one of marketers' class position within the national society.

Several writers stand out for their attention to close, detailed analysis of the work process and social organization of marketing at the same time they take a broad view of the class position and economic role of marketers in the wider society. Only those with such a unified approach can grapple with some of the most difficult issues regarding the changing condition of marketers. For example, Caroline Moser (1978), Chris Gerry (1979), and Alison Scott (1979) all consider whether, given that the number of workers in petty production and commerce is expanding rather than diminishing in dependent capitalist countries, proletarianization may be occurring. Their research reveals the heterogeneity of workers in small-scale enterprises and the varying degrees of autonomy they have over the labor process. Evidence suggests that a large number of these "self-employed" workers in Third World cities are actually commission sellers, outworkers, and the like, subordinated to larger firms.

My emphasis on the importance of linking broad-scale analyses of marketing to further local-level research comes at a time when studies of regional marketing are hailed as the critical field for future research. I take this position for several reasons. First, the concepts and modes of analysis we have for understanding petty commerce at the local level are far from precise. Moreover, most studies have failed to come to terms with the principal participation of women as marketers. This is a substantial problem in the main body of literature on marketing, and it can only be remedied by examining closely the role of women marketers in particular areas and then considering their articulation with the wider society.

Women and Marketing

In her pioneering work on women and development, Ester Boserup noted that "in no other field do ideas about the proper role of women contrast more vividly than in the case of market trade" (1970:87). Yet, despite the diversity of women's participation in marketing throughout the Third World, most writing on marketing pays no special attention to women's role. Social science research as a whole has given little attention to women's social and economic lives, as recent critiques (e.g., Nash 1980) have pointed out and challenged. What is surprising in the case of market studies, however, is that, while it is frequently acknowledged that in many markets women outnumber men, the reasons for this and the consequences it has for women are rarely examined. Marketing is unusual in the prominent role women have traditionally played and continue to play in employment outside the household, and understanding the conditions behind their participation precisely as women is critical.

Some studies that do not set out to investigate marketing specifically in terms of women's role do give attention to the relative participation of men and women, the sexual division of labor in the marketplace, and so on (e.g., Forman and Riegelhaupt 1970; Oliver-Smith 1974; Mayer 1974b; Weldon and Morse 1970; Hartmann 1971). And some rich ethnographic descriptions of the lives and work of individual marketers have occasionally focused on women traders (e.g., Katzin 1959; Jellinek 1977). Here, however, discussion is restricted to research that places marketwomen at the center of study.

Several classics in the small field of studies on women marketers have sought to examine the women's work within the broader framework of their lives in and out of the home. This is a particularly useful framework for considering the productive and reproductive aspects of marketwomen's work, as these are integrated in their daily lives. Marketing is unique in allowing large numbers of women the flexibility to fulfill domestic responsibilities while participating actively in the market economy. Indeed, in some areas marketing is regarded as an extension of women's work in the home. Exactly how women manage to coordinate market work with gardening, fetching water, preparing meals, caring for children, and other domestic tasks varies widely across societies.

Studies from Mesoamerica and West Africa, two areas of the world where women have the reputation of being fiercely independent traders, have considered the interlinkage of women's marketing and family roles. Both Beverly Chiñas (1973, 1975, 1976) and Niara Sudarkasa (1973) find that nearly all the women they studied trade at some time in their lives and that this activity resembles their work at home in many ways; thus, marketing is seen as an extension of their household roles. However, while Chiñas suggests that marketing is considered secondary to housework and child care among Zapotec women, Sudarkasa shows how homelife is accommodated to Yoruba women's trading. Still, the two studies are similar in revealing certain familial constraints on trade, principally a woman's age and the ages of her children.

The concern to examine women's work in production and reproduction can be located within the broader feminist approach to analyzing the sexual division of labor cross-culturally. Chiñas presents a more traditional functionalist perspective, noting that in Zapotec tradition men are the producers (agriculturalists) and women are the processors and sellers. Since farming is not adequate to support a family, households are diversified, and marketing is women's contribution to family income. In contrast, Sudarkasa offers a historical explanation for the division of labor whereby Yoruba women trade and men farm, relating it to settlement patterns and the dangers of the nineteenth-century civil war period. Neither author's approach, however, is entirely successful in going beyond description to provide an analysis of women's market and domestic work that has cross-cultural applicability.

The recent scholarship on women has shown that, even in areas where women are central participants in economic life, they may experience secondary sexual status. Despite the high degree of autonomy of these marketwomen in Mexico and Nigeria, both authors suggest a degree of sexual inequality; Chiñas maintains that while Zapotec women control the commercial sphere men control the political sphere, and Sudarkasa concludes that in Yoruba family life men have greater authority.

Several other studies of marketwomen have examined the interface of trading with women's traditional position in society (e.g., Durant-Gonzalez 1985; Lessinger 1986). While the research mentioned above concerned women who are regarded as relatively powerful in the family and society, even fully secluded Muslim women have played a significant role as traders. Polly Hill's (1969) research on "hidden trade," or women's house trade, in Hausaland is revealing, especially in view of how little we know even of women's public marketing in most areas. As the primary distribution mechanism in the area studied, hidden trade gave secluded women traders considerable control over setting prices, making loans, and so on, adding up to a surprising degree of economic independence.

In peasant societies in which men farm and women trade, women play key roles in linking the subsistence sector to the commercial economy (Mintz 1971). However, "Westernization" is often a disruptive force for change in the traditional division of labor and women's status cross-culturally. Women's internal marketing may be expanding in some areas, but in other areas it is in decline at the same time that marketing for export increases in the hands of men. Even when women continue to market, they often lose social status and economic standing as long as they remain in the internal marketing system and men come to dominate the external trade.

Marketwomen have been recognized not only for their traditional economic independence but also for their political sophistication. Two studies from West Africa consider collective action by marketwomen, in one case unsuccessful and in the other case more successful. Barbara Lewis (1976) found that the intense competition between urban Ivory Coast women from the north and the south of the country prevented them from successfully organizing associations to promote saving and collective buying. She concludes that the forces limiting women's organization were individualism, unequal access to resources, and ethnic differences. Judith Van Allen (1976), in contrast, considers the 1929 "women's war" of Igbo marketwomen in Nigeria. Although they ultimately lost to the British, tens of thousands of women unified to oppose European control of the market economy when they were threatened by rumors that the British planned to tax women. The women's market network enabled them to organize quickly in the market squares and gave them a base of support. To understand why strong market organizations form under some conditions and not others, we will need more studies of marketwomen's active roles.

Few studies of marketwomen have explored the consequences of women's marginalization in the informal sector in Third World countries. Boserup (1970) began to when she noted the domination of men in the modern, or formal, sector of developing countries in which women remained entrenched in the traditional, or informal, sector. While she described the proliferation of women in the services and commerce in cities and towns, she left it to other analysts to dig deeper into the phenomenon.

More researchers are now doing so, using the framework of dependent capitalism and underdevelopment to assess the situation of women in the urban Third World (Arizpe 1975, 1977; Chaney 1976; Chinchilla 1977; Schmink 1977; Safa 1977; Vasques de Miranda

1977; Buechler 1972, 1976a, 1976b; Hansen 1980; Robertson 1984; Rakowski 1987). Their work reveals the widening sexual division of labor as men enter the industrial labor force and women find employment opportunities limited to the services and commerce.[2] As poor and working-class women are increasingly marginalized in dependent capitalist economies, there is little expectation that their involvement in the urban informal sector will result in improved conditions—notwithstanding their valiant efforts to use the system to their best advantage.

Research to date has demonstrated the need to unite Marxism's attention to class and feminism's attention to gender if we are to comprehend the situation of women in the impoverished informal sector. The double exploitation of these women, as marginalized workers and as women, must be taken as basic to further analysis. To carry out this task will be a challenge for future research, for it requires the further development of a theoretical framework (locating petty commodity production and distribution within Third World economies) and the conceptualization of women within this framework. This study is one effort in that direction.

Related Research on Peru

Marketing

At the time of the Spanish conquest, the Andean region, like Mesoamerica, was the location of a highly developed state society.[3] Market activity was recorded by *conquistadores* and early historians, but the role of marketing before and after Spanish contact is the subject of some disagreement among ethnohistorians. While substantivist-oriented writers minimize the importance of market trade, emphasizing instead reciprocity and redistribution, formalists argue that the early markets were full-fledged centers of commerce. John V. Murra (1975) set forth the well-known concept of the "vertical archipelago" to describe the reciprocal exchange carried out by highland communities that controlled various ecological zones in the Andes during the time of the Inca empire. And Enrique Mayer (1974a) added to this a discussion of redistribution carried out by the Inca state. María Rostworowski (1977), in contrast, found market exchange to be quite important among coastal cultures, though diminishing at the height of Inca rule.

Although the debate over the place of marketing in the Inca empire is not closed, certain features of commerce at the time of contact are fairly clear. A number of chroniclers point out the large size of the gatherings that assembled to exchange small quantities of goods (Mayer 1974*a*). In this commercial activity women were prominent, bartering in the plazas (ibid.: 28–29) and controlling intercommunity trade (Silverblatt 1978:43). Indeed, from the earliest time for which there is evidence of commerce through the present day, women have held a long tradition of marketing.

Evidence indicates that commercial activity in the Andes expanded during the colonial period. In many areas this must have meant the continuation of traditional barter, but elsewhere the Iberian influence resulted in regulations to control markets (Bromley 1974:8–9). A letter written by the noble Peruvian Huamán Poma (1978:164–166) to the Spanish Court at the turn of the seventeenth century describes the abuses of royal administrators who set official food prices favorable to themselves. These colonialists bought goods from Indians at low prices to resell at high prices, retaining the difference as a sort of tax. At the same time, these officials charged dearly for the hiring of pack animals and for household provisions to Indians. These unequal exchanges between dominant and subordinate groups in colonial Peru have persisted in the contemporary period.

For the colonial period through modern times, little has been written about marketing in the Peruvian Andes.[4] During the present century, writers, often geographers or ethnologists, have occasionally addressed the marketing system in Peru. Generally, they have provided colorful reports of peasant markets but have not attempted in-depth research (Wrigley 1919; White 1951; Grollig 1964), though there are exceptions such as Gregory J. Scott's (1985) systematic study of potato marketing in central Peru. Most note the active role of women in the markets, but several regard marketplace commerce as a thing of the past, in steady decline. However, Luis E. Valcárcel (1947:477) asserts that based on his brief study marketing has not declined since pre-Columbian times. The disagreement as to whether Peruvian marketing has declined may be due in part to the different times and places in which observations have been made; however, an underlying assumption that with "modernization" the traditional market system is becoming outmoded has surely biased some writers.[5] For more recent observers in Peru, as we will see, it is clear that petty marketing is increasing.

Much of the recent literature on Andean society has dealt with reciprocity as a contemporary form of exchange that has endured since pre-Hispanic times (Alberti and Mayer 1974). The relation of traditional barter, in which goods are exchanged directly for other goods for consumption, to modern market trade is discussed by a number of writers (Esteva Fabregat 1970; Mayer 1974*b*; Concha

Contreras 1975; Casaverde 1977; Flores Ochoa 1977). In areas of Peru where barter has endured and where the market is peripheral to peasant communities, market prices have nonetheless had an effect on customary exchange. The pressure of the national market economy has meant that barter exchange rates have tended to conform to market prices. Local traders have sometimes bowed to the pressure by accepting both goods and cash in partial payment. In some areas younger women marketers sell for cash while older women continue to barter. Whether selling for cash or in kind, the women appear to be seeking a measure of security for their families rather than acquiring wealth. Throughout the Andes, gradual capitalist penetration has had contradictory effects on noncapitalist systems of exchange; where peasants and pastoralists contribute to capital accumulation, systems of reciprocity may persist, while in other regions traditional economies are experiencing dissolution as capitalism intrudes (Lehmann 1982).

In the Callejón de Huaylas, site of the present study, petty traders and merchants have played a significant role in linking rural communities to the wider market economy (Barkin 1961; Stein 1961; Weldon and Morse 1970; Oliver-Smith 1974). Typically, residents of rural communities travel weekly to participate in marketing in nearby towns, while residents of larger towns benefit from daily markets where they may make their livelihood. The work of Anthony R. Oliver-Smith in the community of Yungay examines the post-1970 changes that occurred as a result of Peru's tragic earthquake and the political transition then occurring. In Yungay, as in Huaraz, the modernization of the marketplace and of marketing, which came about with the towns' reconstruction and with the economic intervention of the military government, did not mean better conditions for marketers. Increasing dependence on the market economy and a growing number of marketers during the economic crisis of the 1970s in Peru meant marginalization and poverty for the majority.

The Urban Informal Sector

With the military government's (1968–80) emphasis on capital-intensive industrial growth came a corresponding lack of concern for providing employment opportunities in the expanding cities. Since the transfer of power to Morales's regime in 1975, which ushered in a period of deeper troubles—deeper still with the return of civilian government in 1980—an increasing number of people have been driven into the impoverished petty commodity sector. While these may often be highly motivated individuals, collectively they are rarely able to improve their condition. Furthermore, with the soaring cost of living in Peru, they have not even benefited from the government's modest raises in wage levels since most are self-employed or not protected by official legislation.

The urban informal sector, also called the urban traditional sector (Webb 1975a), in which petty production and commerce thrive, has received scholarly attention in the nation's capital and largest city, Lima, and the large commercial center in the sierra, Huancayo, and its environs. Both are growing urban areas with strategic roles in the nation's economy. Growth in both Lima (Doughty 1976) and Huancayo (Roberts n.d.) is largely the result of migration. While Lima attracts the most Andean migrants—now estimated to make up half of the city's population of eight million—Huancayo has also attracted migrants from the region because of the economic opportunities available there.

The experience of the urban poor, especially migrants, is a difficult one. Aside from settlement problems, becoming integrated in the work force as wage laborers and self-employed may require the greatest resourcefulness (Lloyd 1980; Lobo 1982).[6] The majority who fill the ranks of the "self-employed" for lack of opportunities in the formal sector of wage work frequently meet new problems. In Lima, artisans involved in petty manufacturing frequently lose their independence when confronted with large-scale industrial competition and fall into dependent relationships with merchants who offer credit in return for output at a fixed price. And in the transport and commerce sectors, many workers who have the illusion of self-employment are really commissioned wage laborers for larger concerns. While artisans are declining in number in the face of these changing relations of production, commercial workers are growing in number. Scott (1979) assesses this situation in Lima using the model of petty commodity production, suggesting that small-scale manufacturing and commerce may actually be promoted as an indirect source of surplus under capitalism.

Observers have long noted the substantial Lima population devoted to petty commerce, and one anthropologist has described the lives of residents in the city's market district, La Parada (Patch 1967), but few have examined closely the economic situation of marketers and street sellers. Recently, several Peruvian researchers have conducted more systematic investigations of Lima's street vendors (Osterling 1981; Osterling, Althaus, and Morelli 1979; Osterling and Chávez de Paz 1979; Wendorff 1983; Grompone 1985). They use the framework of the informal sector model in a critical way to consider the expansion of petty commerce in the city, which has become a focus of governmental concern in recent years. Like analysts of petty commerce elsewhere, they demonstrate the need to place small-scale traders within the broad context of dependent capitalism and its consequences for the urban poor. In general, they suggest that despite the dynamism of the informal sector capital accumulation will be unlikely without structural change in the economy.[7]

A somewhat different perspective is offered by scholars who have conducted studies of petty production and commerce in Huancayo and the Mantaro Valley in the central Peruvian sierra. Norman Long and Bryan R. Roberts (1978, 1984) emphasize the active role of small-scale local enterprises in shaping national economic and political development. Countering the model of peripheral dependency in Peru (Quijano Obregón 1974), they argue for a view of individuals as actors, asserting that change derives from the periphery as well as the center. This perspective is a corrective to views of the traditional sector as a passive victim of externally generated change, but the authors' portrayal of autonomous small entrepreneurs might not apply to the majority of marketers in Peru. Significantly, data collection was restricted to the economically active male population, bypassing Huancayo's numerous marketwomen.[8]

Mantaro Valley researchers have been critical of both the informal sector and petty commodity production models, while recognizing their respective contributions (Roberts 1975, n.d.; Long and Richardson 1978). They contend that each model can offer only a partial explanation for the growth of petty commodity production. The informal sector approach is essentially descriptive and must be supplemented by an analysis of the capitalist and petty commodity modes and their linkages. Most problematic, neither approach deals adequately with the internal functioning of the informal or petty commodity sector. To overcome this problem, the authors maintain that analysis should begin at the household level, where critical economic decision making takes place, and then relate this to the whole labor process.[9] Certainly, if analysis of petty commodity production placed greater emphasis on the household, this should have the advantage of focusing more attention on gender relations and women's activities, though this often is not the case in household analyses. Such a development would be welcome because, despite their important role in small-scale activities, women are rarely the center of study in research on petty commodity production (Nelson 1979:299).

Women in Peru

During the past decade, with the growth of cross-cultural scholarship on women, attention has begun to be directed to the situation of Peruvian women. Analysts disagree substantially, however, in their assessments. While most researchers view urban women as socially and economically disadvantaged in Peruvian society, the status of rural women relative to their urban counterparts and to rural men is a more controversial question. This seems to be due as much to different perceptions of history, "development," and women's place as to differences stemming from empirical observation.

Historically, women in Peru participated actively in society, but their experiences varied considerably depending on their status as either elite or peasant women.[10] Before the Inca expansion, a kinship-based division of resources gave women equal access to land and other material goods, and their labor was highly valued (Silverblatt 1978:40). However, gender differences embodied a latent inequality that became consolidated along with class inequalities with the Inca conquest. As a consequence, non-Inca women became alienable property subject to the disposal of the Inca elite (ibid.: 46–47).

The Spanish conquest brought in its wake more severe inequalities for women, despite their resistance to oppressive conditions (Silverblatt 1980, 1987). The loss of rights to their own persons was commonly experienced by all women during the colonial period. This was enforced by elite men who controlled the marriage of women of all races and classes. However, the impact of this control varied significantly. Although the marriage of elite white women was manipulated in the interests of their male relatives, these women received benefits from their marital alliances and also from their superior position in relation to nonelite women. The latter had no such class or race privileges by which to ameliorate the effects of sexual inequality (Burkett 1977).

Less is known about women from the colonial period to contemporary times.[11] Florencia E. Mallon (1987), however, examines the interlinkage of gender relations with precapitalist and capitalist relations in the transition from nineteenth- to mid-twentieth-century Peru. Focusing on household units in the central highlands, Mallon demonstrates that, since the colonial period, women of the region "were a strong presence at all levels of economic activity" (ibid.: 382). While elite women frequently managed commercial properties, women of the popular classes were also active in commercial relations, often as merchants. Yet these precursors to today's petty producers and traders did not enjoy equality with men; the latter controlled access to networks in the broader economy just as they exerted their patriarchal power in the household (ibid.: 384–386).

The social and economic institutions implanted by the Spanish deepened gender inequality through the postcolonial period. For example, the *hacienda* system remained in place through the middle of the twentieth century, oppressing rural people in general but having particular consequences for women. Studies of women under the *hacienda* system in this century (Deere 1977; Stein 1975; Babb 1985) report the unequal rights of women to work, hold property, and engage in community decision making. The intrusion of capitalist relations of production in the Andes, finally resulting in the abolition of the *haciendas*, had uneven effects on women. In some instances, such as in Cajamarca, where Carmen Diana Deere worked, women who lived under the *hacienda* system through the 1940s found a positive change in economic condition—though no improvement in social status—in their new work as milkmaids in a capitalist dairy enterprise. Those who left the *hacienda* for work on *minifundios*, or below-subsistence landholdings, met worse economic conditions but a higher social status. When the Hacienda Vicos in the Callejón de Huaylas became an autonomous community in the 1950s, there was an absolute improvement in the situation of both men and women, but women came to experience increasing inequalities in the areas of education, community leadership, and access to work.

The uneven development of capitalism in Peru has both improved and deteriorated women's socioeconomic condition, yet as men have gained greater participation in the national economy, the widespread result has been growing sexual inequality. Since the Spanish forced Andean men to work on a periodic basis in the mines and later the British and North Americans recruited them for temporary wage work on coastal plantations, rural men have engaged in work as seasonal migrants. While this has often meant a changing sexual division of labor whereby women take on a number of new responsibilities as subsistence producers, women's work in and outside the household has generally been regarded as having less value than men's work (Deere and León de Leal 1981).

Researchers' interpretations of the rural women's situation in Andean communities appear to be linked to whether they regard these communities as basically autonomous or dependent within the Andean social formation. For those who see cultural continuity, the emphasis is placed on the interdependence of women and men, the complementarity of their roles, and the power women exert within the family unit (e.g., Nuñez del Prado Béjar 1975a, 1975b). In this view, women's role in the control and distribution of goods their husbands produce gives them a strong voice in family decision making. Although men have higher political status and acquire prestige as sponsors of fiestas, attaining these positions requires access to

economic resources that women control. In traditional communities that have endured in the Andes, then, women enjoy near
equality with men.

In contrast to this view, others more impressed by the incursions
of capitalism in the Andes suggest that rural women are not only
part of a marginalized social sector in Peru but also further op-
pressed as women (e.g., Carpio 1975). Indeed, dependency analysis
can be extended to women to show that in the social pyramid of Peruvian society rural women are at the very bottom. In spite of the
important productive role of *campesinas*, or rural women, and their
economic control within the family, they are denied all social recognition and rendered dependent on men. Even where rural women engage actively in the wider market economy as petty traders, they are
simply more vulnerable to exploitation in the capitalist system.

Avoiding the potential excesses of either idealizing rural women
or portraying them as helpless victims, Susan C. Bourque and Kay B.
Warren (1976, 1980, 1981a, 1981b) have offered a dynamic analysis
of gender relations in the Andes. They examine the subordination
of women that has accompanied state expansion into rural affairs,
comparing the situation in agricultural and commercial communities. Basing their study on a consideration of the sexual division of
labor and social ideology, they discover that women themselves perceive the substantial contribution they make in their families and
communities; however, men control access to key resources and
social institutions and, perforce, perpetuate a social ideology that
posits the lesser value of women's work. Even so, the authors conclude that greater opportunities are available to women in the commercial town they studied, suggesting that, within the terms of national development and closer integration in the market economy,
women must be seen as active agents rather than passive subjects in
the process of change.

If women have more options where they are more closely integrated in the national society, they also face new problems. Surveys
of the education, employment, health, social and political participation, and legal status of women throughout Peru have found them
to be systematically disadvantaged by differential access to needed
goods, services, and other resources (Figueroa and Anderson 1981;
Villalobos de Urrutia 1975; CONAMUP 1976). The guiding view is
that both rural and urban women are doubly marginalized, by social
class and sex, but that this has not prevented them from developing
a social consciousness of themselves as women. This is shown by
the mobilization of women in Peru in recent years, in feminist orga-

nizations in the cities and also in rural associations, labor federations, and communal kitchens in the *barriadas* (Andreas 1985; Sara-Lafosse 1986).[12]

Current research on rural and urban women has increasingly explored the effects of the economic crisis that has gripped Peru since the mid-1970s. Often taking the family or household as the unit of analysis, scholars have shown the need to examine gender differences to understand strategies for economic survival and long-term prospects for development (Galer, Guzmán, and Vega 1985; Sara-Lafosse 1983).

With few exceptions, research on women in urban Peru has been based in Lima.[13] There, the contradictions of sexist society in the lives of middle-class women have been the subject of several studies (Anderson 1978; Barrig 1979), but more attention has recently focused on the expanding ranks of poor and working women in the informal and formal sectors (Barrig 1985, 1986; Barrig, Chueca, and Yañez 1985). Feminist researchers and activists have explored the living and working conditions of poor women, especially the migrants flocking to Lima's *barriadas*, often with a view to assist in improving them (Figueroa n.d.; Centro de Información, Estudios y Documentación 1981; Perú Mujer 1983; Barrig 1982).

As the most numerous group of Peru's urban women workers, domestic servants are no doubt the best known. They have also been the subject of some lively disagreement, with one major study contending that domestic service can be a route to upward mobility (Smith 1971, 1973) and others pointing to the economic exploitation of servants and the unlikelihood of their moving out of the poorest sector (Rutte García 1976; Bunster and Chaney 1985). There is substantial evidence, however, that the most common move made by domestic servants is a lateral one into street vending or marketing.

Women's work in street vending and marketing—second only to domestic service as a source of female employment—has been examined as part of a major research project assessing poverty's effects on women in urban Peru (Chaney 1976; Mercado 1978; Bunster 1983; Bunster and Chaney 1985). Interviews with domestic servants and factory workers as well as vendors and marketers revealed the marginalization of women in Lima's labor force, which the researchers attribute to women's subordinate sexual status and to Peru's distorted development process. For street vendors and marketers, however resourceful they might be, life is a continual struggle to make ends meet and to carry out the double day of family responsibilities and income-generating work. Many choose petty trade over domestic service because it allows them to take their children along and offers a measure of independence and flexibility. Yet each day they face exploitative wholesalers, punitive market officials, and consumers angry about rising prices as they attempt to make a meager living in the city. They might be a political force for change if they only had the time and energy at the end of their long working day.

Another study of street vendors in Lima (Chávez 1985) attempts to unravel the factors that are conditioning women's rapid incorporation into informal commerce. Family responsibilities clearly limit women's alternatives for outside employment, yet macroeconomic factors linked to the process of capital accumulation are also significant in determining the household allocation of labor. In the present period of crisis, more women are entering the work force to add to family income, and the majority find that the only employment available to them is in commerce and the services. This work is typically precarious, generates low incomes, and requires low levels of skill—making women a second-class category of workers.

The scholarship on women in Peru includes vastly different analyses regarding women's position. While some writers view rural Peru as nearly egalitarian in gender relations and see inequalities as intruding from the "modern" cities, others view traditional Andean culture as the source of machismo, which is only slowly disappearing in the more enlightened cities. These disparate interpretations of women's changing condition may be traced in part to an underlying disagreement as to whether capitalist development is "good" or "bad" for women. Of course, more penetrating analyses have been proposed, such as Deere's (1977), which argues that history proceeds dialectically and has contradictory effects on women.

Future research must pursue the question of the relationship of women's work and status to pressing issues of national development. This study of the situation of women in petty commerce in Huaraz attempts to make a contribution in this direction by examining the lives and livelihood of marketwomen in the marginalized sector of an underdeveloped economy. The need for such research is critical at a time when women in Peru and other Third World countries are participating in the urban informal sector in ever larger numbers.

Four   *The Marketplace*

ALTHOUGH HUARAZ HAS been an important commercial center for some time, commerce receives little attention from historians of this city. In the few pages that P. Alberto Gridilla (1933) devotes to the subject, he portrays the city of his day as a thriving, enterprising center. From his description, one wonders whether the level of large-scale commercial activity may have declined since the time he wrote, perhaps after the disasters of 1941 and 1970. Gridilla (ibid.: 143) notes that several factories were established in the early part of this century, including the soft drink factory that operates today, a chocolate factory, and a brewery manufacturing the beer El Huascarán.

Furthermore, Gridilla (ibid.: 144) comments on the large number of mules and trucks that daily entered Huaraz with agricultural products from the Callejón and elsewhere. In the early 1930s Huaraz had a burgeoning population and growing consumption needs to match. Gridilla points to the manufacture of bread as an indication of the high level of consumer demand, noting that ten mills and eleven bakeries worked day and night to meet urban needs (now there are twelve mills and many more bakeries).

Even before this twentieth-century expansion in the Huaraz economy, the city was known for its active marketplace commerce. Gridilla (ibid.: 145) offers evidence that as early as the end of the seventeenth century the Spanish were impressed by the lively business of marketers entering and leaving the city. Since then, the Huaraz marketplace has had a long history of active commerce.

In a description of the city as it was before the earthquake, Manuel R. Agüero León (n.d.: 26) notes the daily congestion around the main marketplace and surrounding streets as wholesalers in trucks unloaded goods for sale to retailers and as customers soon afterward flocked to make purchases. He (ibid.: 28) recalls the Avenida

Raimondi in those days, when the street's commercial importance was obvious from the number of popular establishments and business offices on it as well as the market sellers who found they could attract customers there. After the earthquake, the street was left "a cemetery," as he puts it, and for several weeks all commercial activity ceased until marketers in the region overcame their fear and began reentering the demolished city.

Before very long, marketers told me in 1977, people from the countryside were flooding the streets of Huaraz as petty traders. While in earlier times the marketers "all knew one another," as several women told me, "now Huaraz is just one big marketplace." When in the course of my fieldwork marketers were asked to describe marketing in the city before the earthquake, the majority stated that things were much better then. They referred to the smaller number of sellers, the stronger friendships and cooperation among them, the more leisurely pace, the easier access to products to sell, and the larger scale of business. Certainly, many of their current problems may be explained in terms of the state of the economy overall, but the situation has been aggravated as more and more people have had to turn to the marketplace as a means of living.

The Huaraz Markets

Until 1970 there were three markets in Huaraz: Mercado Central, located at Plaza de Armas; Mercado Mayorista (Wholesaler Market), located on Jirón Ancash and so named because it was the stopping place of wholesalers as they brought goods to retail marketers; and Mercado Chico (Little Market), located to the east of the plaza.

The earthquake left only Mercado Mayorista standing, and even this market saw enough damage that sellers were forced to trade in the streets until repairs were completed. The market was officially renamed Mercado Central, as it is called here, though people occasionally use its old name. Many of the same people who worked in this market prior to 1970 continued working at the same stalls after the earthquake. Relative to marketers in general in Huaraz, they are more often native Huaracinos and are proud of their urban status.

Three other markets may be identified in Huaraz today. La Parada (The Stop) is an outdoor marketplace covering around eight city blocks between Avenida Raimondi and the Quillcay River and bounded to the east by Avenida Fitzcarrald. In Peru it is customary for the place where *mayoristas,* or wholesalers, come to sell to *minoristas,* or retailers, to be called La Parada. Because of the reconstruction of Huaraz, La Parada has moved several times since 1970 but has been in its present location since 1976. Unlike the other markets in Huaraz, where shelter is provided by a roof and stalls are permanently constructed, La Parada offers only dirt streets where people settle and spread their goods or build makeshift stalls that must be assembled daily. This is the marketplace to which most newcomers to Huaraz and most occasional marketers come.

Two new markets were built after the earthquake in the outskirts of Centenario and Nicrupampa, where the largest number of people settled after the downtown area was destroyed. Unfortunately, people soon returned to the center of town, and most people preferred to attend the large markets downtown where prices are lower and the selection greater. The new markets are cleaner and more modern, but they are underutilized, most stalls remaining unoccupied. Mercado Centenario was built in 1974 and is an impressive structure with a tiled meat and poultry section, roomy vegetable stalls, rows of attractive stalls for staple items, and a separate room for small restaurants. Nevertheless, it is not well attended by marketers or their customers. Nicrupampa's market, built in 1972, is a very small, simple one with counter space designed to accommodate around sixteen to twenty sellers. In 1977 only four marketers attended regularly and customers were few and far between.

All the Huaraz markets operate on a daily basis. In contrast to areas of the world where marketing is cyclical, in the Callejón de Huaylas markets are customarily held on Sundays in provincial towns and villages and daily in the commercial centers. Though the Huaraz markets operate every day, there is more *movimiento,* or business traffic, on weekends and in midweek, when many wholesalers arrive with goods from the coast.

Let us return to consider each of the four Huaraz markets in greater detail in order to have a sense of their physical layout and of the activity that takes place in them.

Mercado Central

Mercado Central, formerly known as Mercado Mayorista, has been in Huaraz as long as any of the marketers I questioned could remember.[1] Significant changes have been made; for example, part of this market served as the city's slaughterhouse before a new one was built after the earthquake and wooden stalls have been replaced by concrete stalls, but the old structure remains. The market fronts on Jirón Ancash, where a wide gate is swung open to admit customers, who begin to arrive in large numbers by eight or nine in the morning. Marketers and customers have access to several other en-

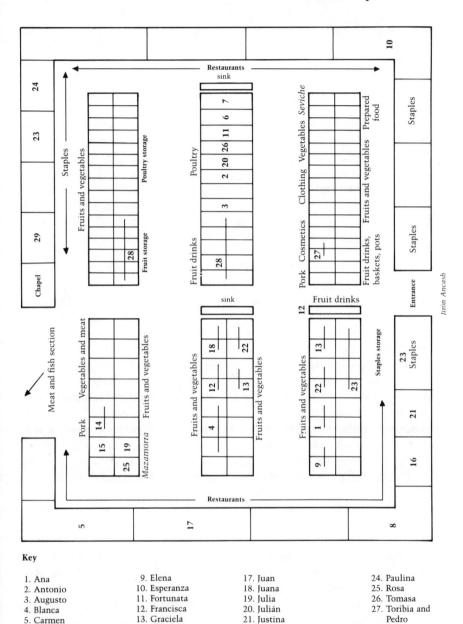

Key

1. Ana
2. Antonio
3. Augusto
4. Blanca
5. Carmen
6. Dominga
7. Donicia
8. Señor Eduardo
9. Elena
10. Esperanza
11. Fortunata
12. Francisca
13. Graciela
14. Guillerma
15. Inez
16. Isabel
17. Juan
18. Juana
19. Julia
20. Julián
21. Justina
22. María
23. Mónica and Mario
24. Paulina
25. Rosa
26. Tomasa
27. Toribia and Pedro
28. Víctor
29. Victoria

Mercado Central (interior).

trances to the side and back of the market, which extends a block to the west.

As we enter by the main door, we pass women, both outside and inside the market, seated by baskets of bread. Some sell brightly colored plastic bags to urban shoppers who can afford this luxury. Continuing on into the center aisle of the market, we have a view of the principal part of Mercado Central. It has the appearance of a pavilion, a roofed but not entirely walled structure that admits sunlight to the earth floor and cement tables where marketers display their goods.

The largest single group of sellers in this part of the market are the vegetable and fruit sellers, all women, who dominate the interior. Of a total of fifty-nine regular sellers, the vegetable and fruit marketers number twenty-one. At both ends of the market, to the left and to the right, small restaurants line the walls. Eight women and three men operate these eating places, which serve simple meals mainly to other marketers and sometimes to shoppers. Each restaurant has seating for from three or four to a dozen customers. Located along the front and back walls of the market are small stores selling staple grocery items, or *abarrotes*. These stores stock everything from flour, sugar, rice, salt, noodles, peanuts, parched corn, honey, candy, some canned goods, and other nonperishable foods to soap, oil, kerosene, shopping bags, and other household items. Five women and two men run these stalls where they sell what are referred to as articles of primary necessity (*artículos de primera necesidad*). From the center aisle, we see the chicken sellers to the right, seven women and two men who sell at a long tiled counter. Finally, a few scattered sellers specialize in such items as roast pig, marinated fish (*seviche*), fresh fruit juices, cornstarch pudding (*mazamorra*), cosmetics, and knitted clothing.

Beyond this section of Mercado Central, other areas still within the interior of the market are devoted to the sale of meat and fish and to the preparation of meals. For now, however, we will consider only the section I have described, which became my fieldwork base. I had informal interviews with all but a couple of people there, and many of the sellers became my close friends.

A sense of community seems stronger in Mercado Central than in the other markets in Huaraz. This may be explained by the longer tenure of the sellers and by the common background many of them share as residents of Huaraz. Although marketers retain a degree of privacy even when they have close stall neighbors, there is still continual interaction in this workplace they share. With the exception of some restaurant workers who have the privilege of their own water source, people congregate as they use the two large sinks in this market. They share information concerning actions taken by the Ministry of Food and by market officials, and they frequently help one another. Once a year, on May 13, they hold their market fiesta and mass to honor the Virgin of Fatima, whose figure resides in the small chapel within the market.

Mercado Central receives less business than La Parada or the numerous street sellers throughout downtown Huaraz. Customers looking for the best buys on fresh produce generally go to marketers on the street, who are able to charge somewhat less because their expenses are lower. Sellers in Mercado Central complain that the proliferating number of marketers in the streets has taken away their business. Nevertheless, many prefer the indoor market because it offers a place to store and protect their goods at night, because it provides shade from direct sunlight, which could spoil their fresh foods, and because it is considered more respectable (*más decente*) than the street. Their customers include members of the urban middle and working classes who come to purchase meat or fish and stay to buy produce, even if it means spending a few cents more. Most marketers have some regular customers, although they just as frequently sell to people with whom they are not acquainted.

We may begin with the fruit and vegetable sellers in the left side of Mercado Central and take a brief tour through this market. Elena, whose workday was described in the first chapter, is characteristic of hardworking marketers whose efforts are rewarded by very small earnings and, occasionally, some unsold food to take home. Elena only stays at the market until around 11:00 A.M. since her work at home demands her time, but she remains busy during the morning hours at her stall (*puesto*). Since the number of small traders like Elena is growing so rapidly, she often has difficulty finding goods to stock her table. Much of her time is consumed in locating goods to buy from wholesalers. Then, once she arrives at her stall, she must sort, clean, and prepare the goods she has for sale.

Sometimes she and her sister-in-law, María, who works at a stall a few meters away, assist each other by sharing the goods they have found for sale or by helping to clean each other's vegetables. María's back troubles her at times, and Elena comes to her aid.

Between Elena's and María's stalls is that of Ana, a seventeen-year-old who has just begun working. She sells fruit from her table, but her major customer is her elderly aunt, Francisca, who uses the fruit to make fresh drinks in the market. Francisca is in this way helping Ana to establish herself in the market, and she herself is assured a supply of fruit for her trade. Francisca's main concern is with the uncertain electricity in Huaraz, for when the city is without it she cannot use her blender to produce her drinks.

Graciela's stall is adjacent to María's. Both women have occasional problems when the sunlight enters and spoils their produce, so they rent additional table space, where they can protect their goods, on the other side of the aisle from where they sit. Graciela is an unmarried woman in her fifties, and like other single women marketers she often works longer hours than women with husbands, until 3:00 P.M. or later. Some sellers criticize these women for being overly ambitious or competitive, but in reality women like Graciela, whose experiences include a long period as a domestic servant in Lima, need to work harder because they have no other source of livelihood.

Sitting in the next aisle of fruit and vegetable sellers are two women who, like Elena, became my special friends and opened their homes to me. Blanca and Juana differ from Elena in that both have been to school and are literate, articulate women. They are among the few sellers who can be seen during their rare idle moments reading (often *fotonovelas*, or fiction in comic book format using photographs). The similarity of the two ends here, however, for their economic situations are quite different. Blanca's husband has an office job and makes enough money to support their three children and even pay *peones* (hired farm laborers) to work in their fields. Blanca's earnings help make it possible to send their son to college in Lima, after which she says she will rest. Juana, in contrast, is a widow with eight children and three grandchildren to raise under one roof. Her two oldest daughters work, one as a marketer and the other part time in a bookstore, but the family is primarily dependent upon her small earnings. During the time I was in Huaraz, they were able to move from a one-room to a two-room home, but their problems with poverty and illness remained severe. Ten years ago, Juana was elected vice-president of the major market union, making her one of the few women to reach such a high position in the union bureaucracy. She is critical of the present leadership, and she continues to be one of the more politically conscious and vocal people in the marketplace.

Most marketers have had little or no schooling and some know little Spanish. Even in Mercado Central a fair number of people are from the countryside, where only Quechua is spoken. Consequently, I needed the help of a bilingual speaker to talk to vegetable sellers Rosa and her sister Julia and others. Four women who sell vegetables on the other side of the center aisle, behind a large fruit-drink counter, also come from outside Huaraz and commute daily from their community. The oldest woman among them speaks little Spanish, while the youngest is fully bilingual. These women have not sold in this market as long as the women described above, and they sit in a less desirable area, partially obscured by the fruit-drink bar. In an effort to overcome this disadvantage, the women have added small tables in front of their stalls to attract more attention, and they offer the service of preparing packets of chopped, mixed vegetables for their customers' immediate use in soups.

Turning to the small restaurants that ring the market, we find that the first, located in the left rear corner, is a small-scale venture with only one table for customers. It is run by a woman who is monolingual in Quechua and also quite hard of hearing, and we never managed to exchange more than a few words. Next to her, in contrast, is a restaurant boasting three tables and run by a woman who appears younger than her twenty years. Carmen "inherited" this selling space from an older woman relative who died recently. She is originally from the department of Amazonas and came to Huaraz with her family just after the earthquake. She married at seventeen, and she and her husband, a topographer with ORDEZA, soon had a daughter. Carmen had hoped to be a singer, but her husband did not like the idea, so she works here.

Carmen's father-in-law, Señor Eduardo, who has a small restaurant not far from here, helped her get started, but she does not get along well with him and they rarely speak. She says there is competition between them. Her feelings are clearly based in part on the fact that Señor Eduardo (as he introduced himself) has another daughter-in-law, Isabel, who works right next to him and to whom he offers frequent assistance. Like Carmen, Isabel reached the third year of secondary school, she married an employee of the city government, and she has a young child. She has less business, however, at the single table at her restaurant and often relies on her father-in-law to supply her with items requested by customers. Isabel is filling in for her mother, who generally operates this stall, and she hopes one day to have a business of her own.

Reliance on family connections in the market is not uncommon. Another man who runs a small restaurant, Juan (who happens to be an uncle of Carmen), depends upon the assistance of his wife, Julia, and her sister Rosa, mentioned above. Julia leaves her vegetable stand during periods when her husband is busiest to help him cook and to serve customers. Rosa's specialty is *mazamorra;* she makes use of her brother-in-law's stove to cook it and then offers some to Juan's customers. Marketing for these people is truly a family affair, as they generally bring a half dozen or more young children with them.

Marketers without family members they can turn to sometimes depend on their market neighbors for help. For example, a woman with a modest restaurant next to Juan's has the assistance of Elena. As mentioned before, they have an arrangement whereby every day Elena sells the required amount of potatoes, carrots, and onions to the woman for her restaurant, and she provides the additional service of peeling them. In return, Elena is offered a breakfast of tea and bread or occasionally soup, and she keeps the peels to take home and feed her animals. Both women are satisfied with this cooperative relationship. Surprisingly, Elena told me that, although they have had this arrangement for some time, she does not know the other woman's name.

Women living without men often turn to running small restaurants or, very commonly, preparing simple meals on the street. How these independent women fare depends on a variety of circumstances that will be discussed later. Two women with restaurants in Mercado Central described their experiences to me. Justina, who grew up in a nearby valley, explained that first she was abandoned by her parents and then by her husband. She came to Huaraz after the earthquake and worked as a maid for a couple of years before coming to the market. Now she comes to Mercado Central every day with her young son and appears to be struggling to get by. Esperanza, who works on the other side of the market, says that sales are down and making a living is difficult, but her independence is important to her, so when her husband tried to control her activities she rebelled and left him. Her determination to get by in the market may come from the long experience she has had. As she puts it, she "grew up in the market" in Huaraz, working alongside her grandmother and mother.

The poultry sellers in Mercado Central work at a brand-new tiled counter that stretches across the right side of the building with ample table space behind, which they use as a storage area for their chickens. Having used small wooden tables before this counter was completed, they were pleased with the improvement. They had planned a traditional inauguration of their new market stalls with *padrinos* (godparents, or sponsors of the stalls) and a fiesta, but this was not carried out for lack of sponsors. These sellers work virtually shoulder to shoulder and they are a friendly group.

Most of the seven women and two men who work here rely on the help of spouses to kill and prepare the chickens for the market (as is true of the meat sellers in the other section of the market). For example, Augusto, who is the old-timer of the chicken sellers here, counts on the help of his wife, who has a nearby stand where she sells prepared vegetables, to butcher his poultry. Similarly, Donicia, who at twenty is the youngest poultry seller, has the help of her husband every morning when she comes to market. Two sisters, Tomasa and Fortunata, say they work independently of each other, but they seem to help each other from time to time. Tomasa also has the assistance of her husband, who took over her work entirely when she left to have a baby. One man, Antonio, sold chicken regularly during the time I was in Huaraz, although the stall is in his wife's name. A few sellers, like a woman named Dominga, work alone to prepare and sell their chickens. This is quite possible but means harder work and usually a smaller scale of business.

With beef on sale for only two weeks each month in 1977 and the price doubling in the month of June alone, those who could afford to buy meat for their families bought chicken. Although the price of poultry rose somewhat that year, business did not suffer too much. Since all the sellers depended on the same suppliers from the coastal city of Chimbote and the price of chicken was officially controlled, the variation in sales that existed among different marketers must be attributed to other factors. One man, Julián, had a clear advantage since he owned a refrigerator, which he stocked against periodic shortages; on several occasions when suppliers did not arrive, he was the only one left with chicken to sell. Some sellers were beginning to sell local chickens, which were considered inferior but cost less and attracted some customers. Beyond these considerations, differences in sales depended in part on the loyalty of the sellers' clientele and on their ability to attract new customers. Tomasa, for example, seemed to have somewhat more business than the other sellers when they were at their old stalls. This could be attributed to the strategic spot she held along the market's center aisle, to her skills as a marketer, or perhaps to the pleasant way in which she conducts her sales. When the new stalls opened and Tomasa was no longer in an especially advantageous position, her sales appeared to remain slightly above average, suggesting at the very least that her customers continued to seek her out.

The final group of any size in this part of Mercado Central are the sellers of staples, whose small shops are found along the front and back walls of the market. Selling these grocery items is considered appropriate for both men and women. Two of the sellers in this market are a husband and wife who operate independent stores at opposite ends of the building. Mónica and Mario buy from wholesalers together around once a month and then sell in their very similar shops. They say they do equal business and work in two places in order to increase their chances for sales.

Several women working alone selling staples discussed the growing difficulties entailed in their work. Formerly, wholesalers bringing goods to Huaraz allowed marketers to buy on credit, paying after they had time to sell the goods. Now, buying on credit is common for only a few items, posing real problems for small sellers. Furthermore, several large intermediary houses in Huaraz have begun taking most of the business of the wholesalers, squeezing out many smaller wholesalers and forcing petty retailers to deal with the local houses. While men like Mario may still be able to settle business deals *con tragos* (with a few drinks), women are becoming more dependent on a few powerful Huaraz intermediaries.

The oldest woman in this section of the market is Carmen's grandmother, whose business career spans sixty years. Although she did not go to school, she is very proud of her shrewd abilities as a merchant. Her experience is no help, however, when it comes to the decline in business that has followed recent sharp hikes in the official prices of her goods. Another woman, Paulina, who is in her fifties, cannot rely on the business of her store alone to support herself. After the long hours she puts in at the market, she returns home to earn a little bit more by taking in clothes for ironing. One younger woman, Victoria, has taken over her husband's store since he left for Lima, and she is somewhat more successful in her work. This is probably due to her strength and good health, which allow her to go directly to the wholesalers who come from the coast, bypassing the powerful city merchants. In addition, the store she manages is twice the size of the older women's stalls, giving her the opportunity to carry a large variety of goods and draw more customers.

Among the remaining sellers in this part of Mercado Central is, very prominently, Víctor, whose fresh fruit juice counter, Eight Flavors, holds a favored central spot and occupies the space of five small (two meter) stalls. Víctor's signs greet the customers as they enter the market and his fruit display is impressive. The scale of his business is much larger than that of most marketers, and he hires three young men to prepare and sell drinks. He owns his own generator, so that when there is no electricity his business does not suffer as Francisca's does. The chief symbol of his success, however, is his cash register, the only one in the market. Víctor is an unusual marketer, an educated man who had experience in several careers before beginning this one. He is a past union president and still has a lot of influence in Mercado Central. Other sellers include Inez and Guillerma, sellers of smoked pork who could not find space at the

This young woman began selling staples in Mercado Central after her grandmother's death left the stall vacant.

new stalls built for pork sellers in the adjoining section of the market. Another is Toribia, who comes periodically to this market as a traveling seller of cosmetics, often with her partner, Pedro.

If we spend the day in this market, we find that by noon the level of activity is much reduced. Many of the fruit and vegetable sellers are returning home by this time, especially if they have families to feed. Until 2:00 P.M. or so, the poultry sellers are on duty at their counter. Those who remain in the market later, until around 4:00 P.M., include restaurant operators, who stay to clean up after the midday meal and to prepare for the next day, and staple sellers, who sometimes stay open until closing time. Leaving through a back entrance that faces toward the Frigorífico fish distribution center, we pass a large scale and latrines as well as the stalls of beef, pork, and fish sellers, most of whom have left by midafternoon. A few casual sellers sometimes remain seated on the floor in this section until late in the afternoon, but by 5:00 P.M. the doors are swung shut and the market is quiet until the next day begins twelve hours later.

Now that we have observed one part of the Huaraz market in some detail, let us take a more rapid tour through the places where other marketers work. Many interviews were conducted in these markets, the content of which will be discussed in later chapters.

The streets surrounding Mercado Central are full of marketing activity, and sellers there identify themselves in terms of their location outside the market and the Frigorífico. Those to the west of the market are for the most part fruit and vegetable sellers who have constructed wooden stands of their own or who sit along the sidewalk facing the street. Some of these marketers formerly worked inside the market but now use the stalls only to store their goods, having found business brisker outdoors. This area also has a number of small grocery shops for the sale of staples as one looks in the direction of Avenida Raimondi.

Along the southern side of the market and across from the Frigorífico, a number of sellers, many from the countryside, sit with their backs against the wall of the market building. Here one may purchase wheat, barley, fresh and dried *ají*, garlic, eggs, live guinea pigs and rabbits, bundles of alfalfa for animal feed, and a variety of other products that often come directly from the sellers' fields.

Rounding the corner to Jirón Ancash, and continuing on this street to Raimondi, we find that most of the sellers here deal in clothing. Stalls are set up in the street and display blouses, skirts, slacks, socks, sweaters, and ponchos. Some of the stalls belong to storeowners along Jirón Ancash who call attention to their stores by displaying some goods outside. There are also occasional sellers of pots and pans, herbs, and dyes along this street as well as some small restaurants.

La Parada

Once we cross the Avenida Raimondi, we have entered the open air market known as La Parada. Here in these streets, wholesalers and retailers come between 3:00 A.M. and 6:00 A.M. to make their transactions. During the chilly, early morning hours in La Parada, the transactions are quick. The pace picks up as more marketers arrive and *cargadores* (porters) and *triciclos* transport retailers' goods to places throughout the Huaraz markets.

Later in the day, the marketers who settle in La Parada to sell their goods present a confusing picture to the uninitiated observer. However, a closer inspection reveals a definite order to the way sellers of particular kinds of goods position themselves. Walking along the busiest street, San Cristobal, we see a rough division. From the Quillcay River bank to a point slightly more than halfway to Raimondi, sellers of fruits and vegetables and prepared foods sold by the plate predominate. An occasional seller of pots and pans or staples may also be found here. In sharp contrast, from this point on up to Raimondi, clothing sellers spread their wares, with a rare seller of staples among them. The street is lined with small restaurants and, in several places, with artisans' stands selling baskets, pots, saddlebags, hats, sandals, and other goods made in the region.

A block to the west on Hualcan there is somewhat less activity. Most sellers are concentrated in the half of the street toward Raimondi, and they sell primarily fruits and vegetables. A group of bread sellers station themselves at the corner of Raimondi. Another block to the west is the street named for Peru's highest mountain peak, Huascarán. This street is still less active than Hualcan, but a number of sellers of fresh produce may be found there. Sometimes, trucks that come early in the day remain stationed in this street all morning.

The streets cutting across those described above, 13 de Diciembre and Caraz, have a fair amount of commercial activity, particularly where they approach the Avenida Fitzcarrald. They support a considerable variety of business, including hatmakers selling their creations outside their shops, traveling sellers of yard goods displaying large bolts of fabric, and dealers in live chickens showing off their fowl. Finally, along the riverbank to the west of the Quillcay bridge, many semipermanent stands have been established for the sale of produce and simple meals. In addition, a number of wholesalers remain in this area long enough during the day to sell to the public whatever is not bought by retailers. Itinerant sellers of blankets, kitchen items, and other household goods often favor this area, too, for the large number of customers that pass this way.

La Parada is the market that draws the heaviest commerce and the most diverse sellers and customers in the city. The orderly manner in which hundreds of sellers are able to organize themselves is surprising, given that most do not have permanent stalls and must contend with bringing their goods and arranging them daily. Storage is available for a fee in some buildings in the market area, but space is scarce and many sellers must pay porters to take their merchandise to and from the market every day. Other difficulties faced by La Parada marketers and street sellers generally are the lack of sanitary facilities and access to water. Despite these problems, the sellers take pride in their market and organize themselves into groups by the products they sell to create a pleasing assemblage and to make shopping more efficient for consumers and marketers alike. The marketers are largely self-regulated in this respect, but local officials sometimes intrude to enforce compliance with policies designed to control the sellers' whereabouts.

Mercado Centenario

The greatest contrast to La Parada is provided by Mercado Centenario. Where the former is a sprawling outdoor market bustling with activity, the latter is an enclosed market with little commercial traffic. Where the former attracts marketers from the countryside as well as the city and customers of all social backgrounds, the latter generally brings marketers from the Centenario barrio and a middle-class clientele from the same neighborhood. People say that when Mercado Centenario first opened four years after the earthquake marketers filled it and business was good. Then, when downtown Huaraz was rebuilt and its population grew, commerce in Centenario declined. Since then marketers here have asked local officials to encourage downtown sellers to move to this market, but none of them have moved.

A chief concern of marketers in Centenario is the additional expense they incur in transporting the goods they buy from wholesalers in La Parada to their stalls here. While sellers in Mercado Central might pay S/.5 or S/.10 to have a sack of potatoes carried a couple blocks to their stalls, sellers in Centenario would pay around S/.20 to have the same sack transported over the river and eight blocks to the market. This expense translates into slightly higher prices and serves to discourage shoppers. Centenario marketers have asked officials to force some wholesaler trucks to stop by their market, but in this, too, they have been unsuccessful.

With these constraints on marketing in Centenario, most marketers prefer to trade downtown even if it means having to travel farther to get there. When I asked the Centenario sellers why they work in this market, their responses were revealing. A number of women work here because they have young children and find that if they sell near home in Centenario they can get back and forth quickly between market and home to give their children breakfast, send them to school, care for infants when their older children go to school, and so on. Of course, women in the other markets often have young children, too, but they are more likely to take their children along to the market or to make other arrangements. I observed children with marketwomen in Centenario on only a few occasions.

Another reason why some women choose to sell in this market is suggested by the response several marketers gave when asked why they started to sell. In general, women in Centenario answered very differently from marketers elsewhere, often explaining that exceptional circumstances forced them to work in the market. For example, their husbands died in the earthquake or suffered accidents that prevent them from finding work, or their families' declining standard of living became a hardship. Most of the sellers have only worked outside the home in recent years, many beginning in 1974 when this market was built. What unified the responses of these women was an apologetic quality, a certain need to explain why they were doing the work of lower-class people. A fish seller told me that, although it is humiliating to have to sell, she is at least selling something more respectable than fruits and vegetables. Others pointed to a factor that appears to be important to most of the sellers at this market, that it is the cleanest and most attractive of the Huaraz markets.

Sellers in Mercado Centenario are, for the most part, of a higher social status than those in the downtown market, and they are willing to accept a lower level of business for the advantages they see in working at a more tranquil, respectable market near their homes. Their customers, too, reveal a willingness to pay a little more for the convenience of shopping near home and for the hygienic surroundings. Many middle-class women in Centenario go to the downtown markets or send their servants to shop there, but others make up a small clientele at Mercado Centenario. These shoppers are discriminating in their selection of foods, and the marketers bring only the freshest produce and meats they can find. Several sellers commented on this, saying that their customers do not want the overripe bargains that the *campesinos* who shop downtown are always seeking.

Mercado Centenario was built to accommodate 104 marketers at stalls and eight workers in small restaurants. Like Mercado Central, this market has its own small chapel, access to water, and sanitary facilities (in this case, flushing toilets rather than crude latrines). The fruit and vegetable section of this market, located at the far side of the building, is the only area that is occupied to near capacity; in 1977, twenty-five women worked at stalls built for twenty-eight, and two more women preferred to sit in the aisle. Almost half of this market was designed for small grocery stores, but this was the most underrepresented section with four men and four women selling staple foods, leaving thirty-six stalls unoccupied.

Two men sell fish independently, and a woman sells on commission for the Frigorífico. Since the latter's sales are far lower than those of Frigorífico employees working downtown, she is allowed a slightly higher commission. Sellers in meat and poultry include five women dealing in beef, whose husbands work in partnership with them to locate and purchase animals to be slaughtered, and a single seller of chicken, working by herself.

The pricing and sales of the meat and poultry sellers in Centenario deviate somewhat from what was described above. Beef sellers point out that although their prices are controlled they often need to sell for slightly under the official prices in order to compete with downtown sellers. And the chicken seller finds that working as the sole poultry trader here makes good sense since her sales are comparable to those of most of the Mercado Central sellers. The meat and poultry marketers in Centenario are in closer communication with their sister sellers in Mercado Central than are the other sellers here. The beef sellers are part of the same union, and they are in contact through other aspects of their work as well. The chicken seller is also in frequent contact with those working downtown, as I realized when she corrected me on the number of poultry sellers there and told me she knew some of them personally.

Finally, in this market are two sellers of fruit drinks, a woman and a young man. The latter attends a nearby high school in the afternoons and expects to have a more lucrative business career when he finishes his studies. He started here with the help of his mother, who has a restaurant in the adjoining section of this market. Two other women work in small restaurants but have little business despite the attractive setting. The added expense of transporting supplies to this market means that they must charge one or two soles more for each item they sell than the downtown marketers charge.

Mercado Nicrupampa

The fourth Huaraz market is so small that some people would not refer to it as a *mercado* proper but as a *mercadillo* (little market). It was designed to accommodate about twenty sellers, but when I first attended in 1977 it was largely unoccupied, with just four women selling there regularly. The structure of this market is much simpler than either of the two market buildings already described. A roof and counter space are provided, but no walls enclose it or protect the marketers' goods overnight.

The sellers who come to the Nicrupampa market are from this barrio. Two are older women who come here because it is not far from their homes. They count it as an advantage that they can carry their unsold goods home at night. (Of course, they have the same problem as the Centenario marketers in paying the relatively high cost of transporting goods from La Parada.) Another seller is an employee of the Frigorífico, a nineteen-year-old woman who told me her nine-year-old sister began selling fish here before she took over. She has completed high school and says she would like to go to

A vegetable seller in Mercado Centenario, where many stalls remain unoccupied.

medical school, but since her father is not able to support his nine children she must work to help out. Her sales here are low, but like the woman in Centenario she receives a slightly higher commission to help compensate. The fourth woman who sells here is around thirty and sells an unusually wide variety of goods, including fruits and vegetables, cheese, and often a little meat or fish. Sometimes her husband and daughter accompany her to help set up the goods in the morning. This young woman chooses to sell at this small market for several reasons; for one, unlike many marketwomen, she views her earnings as supplemental to her husband's income rather than as a chief source of family support, and, for another, the diversity of the products she sells assures her of a certain amount of business as long as there is no significant competition.

People who shop in Nicrupampa are mainly women of the barrio who, for one reason or another, find it difficult to shop downtown. This includes the elderly and the infirm, but it also includes other women who come to the market when they have forgotten something in the downtown markets or when they need an item in a hurry. In contrast to the other markets, Nicrupampa's begins fairly late, at around 9:00 A.M., and business picks up toward afternoon.

The Social Organization of Marketers

Huaraz marketers frequently comment on the changing physical structure and appearance of the city markets, especially since the reconstruction of the 1970s; they judge the situation to be better or worse based on their recollections of the past and their recent personal experiences. Yet marketers rarely question many of the aspects of social organization that draw the attention of outside observers, viewing them as customary and unnoteworthy. Consequently, for the investigator interested in market organization or the sexual division of labor in the markets, it is often easier to record observations than it is to elicit the opinions of marketers themselves.

Huaraz officials seem surprisingly uninformed about the people on whom they depend for the urban food supply and for a major source of revenue generated through the collection of market fees. Municipal records were unreliable since they only include marketers with stands, leaving out the many sellers without stands. In order to determine how marketers are distributed throughout the Huaraz markets, I had to count them.

The information in Tables 1 and 2 was collected by a simple head count of marketers in Huaraz, which I carried out in 1977 with the assistance of Tomás Camino. We counted sellers in the downtown markets on a Saturday morning when marketing was in full swing. Sellers in the other markets were counted on two weekday mornings during hours when the number of sellers was assumed to be at its maximum. An effort was made to count as accurately as possible, recording the number of sellers by sex and by product sold, but our data should in no way be viewed as representing the full number of persons trading in the city. First of all, having counted in midmorning we did not include the number of wholesalers who come in with goods to unload quickly to retailers and who leave early in the day. Nor could we count all the periodic sellers who come to Huaraz regularly but not daily. Second, inevitable problems arise in sorting out sellers and customers in the crowded marketplace, and we no doubt erred in underrepresenting the number of marketers. Furthermore, some sellers are found scattered along streets of Huaraz beyond the limits of the markets and are not included here. Nevertheless, the tables offer some idea of the number and activity of women and men trading in the markets at a given time—a rather busy time but not as busy as Sundays, when more trucks carrying produce arrive from the coast and more sellers from the countryside enter the city.

Table 1 presents a summary of the number of marketers by sex in

Table 1
Huaraz Marketers by Market and Sex

	Female	Male	Percentage Female
Mercado Central	352	103	77
La Parada	501	165	75
Mercado Centenario	42	7	86
Mercado Nicrupampa	4	0	100
Total	899	275	77

Source: 1977 count by Florence Babb and Tomás Camino.

the four Huaraz markets (figures for Mercado Central include sellers in the streets surrounding the market) and the percentage of women working in each of them. The total number of marketers of both sexes counted was 1,174, but for the reasons stated above this count is likely to be conservative, and it is reasonable to assume that the actual number of marketers present on busy days may be considerably higher. Clearly, although marketing is most often identified in Huaraz as women's work, men make up a good number of sellers in the city. In Mercado Central and La Parada, where the bulk of marketers work, the ratio of women to men is similar, with women comprising 77 percent and 75 percent of sellers in the two markets, respectively. In the two less popular markets in outlying barrios, Mercados Centenario and Nicrupampa, women appear in much higher proportion to men. Before considering further the question of female and male participation in the markets, we will examine the broader social division of labor among marketers in Huaraz commerce.

The Division of Labor in the Distribution Process

The principal distinction between the various kinds of Huaraz marketers, based on their place in the distribution process, is that between wholesalers and retailers. Marketers can also be classified according to their status as producer-sellers, itinerant sellers, transport workers, and service workers. Some of these categories overlap, as certain people carry out several roles in market commerce. Furthermore, there is disagreement over the identification and extent of the categories. Accordingly, the division of labor by distributive roles is much less clear than the division of labor by products sold. In the following examination of workers in the distribution process I do not attempt to establish a rigid typology but only to describe the distinctive features of various marketers' work.

Wholesalers and Retailers

There is no absolute separation between the roles of wholesalers and retailers in the Huaraz markets, and many sellers display features of both. I will assess the two together, keeping in mind that from the largest wholesaler to the smallest retailer there is a great difference in wealth and power in the market.

Wholesalers and retailers represent links in the chain along which most goods pass on their way to the market. As intermediaries, or middlewomen and middlemen, they facilitate the transport, preparation of quantity (bulking and bulk-breaking), storage, and sale of articles destined for customers. Wholesalers may be identified as those who generally purchase goods as close as possible to the place of production in field or factory and who carry them to the markets, where they are passed on to other marketers to sell to the public. Retailers, in contrast, are for the most part individuals who buy their goods from wholesalers in the marketplace and sell directly to urban consumers. What this general pattern overlooks are the wholesalers who buy from other wholesalers and act as transport agents between marketplaces as well as the "wholesalers" who spend time selling retail to the public. Additionally, it leaves out people who define themselves as retailers yet travel a considerable distance to purchase goods at better prices closer to their source and also those who are occasionally willing to sell their goods in bulk at reduced prices to other retailers. In other words, the kinds of market commerce known as *al por mayor* and *al por menor* (wholesale and retail) are not always restricted to one or another group of sellers.

I first realized that the distinction between wholesale and retail sellers was problematic when I began asking about the number of female wholesalers. Responses ranged from "most wholesalers are women" to "there is an equal number of female and male wholesalers" to "there are no female wholesalers." Further questioning revealed that the defining criterion is one of scale, and while some would consider a woman selling ten sacks of vegetables a wholesaler, others reserve the term for the few male entrepreneurs who have their own trucks and transport thousands of kilos of goods.

Some self-identified wholesalers were specific about the qualifi-

Most of the largest wholesalers are men.

cations for wholesaler (*mayorista*) status. One man defined whole-salers in terms of the quantity they deal in, saying one must sell at least 1,000 kilos to be called a wholesaler (he himself deals in be-tween 1,500 and 2,000 kilos each week). He asserted that this crite-rion holds true whether or not a seller buys directly from producers or sells at wholesale prices to other marketers. "Real wholesalers," he argued, "are those who buy in large quantity and go right to the fields." Another wholesaler, a woman, who incidentally meets the scale criterion suggested above since she deals in forty to fifty crates of tomatoes weekly but who buys from intermediaries rather than producers, defined wholesale commerce in terms of the capital needed. She maintained that to be a wholesaler one must have at least S/.10,000 to S/.20,000 in capital.

When I spoke to smaller-scale marketers on this subject, they agreed that one must pass a certain threshold to be called a whole-saler. One woman, whom I believed to be a wholesaler since she traveled to buy from producers and had a fair number of sacks of vege-tables for sale, surprised me by saying she was a retailer (*minorista*). She explained this by saying that she only sells a few sacks *al por mayor*, while true wholesalers have S/.30,000 capital as well as trucks and stores of their own. Her notion of wholesalers' business success may have been exaggerated, but her view was shared by most sellers I spoke to.

When I asked Elena if a person selling four or five sacks could be considered a wholesaler, she said no, that wholesalers sell around one hundred sacks of goods at a time; then I asked if a person selling twenty or twenty-five sacks could be a wholesaler and she said yes. She herself will occasionally sell a whole sack or a large part of one to a regular customer at a reduced price, although this means a loss of income. This is done as a convenience for loyal clients. Customers know that she cannot sell as cheaply as wholesalers, but they go to her because she will sell part of a sack, or because she is in the market later than most wholesalers, or because she knows them and may extend credit for a day or two.

This discussion of the problems involved in defining the role of wholesalers and retailers suggests that the real differences among marketers do not fall neatly along a line between those selling at wholesale prices to retailers and those selling at retail prices to the public. There are marketers who sell *al por mayor* who are just as impoverished as those selling *al por menor;* these are very often women and probably compose the "mostly female" group of wholesalers that some informants referred to. When we consider the composition of the group of sellers who have more capital and sell in large quantity, the "true" wholesalers, we find a much smaller group and one dominated by men.

Producer-sellers

It was noted earlier that the families of marketers in Huaraz often have small plots of land, or *chacras,* which they farm for family use. Few of them grow enough in these fields to sell the product in the market, and their crops are intended for immediate consumption (*para comer no más,* only to eat, they often told me). However, some people with larger fields outside the city regularly sell their surplus and sometimes take the product to market themselves. They may then be considered part-time sellers. Unlike large producers, who sell to wholesalers directly from their fields, these are usually small producers whose harvest exceeds family need but does not always attract wholesalers. In the marketplace, these producer-sellers often want to sell as quickly as possible to retailers and return to work in their fields, but they may choose to spend a few days in Huaraz selling to the public at somewhat higher prices.

For example, on a trip to the town of Carhuaz, north of Huaraz in the Callejón, I met a woman who sells the surplus of her small corn-

Women wholesalers also sell directly to the public.

field. She explained that sometimes wholesalers come to her and buy her corn, saving her the trouble of going to the Huaraz market. But when wholesalers do not come or when she needs something in Huaraz, she goes to the city herself. She considers this to be time-consuming and bothersome (*fastidioso*), particularly because with the cost of transport she earns no more by taking the corn to the market herself. When she goes, she prefers to sell wholesale to other sellers but occasionally must stay to sell retail to unload all of her product.

Other producer-sellers in the Huaraz markets include artisans and others who create their own products to sell. Some of these marketers have an advantage in being able to produce their goods as they sell so that time is not lost away from production. Those in this category include seamstresses, hatmakers, shoemakers, artisan-producers of sweaters, ponchos, baskets, and the like.

Itinerant Sellers

Itinerant sellers, or *ambulantes* as they are called, form a group of chiefly retail, sometimes wholesale, marketers who come to the Huaraz markets daily or less often, but whose distinguishing feature is that they do not have permanent selling places. Many *ambulantes* return regularly to the same place in the streets around Mercado Central or in La Parada and even attempt to guard their spots against others' encroachment. Yet for various reasons they do not work at permanent stands and, accordingly, are not registered with the Provincial Council.

The nature of some sellers' work makes it impractical to pay the daily fees for a stall and the annual registration fee. As *ambulantes*, they pay a fee only on the days when they attend the market. Many *ambulantes* are *campesinos* who come to sell on a casual basis, when they have a surplus after a harvest or when they need cash or the items it buys in the marketplace. A number of urban sellers, notably the clothing sellers, leave Huaraz periodically to purchase goods in Lima or elsewhere; when they return to sell, it is as *ambulantes* in makeshift stalls or on the ground along the streets.

Some sellers choose to be *ambulantes* because selling in the streets suits their needs, and they feel the business is better there. One woman commented that she likes the hustle and bustle of the streets in La Parada and has a chance to meet her friends as she moves around. For most, *ambulante* status is a second-class status but one that economic necessity dictates. It is notable that, while some *ambulantes* talk about eventually acquiring fixed selling places, a number of sellers with indoor market stalls are leaving them to work in the streets as Peru's economic crisis worsens.

Special mention may be made here of a group of *ambulantes* who sell during the nighttime in Huaraz. These people generally sell snacks on the streets, often at regular locations around the movie theaters and at busy intersections. From trays and carts they offer sandwiches, usually sold by women, and hot drinks called *emolientes*, sold by both men and women. Some sellers prefer to sell at night because there are fewer competitors or because, with children to look after or other work to do, there is no time during the day. They point out, however, that the risks are greater at night, when customers may be drunk and threaten the sellers.

Transport Workers

Workers who transport goods and sellers to the Huaraz markets and move goods through the city to various locations are an important presence in the marketplace. Although they sell nothing but their own ability to move goods and people, they are an essential part of the distribution process. Few interviews were carried out with these workers because they are not principally engaged in the selling of goods and because, to my knowledge, they are an exclusively male group. Still, I talked to several truck drivers as well as to porters.

Owning a truck is a symbol of considerable wealth in Huaraz, and few men have the capital to buy one. Some collaborate with one or more friends to purchase a truck for the transportation of goods and passengers. Others do not own their own vehicles but rather are the hired drivers for transport enterprises or for independent suppliers. Many truck drivers engage in some commerce of their own, taking advantage of trips between marketplaces to participate in whole-sale trade.

A number of local Huaraz men serve as *cargadores,* who transport goods between the marketers' points of purchase and sale or, some-times, to and from the marketers' homes and the marketplace. These men fall into two significantly different groups: young men who work as transporters with *triciclos* and older men who work as por-ters with nothing but a length of rope to tie the goods to their backs.

Owning a *triciclo* represents an investment of around S/.18,000, and many of the younger men who operate them received loans or gifts of money from their parents to acquire them. Boys as young as eight or nine may be seen transporting goods on these bicycle carts, while men over thirty-five are rare. The majority of the 305 regis-tered *triciclo* transporters appear to be teenage schoolboys. They commonly work mornings and attend school in the afternoons or evenings.

In contrast, the porters with ropes are generally men over forty, often closer to sixty. They are uneducated men and among the very poorest people in the marketplace. In fact, they may frequently be recognized by the tattered clothes they wear, more patches than original fabric, which are given to them as hand-me-downs from sympathetic customers.

Service Workers

A small number of people identified with the marketplace have as their particular role not handling goods for sale but providing spe-cific services to customers. They include persons who repair shoes, watches, tools, or other goods; haircutters; shoeshine boys; and, in one case, a man with a scale used to weigh people for a nominal fee.

The Sexual Division of Labor in the Markets

In general, women in the Huaraz markets are concentrated in the sale of agricultural products and prepared foods, and men are concentrated in the sale of manufactured goods and items brought in quantity from the coast. Furthermore, the scale of men's business is often larger than that of women's regardless of the products sold. Nevertheless, there is a good deal of overlap in the kind of commercial activity in which men and women participate and in the scale of their commerce, and, consequently, we must regard the sexual division of labor in the market as rather flexible.

Men make up almost a quarter of the sellers in the downtown markets, but closer examination reveals that the participation of male and female sellers varies widely depending on the area of marketplace activity considered. Table 2 shows the number of male and female sellers according to the products they sell. If there were no difference between the items sold by women and men, we would expect female participation in each case to approximate the overall market participation of women as 77 percent of sellers. However, it is clear from the table that the sale of some types of goods attracts women in much greater numbers than this, while the sale of other items draws more men than we would expect based on their number in the marketplace.

The best and probably most important example, since it involves the largest group of marketers, is the case of the vegetable and fruit sellers. These traders of agricultural produce include almost half of all marketers in Huaraz, and 92 percent of them are women. This may help to explain the strong identification of marketing with women, since the provisioning of agricultural products to the city is fundamental. When men engage in the sale of fruits and vegetables, they rarely sell in the indoor markets; men prefer to sell in the streets outside Mercado Central or, especially, in the streets of La Parada. The scale of their trade is typically, but not always, somewhat larger than that of women sellers of the same product, whether they work as wholesalers or retailers.

A second group of marketers in which women make a strong appearance is that of sellers of meals and snacks. I include those who prepare a single item on the street for sale by the plate or glass along with those who operate small restaurant stalls, since there is no sharp division between the two types of business. Women make up 85 percent of this group, and they are particularly numerous among the street sellers of snacks. Thus, we see that the sexes are not divided spatially in terms of indoor and outdoor markets, for male vegetable and fruit sellers work outdoors, while male sellers of prepared food for immediate consumption are more likely to be found inside the markets.

Several areas of market activity are marked by a high degree of

Table 2
Female and Male Sellers in Huaraz Markets by Items Sold

Item Sold	Mercado Central		La Parada		Mercado Centenario		Mercado Nicrupampa		Total		Percentage Female
	F	M	F	M	F	M	F	M	F	M	
Alfalfa	14		21	1					35	1	97
Meat	26	2			5				31	2	94
Veg./fruit	185	9	311	34	27			3	526	43	92
Meals/snacks	43	8	70	12	4	1			117	21	85
Bread	5	1	11	2					16	3	84
Poultry	7	2			1				8	2	80
Farm animals	2		1	1					3	1	75
Handicrafts	3	1	13	5					16	6	73
Staples	7	5	11	2	4	4			22	11	67
Clothing	43	31	36	33					79	64	55
Fish	8	8		1	1	2	1		10	11	48
Hats	2	3	2	8					4	11	27
Housewares	4	29	20	42					24	71	25
Shoes		3	2	15					2	18	10
Other	3	1	3	9					6	10	38

Source: 1977 count by Florence Babb and Tomás Camino.

sexual segregation, with women controlling the bulk of sales. Examples include the sale of alfalfa and of meat, with 97 percent and 94 percent female sellers, respectively. In the case of the alfalfa sellers, among whom thirty-five women and one man were counted, we have an example of a market item handled almost exclusively by women. So closely is the sale of alfalfa identified with women that it is surprising that even one man entered the ranks of these marketers (unfortunately, I did not have the opportunity to speak to him). The alfalfa sellers are among the poorest of marketers, most of them *campesinas* who sit together in the downtown markets. They may be compared with the exclusively male porters, the poorest men in the markets, who look for work carrying goods, which they strap to their backs.

The table shows a large percentage of female meat marketers, with women representing 94 percent of sellers of beef, pork, and mutton. This is somewhat misleading, however, since many of these women are able to carry out their trade only with the assistance of men. Because the women in such partnerships are usually responsible for the selling end of the business, they are the ones represented in the count. Prior to the marketing, time-consuming work goes into locating livestock, taking it to the slaughterhouse, and then butchering the meat for sale. This is ordinarily carried out by men, who leave the meat with their wives or sisters in the market to sell. In contrast to the preparation and sale of poultry, and even pork, which some women manage to carry on independently, the sale of beef involves more labor and more capital than most women can furnish by themselves.

Turning to the areas of market trade that draw more men, we find these include the sale of staples (*abarrotes*), housewares (*mercería*), fish, clothing, shoes, and hats. Although more than half the sellers of staples are women, men are well represented; this is an area of trade considered appropriate for both men and women. Men number just over half the fish sellers, and they make up the majority of those traveling directly to the coast for their fish. Housewares, often sold by men, include all kinds of small manufactured goods for the home, such as tableware, plastic washing basins and kitchen utensils, knives, scissors, needles and thread, combs, mirrors, and the like. The sale of clothing, too, is an area of commerce that men frequently enter (the number of male sellers counted outside Mercado Central may be slightly inflated, however, since some storeowners along Jirón Ancash who have stands outside their shops may have been mistaken for marketers). Finally, the production, repair, and sale of shoes and hats are generally the business of male artisans and dealers; when women participate it is usually in partnership with their husbands. The "other" category, in which men predominate, includes such diverse marketers as a book seller, a jewelry seller, several cheese merchants, and herb sellers.

Certain patterns begin to emerge in the division of labor by sex. The majority of women (526 of 899) in the markets are engaged in the sale of fruits and vegetables, which are brought in from the region of the Callejón de Huaylas and from the coast. Women can usually buy these goods on credit, and they are thus able to operate with little or no capital. Men are more often engaged in the sale of manufactured products brought from Lima and other cities on the coast, which requires a larger capital outlay. Some of these goods may be purchased on credit, but to begin such an enterprise generally requires capital to cover transport and other costs. For example, clothing may be obtained in Lima on consignment, but men, more often than women, form the personal connections necessary to receive these goods and can afford the high delivery costs and market fees. Consequently, women selling clothing are concentrated among those dealing in items produced locally (sometimes by the marketers themselves) and often intended for sale to *campesinos*, while men specialize in the sale of clothing mass-produced in coastal factories and designed to appeal to urban customers. In a similar way, women occasionally sell locally produced pots, baskets, and other items for the home; but men control the sale of manufactured household merchandise, which requires a considerable capital investment.

The tendency, to be sure, is for the division of labor in the marketplace to reflect the division of labor in the society as a whole. In a society in which women are primarily responsible for seeing that their families are fed and in which men are at least formally viewed as the chief breadwinners, it is not surprising to find women selling foodstuffs and men selling products identified with the "modern" economic sector. Clearly, the social expectations of proper male and female behavior influence the areas of marketing chosen by sellers and the acceptance they receive. To what extent the constraints on women's and men's marketplace activity are social and to what extent economic is suggested by the marketers themselves.

During my first weeks in the markets, I asked many marketers why more women than men sell and why women sell certain goods and men others. Their responses varied considerably. A number of women who were asked said that, while women market, men want to work (*hacer algo*, literally, "to do something"); as one woman put it, "Men have to do something, while women just work in the market." Several sellers explained that most men are farmers, workers (*obreros*), or employees (*empleados*), and women normally work at home or in the market. For these marketers, the work of marketing is not viewed in the same way as the work of men in the fields or for wages, that is, as "real" work. Some sellers, like Víctor, the fruit-drink seller in Mercado Central, point to the conditions behind the influx of women to the market; he emphasized the unequal education of women and men, which favors men and prepares them for skilled occupations while it restricts women to unskilled or semiskilled work. Most informants, however, accounted for the concentration of women in marketing by reference to tradition (*es la costumbre*, or "it is the custom," was a very common response). As one man said, "Women have women's work and men have men's work."

Several cases suggest that more men than women are convinced that the marketplace is uniquely suited to women. We discussed the case of Carmen, whose husband rejected her plan of becoming a singer and insisted that she run a restaurant in Mercado Central. Similarly, the husband of Fortunata, a poultry seller in the same market, imposed his will by insisting that she leave another job and sell instead. With a primary school education, Fortunata had found a job as a substitute teacher, but her husband objected because she traveled and worked with other men. He is suffering for his jealousy, says Fortunata, because she used to have a good job and wages and associated with *gente decente* (respectable people), and now she works with *gente baja* (people of lower moral character).

Several women I questioned about the large number of female marketers attributed the situation to male deficiencies. These women, often the sole or primary supporters in their households, see their work as important and emphasize that if there are few men in the markets it is because men are lazy. One woman summarized the words of others when she said simply: "Men are lazy; women don't like to be lazy. Women work harder in the market and in the home." A few added that it is better to live alone, especially when a husband drinks and does not contribute to the family income. For these women, men are in a minority in the markets because they do not like to work—not because they are engaged in "real work" elsewhere.

A few women informants stressed the positive aspects of marketing for women when they considered why so many are employed in petty commerce: Women's work in the market is more secure (*más seguro*) than any kind of work men do, and they can depend on a small but regular income. When men engage in marketing, they are not as successful as women; men lack the skills, and, besides, the housewives who are the customers prefer to buy from other women.

When I asked marketers about the division of labor among female and male sellers in the markets, many maintained that men and women sell the same things and have the same degree of success. When the question was pursued, however, informants suggested reasons why a sexual division of labor in marketing may occur. Some called forth the issue of tradition, saying, it is not the custom for men to sell vegetables. As one woman explained, "Men are ashamed to sell vegetables; women like it better." A man who sells yarn with his wife in La Parada was asked why more men sell clothing and staple goods and few sell fruits and vegetables; he smirked at the idea of selling the latter and said: "Fruits and vegetables are for women. Men work in goods that sell better. How is a man going to sell fruits and vegetables? That's for women." When I asked another man, a seller of small household items, if he would like to sell vegetables, he answered that he did not know the business and had never tried, but he would not want to; he added that "men must look for a business that is more or less decent."

Although these sellers called attention to the sex role expectations underlying the division of labor, they also noted certain economic constraints on marketers that affect men and women differently. First, men are publicly recognized heads of families, and it is expected that as marketers they will sell products that result in the largest possible income. Second, the sale of such goods requires an economic base that men have access to but that women usually lack. For example, one female seller of clothing explained that more men work in this trade than in the sale of vegetables because they earn more selling clothes. When I asked why women do not choose to sell clothing more often, she answered that considerable capital is needed and women rarely have it unless they work in partnership with their husbands. As a further illustration, we may consider the case of Mario and Mónica, the couple who operates two stores selling staple groceries in Mercado Central. He began selling first, and after he was established he helped Mónica open her own store; now they say their sales are equal and they share their work and earnings. But it was socially and economically necessary for Mario to begin his store first since, as he says, the earnings of the man in the family are the most important.

It may be noted here that the capital men use to begin marketing often comes from outside the area of commerce, from their earnings as wage laborers or sometimes as a loan from male relatives. In addition, males appear to have the opportunity to work as apprentices more often than females, learning the skills of artisans and merchants and acquiring the means to begin their own businesses.

Some sellers point out the physical constraints on women's movements in certain areas of marketing activity. For example, a woman who brings fish to sell from Chimbote described the difficulties faced by women who work alone in this trade. She noted that to carry baskets of fish requires a lot of strength. Men handle them with greater ease, and some who have enough capital own trucks, which reduces the problems of transporting fish. Women must struggle on their own or hire assistants. The difficulty of handling large sacks of agricultural produce was mentioned by informants in reference to the work of women wholesalers. These women are at a disadvantage relative to male wholesalers since they must often pay assistants or bypass the producers' fields and buy from intermediaries at higher prices. The physical difficulty of this work is of course increased when women are pregnant or when they have small children along with them. Some women are, nonetheless, active wholesalers, and the man who said, "To go to the fields, carry sacks, take a burro . . . women are useless for these things," was not considering the reality of these women's work lives.

Five

The Work of Marketwomen

HOW DO MARKETERS begin their careers and what kind of livelihood results from their work? Is marketing an avenue to commercial success or an occupational deadend? How are marketers regulated by local authorities and how does this affect their work? These questions will guide us as we consider the work of marketwomen in Huaraz. Following this discussion, we will pay closer attention to the productive activity of marketers in order to understand better the role of marketwomen as workers in the local economy.

Beginning to Market

Among the sellers I interviewed in Huaraz were women who "grew up in the market," learning to sell at their mothers' or grandmothers' knees, and others who began selling later in life, in a few cases as recently as a few weeks before I spoke to them. They offered diverse responses to my questions concerning how they began marketing and how difficult it was. Depending on the type of marketing that sellers engage in and the resources they have available, beginning to market may be as easy as obtaining a few goods on credit and sitting in the street to sell them, or it may be a difficult period of acquiring a suitable selling place, a stock to begin selling, and the necessary commercial skills.

Generally, women who began selling during their childhood said that the process of starting to market on their own was not difficult. They had already learned where to obtain stock, how to judge its quality, and how to prepare the goods for sale. Many women had a small clientele from the years they accompanied their mothers, and some were able to take over their mothers' or other relatives' stalls when they retired from marketing. Furthermore, having begun to market before the number of sellers swelled the marketplace, they avoided some of the problems faced by those who began selling recently. These women often took for granted the process of learning to market as part of their way of life.

Women who began to market later in life, either because they recently migrated to Huaraz or because marketing only became an economic necessity in recent years, had more to say about the problems involved in entering petty commerce. Since these women are often first-generation marketers, they do not have the assistance of female relatives when they start selling. Sometimes they have friends in the markets who will help them find a place to sell or lend them a few soles to begin trading, but many sellers who began selling in their adulthood told me that they learned entirely on their own.

Beginning marketers who want to find permanent selling places (or, for that matter, older sellers who seek a change of location) have several options. They may choose the formal way, going directly to the Provincial Council to request selling space. There are unoccupied stalls in Mercado Central, as well as in the Centenario and Nicrupampa markets, to which they might be assigned. However, some women feel that the best stands are those constructed along the streets outside Mercado Central and in La Parada, where more consumers come to shop, but these are generally occupied. Thus, if a seller is eager to work in one, she is better off making contact with current stand holders and then waiting for a stand to become available. Many desirable stands are transferred in this manner. The new seller informs the council of the transfer, and the stand is generally registered in her name with no problem. Nevertheless, securing this kind of arrangement may take years, and a number of women have sold in the streets or at less desirable stalls for a long time without successfully acquiring space in the areas they prefer. Occasionally, these women take advantage of the temporary absence of marketers from desired stalls, agreeing to pay the required daily fees (discussed below) in return for the use of the stalls for a limited time.

Besides settling on a place to sell, marketers must concern themselves with acquiring stock. For all but the relatively few producer-sellers who do not need to buy in order to sell, this brings up the question of access to capital and credit. In the case of most small traders, the concept of capital has no significant meaning since they do not have capital and rely instead on the ready availability of credit, which is extended by most wholesalers. For example, the fruit and vegetable sellers and other small traders, who make up the bulk of sellers in Huaraz, have some difficulty in obtaining the money required to meet their initial expenses, such as the cost of a

Women and produce come in daily from the surrounding valley.

knife, a scale, a small chair to sit on, and an apron (and not all sellers can afford to purchase even these items). When it comes to buying their stock, most beginning sellers (and experienced ones, too) seek out wholesalers who will give them goods on credit. This may be difficult for the new sellers with few contacts and no established reputation for reliability; but they may be introduced to wholesalers by friends, or wholesalers may be willing to take a chance on them as potential new customers.

Petty traders are familiar with the word "capital," and while many told me that they operate without capital, others said they have S/.100 or S/.200. However, for most sellers with S/.100 or S/.200, this money does not function as capital since it is neither reinvested in their trade nor expected to grow in the future. Rather, most small sellers try to have a certain minimal amount of cash on hand to pay their fees, to use as change for customers, and to buy goods when credit is not offered; any extra is used to meet their families' immediate household needs.

Although it is possible to begin selling foodstuffs with scant resources, sellers who can draw on larger loans from family or friends or who have savings from past work experiences have more options in marketing. One retailer, Blanca, of Mercado Central, compared the economic resources necessary to enter commerce at various levels. Small retailers, she said, do not need capital since they may buy on credit; they need only enough to purchase their scale, weights, and knife (she said this would require S/.2,000 or S/.3,000, but this is more than many sellers have to start). In contrast to registered sellers with stalls, who can obtain goods on credit, *ambulantes* need a few thousand soles to operate (wholesalers cannot be certain of locating them and offer credit less often). She suggested that to be a wholesaler requires S/.20,000 or S/.30,000 to start, and to operate a restaurant or a store requires even more, around S/.40,000 and S/.50,000, respectively. Others might suggest different figures from Blanca's, but hers give a general idea of the requirements for entering commerce at various levels.

Huaraz marketers do not often work their way up from petty retailing to larger, more capitalized enterprises. Instead, most people in those enterprises entered business at or near their present level. Most had savings from other economic endeavors or considerable assistance and loans, which they applied toward their work in commerce. Not surprisingly, more men than women are found in this market elite. Two cases of successful male marketers provide a useful comparison with women marketers. Víctor, who has the lucrative fruit-drink bar in Mercado Central, was first in business raising poultry and then had the opportunity to study agricultural technology in Argentina. He considers agricultural technology his profession, but he was not successful, so he turned to the market in Huaraz. With his savings and business experience, he was able to rent ten contiguous meters of counterspace and begin working on a scale few sellers ever attain.

Carlos, an *ambulante* in La Parada, also entered commerce at a high level. Having dropped out of the normal school in Huaraz, Carlos found that the easiest thing for him to do without a profession was to sell in the market. It was especially convenient since his mother is a seamstress with a small business, and she gave him clothing valued at S/.30,000 to begin selling.

Marketwomen who begin selling in the more capital-intensive areas of marketing include those who begin selling groceries or manufactured items with loans from their husbands, and wholesalers who start with advances and assistance from family or friends already in the business or who work on commission for coastal factories. The tendency of this small group of sellers to enter these areas directly rather than rise in the marketing ranks will be explored further when we consider the question of social mobility in the marketplace.

Having access to credit and loans is essential to most marketers throughout their careers (since their business rarely grows), but it is especially important for new marketers getting established. As noted, the personal loans of family and friends are often a new seller's means of entering marketing. In Huaraz, however, I discovered none of the elaborate savings and credit associations established among sellers that have been observed among marketwomen in West Africa. Assistance is provided only on an individual, not a collective, basis.

Most wholesalers of foodstuffs are willing, as mentioned, to extend credit to their regular customers. New retailers must win the confidence of wholesalers by meeting their terms for repayment. Wholesalers offer goods on credit for two or three days, but if a retailer has not sold out and cannot repay, the wholesaler will generally wait another few days. Many wholesalers have a regular schedule, and the retailers they deal with know when to expect them to come around to their stalls. For example, two sisters regularly make trips to Chimbote for tomatoes, which they bring to Huaraz on Mondays. They sell wholesale as quickly as they can and then remain in Huaraz several days to sell the remainder of their tomatoes at retail prices. By Thursday, they are usually ready to leave, and they make their rounds collecting from clients before they go.

Wholesalers expect to give their product to retailers on credit, and they do not charge interest for the service. At the time when the retailer obtains goods from the wholesaler or soon after, each party normally records the price of the quantity of goods to be paid at a later time. Retailers seem to have a very good memory for the quantities and prices of items they buy and do not need to refer to their notebooks when the wholesaler comes around, but most keep a record in case of any disagreement. I have heard retailers insist to wholesalers that a record be made of their purchases. Elena once made a point of seeing that a woman from whom she regularly buys apples recorded her name as well as the amount of apples she purchased. Wholesalers are legally responsible for giving receipts to their retail customers, but if any do this I did not observe it, nor did I see any retailers request receipts.

Although *ambulantes* are a bad credit risk because they may leave the city without paying, some can obtain very short-term credit, for two or three hours. One *ambulante* who does business this way complained that sellers with capital and stalls can obtain more credit for longer periods, while she and others like her cannot.

Another source of financial assistance for marketers is the banks, but bank loans are available only to a privileged few. One couple who sells yarn in La Parada obtains loans occasionally by going to three different banks, trying one after another in succession. Another woman told me that she used to be able to get loans from her bank, but, once, she could not repay and no longer has access to loans.

The Regulation of Marketers

All marketers are required to pay one or more fees in Huaraz, whether they are daily urban marketers or casual sellers from the countryside. They are also subject to certain regulations, which are enforced under penalty of fines issued by local authorities. Although authorities keep a rather low profile, they maintain fairly strict control of the marketplace.

All marketers, *ambulantes* as well as those with stands, must have photo identification cards to show that they have passed a medical exam. The cards, bearing the title Carnet Sanitario (health card), are issued by the Provincial Council. In addition to paying for the cards, sellers have to pay for their medical exams. Many of them object strongly to the blood tests they must undergo, believing that it is unhealthful to lose blood. Their concern over the tests and the expense keep some marketers from obtaining their cards. Accordingly, they risk being fined.

Annual registration fees, which are of growing concern to marketers recently, must be paid by all sellers with permanent stalls (they are paid by all commercial establishments and transport agents in Huaraz as well). These fees, called the Derecho de Matrícula (matriculation right), vary in amount based on the products sold and the space that sellers occupy. For example, in 1976 sellers of vegetables, fruits, prepared food, and bread paid S/.50 for each meter of space they occupied (most have two meters of table space), while sellers of staples paid S/.70, and meat sellers paid S/.150 per meter. When the fee is paid, marketers are given receipts indicating the location and size of their stalls and stipulating their daily fees. Some sellers cannot, or choose not, to pay the fees, risking fines instead. Several, like Elena, expressed their concern that if they pay one year it may be discovered that they did not do so the year before.

Daily market fees are collected from all sellers and, like the registration fees, they vary by product sold. The fees, called Derecho de Puesto (stall right) or Arbitrios (rates or taxes), also vary slightly by market. In Mercado Central fees ranged in 1977 from S/.2 per meter for sellers of vegetables, fruits, groceries, and bread to S/.5 per meter for sellers of prepared food, fish, and household merchandise to S/.10 for meat sellers. Sellers at the Centenario market are charged somewhat more, presumably because of the attractive quality of their stalls. Those at the Nicrupampa market pay somewhat less for the simple counter space they use, and the fee collectors only bother to make the trip to collect from the four sellers there around once a month. *Ambulantes* in La Parada pay about the same as sellers in Mercado Central pay for one meter, though street sellers generally use more space than this. Again, some sellers manage to escape paying these fees. *Ambulantes* sometimes appeal to collectors, saying they have not yet sold anything and cannot pay until they do—and then move to a different spot. *Ambulantes* are easy to miss anyway, and some rarely pay any fees at all.

Marketers must pay a number of other fees from time to time. Those with scales must pay S/.30 or S/.50, depending on the scale's size, twice yearly to have the accuracy verified. Each time sellers use the large platform scale in Mercado Central they pay S/.2 for the service. Perhaps the most annoying fee is the S/.2 people must pay each time they use the latrines in that market.

Special fees pertain to certain sellers. For example, when sellers of beef, mutton, or pork take their animals to the slaughterhouse, they must pay veterinary fees and slaughtering fees. And sellers of grains pay mill owners to prepare their product for sale.

Wholesalers pay fees based on the quantity of goods brought in and taken out of the city (*ingreso* and *salida*, respectively). They are usually charged in accordance with the number of sacks or crates they have, say, S/.5 per sack of potatoes, or occasionally by the truckload. Since wholesalers must generally pay *salida* on the goods they take from regions outside Huaraz and *ingreso* on the same goods once they reach the city, they pay twice before the products are sold to retailers in the markets.

All the fees discussed here were undergoing consideration in the council in 1977, and tentative increases were suggested. The market fees are a chief source of revenue for the city, as revealed by the mayor's attention to them and by the marketers' understanding of their own power in threatening to withhold the fees (and their labor). Sellers are particularly angered by proposed fee increases because they know that market taxation supports the city bureaucracy and does not result in improvements that benefit them. As one seller put it, "If the increases were to build industry and create jobs—to give more work to people—it would be one thing, but we don't see anything of that."

As noted before, the wholesale and retail prices of basic foodstuffs and "articles of primary necessity" were under the control of the Peruvian Ministry of Food during this period. The ministry's offices in the department capitals established prices on a regional basis. These prices were subject to change biweekly when the ministry issued new price lists based on supply and the distance that goods traveled to reach their destination.

In Huaraz, lists were distributed to marketers every two weeks, and both wholesalers and retailers were responsible for selling at the official prices. Included in the lists were around fifty to sixty types and qualities of vegetables, fruits, and grains, depending on the season, with wholesaler and retailer prices by the kilo (or by different measures or units for some products).

The prices of such items as meat, bread, milk, butter, sugar, rice, flour, noodles, and oil were also officially controlled. The national government's announcements of rising prices were generally made on the radio and passed by word of mouth even before the local ministry issued notices. Such announcements came with alarming frequency during and after my 1977 field research.

Along with the controls on prices, the Ministry of Food in Huaraz set several other regulations against speculation in goods and the alteration of prices. Retailers were legally required to obtain receipts of wholesalers (though they did not appear to comply in this), and wholesalers who sold products directly to the public were required to sell at wholesale prices (actually, goods marketed this way are usually sold at prices between the official wholesale and retail prices).

The local authorities who enforce the regulations include inspectors from the Provincial Council, city police, and the PIP, the Peruvian Investigative Police. At the inspectors' stations in Mercado Central and Mercado Centenario, officers work on a rotating basis for several weeks at a time, as directed by the council. These officers act in a supervisory capacity, and they serve as intermediaries between marketers and higher levels of law enforcement. The officer who was most often in Mercado Central during my fieldwork appeared to be an easy-going, sympathetic man, who tried not to make problems for anyone. When marketers came to him with their troubles, he seemed concerned, spoke with them in Quechua, and tried to solve their problems. Nevertheless, as a representative of local government, he passed down regulations from above, issued summonses, and occasionally reported sellers to the council. In his capacity as an intermediary, he acted as a buffer, making it easier for higher authorities to control the marketers.

To the extent that they were able, the officers in Mercado Central and Mercado Centenario disregarded minor infractions of market regulations. In Mercado Centenario, marketers were often allowed to charge a little more than the official prices because it was under-

Table 3
Sample Wholesale and Retail Prices in Mercado Central

Product	Wholesale Price	Retail Price
Potatoes	S/.10	S/.12
Ollucos	S/.17	S/.20
Yucca	S/.9	S/.11
Sweet potatoes	S/.9 (S/.10)	S/.12
Cabbage	S/.4	S/.7 (S/.6)
Onions	S/.15	S/.17
Tomatoes	S/.7 (S/.11)	S/.15
Squash	S/.12	S/.15
Carrots	S/.12 (S/.8–9)	S/.15 (S/.10–11)
Limes	S/.450 bag of 800 (S/.500)	S/.1 each (S/1.50)
Corn	S/.25	S/.30
Apples	S/.20 (S/.22)	S/.25
Bananas	S/.2 each	S/.2.50 each

Source: 1977 survey by Florence Babb.

stood that their expenses were higher. When I asked an officer there if the prices were the same in that market as elsewhere, he said they were; since it was common knowledge that they were not, his response suggested to me the protective role these officers sometimes play in relation to the sellers.

In the markets generally, some flexibility was allowed in pricing. A list of products and their prices that I recorded one day at Blanca's stall in Mercado Central can serve as an example of the sellers' degree of conformity to official prices. Table 3 lists the products she had for sale, the prices she paid wholesalers, and the prices she charged consumers. Where prices differ from the official ones for the time period, I have put them in parentheses. Prices are per kilo unless otherwise noted. Blanca expressed some surprise when I pointed out how these prices deviated from official ones. But she explained that the question of quality must be considered and that, when goods are of higher or lower than average quality, the price may be altered. This is particularly true as goods begin to spoil, and prices drop accordingly. Sellers claimed a certain degree of ignorance of changing prices (and it was clearly hard to remember because they changed so often), and they also emphasized that they have a right to readjust prices in line with the desirability of their product. Market officers understood this and seldom imposed fines if the sellers' prices were reasonable.

Higher-level authorities, however, show less sympathy with sellers, and many informants related experiences of having been fined and treated harshly. The most feared and disliked are the police from the PIP. A number of women told me they had been fined by the PIP for such minor violations as failing to display a sign posting a price or charging prices a sol or two above those set by the ministry. Elena described PIP officers as "cunning, ruthless, and brutal . . . striking out at the innocent." They come around the markets and give fines arbitrarily to marketers, she said. She bitterly described the time she was taken to their office simply because she had neglected to post a price. She had her daughter Pilar with her, then seven months old, and they were kept late into the night, the officers showing no compassion when Pilar cried. In the end, Elena was not fined, but a lot of information about her was recorded, and she felt humiliated by the experience. "There's no justice for the poor," she told me. Another woman had to pay a fine of S/.2,000 (equivalent to weeks of market earnings) because, she said, her price sign had fallen down. She had to borrow money after a lawyer told her there was nothing she could do but pay. Many other sellers had similar stories.

Some authorities from the Provincial Council are also known for their insolence and condescending way of dealing with sellers. Fee collectors, for example, have the power to remove sellers from their stalls if they do not pay the Derecho de Puesto for three consecutive days, and impoverished marketers can only hope to appeal to the collectors' better nature. Sellers are also wary of the inspector of hygiene and the inspector of weights and measures, both of whom issue frequent fines for small infractions (e.g., improper protection of foods, inaccurate measures). A common complaint of small retailers is that they receive a disproportionate share of fines, while the larger violators, wholesalers, are less often apprehended and penalized.

The Livelihood of Marketers

The first thing that may be said about the livelihood of the majority of small traders is that it is a very poor one. When asked how much she earns by the day or by the week, a marketwoman's immediate response is likely to be: "How much do I earn? Better to ask how much I lose!" or "Earnings? I can tell you about expenses.

There are no earnings." While these comments accurately reflect the frustration of many sellers who, in fact, do lose money from time to time and who have been undergoing a period of real hardship since the mid-1970s as a result of the economic crisis, sellers must, of course, earn something or they would stop selling. No marketers I spoke to kept records of their incomes (they only recorded what they owed wholesalers or the amounts owed them by customers), but I found that by observing and talking with marketers I could arrive at some idea of their earnings.

There are several ways to try to calculate the incomes of marketers. The first, by observing and recording the sales of an individual seller for a set period of time and subtracting expenses, is difficult since transactions are sometimes rapid, and accurate recording requires interrupting the seller in her work. A second way is to keep track of a seller's stock, how much she paid for it and what her prices are, and then observe how quickly the stock is sold, thereby figuring her earnings. This method, too, is difficult and open to error. I decided, on the basis of initial questioning, that simply asking sellers for estimates of their earnings might be as accurate as the other methods.

When I asked numerous vegetable and fruit sellers about their earnings in 1977, there was considerable agreement in their responses. After the initial denials, most said they make between S/.20 and S/.40 daily, but that some days they make nothing and some weeks they make as little as S/.100.[1] Low as this seems, the consistency of their responses and my own observations lead me to believe that these estimates are probably accurate. Some produce marketers selling in the streets do better, earning S/.50 or more daily, and clothing sellers told me they earn around S/.100 daily. The earnings of prepared food sellers vary widely depending on the size of their operations, from the level of vegetable sellers to well above it. Sellers of manufactured housewares seem to make in the range of S/.100 or more daily.

With earnings as low as these generally are, it is no wonder that few marketers envision the expansion of their businesses and more often struggle just to keep the level of their trade from contracting. Their "profit," taken home in the form of a small amount of money or some leftover food, is hardly enough to support themselves and rarely enough to support a family. The goal of most of these small marketers is to maintain trade at its present level and to bring home a modest, but steady, income—that is, to reproduce their present conditions. How many of them are successful even in this is difficult to ascertain, but clearly the majority need to rely on various sources of family livelihood. Notwithstanding the resourcefulness of marketers, a frequent comment heard about market income is, *"No alcanza,"* which means literally "it doesn't reach," or it is not enough to meet family needs.

When asked about their earnings, a number of women say, "We make enough to eat, that's all." Many of them measure their success by the food they can afford to take home from their stands, like one woman who said, "I don't really make a profit, I just have some food left over." Bread sellers are a good case in point. These women buy from bakeries, which typically give them twenty extra rolls for every one hundred they buy. For women doing business on a small scale, this can mean that their efforts keep their families supplied in bread but little more. Women, like Elena, who sell bread from their homes as a sideline, do not view it as gainful employment but simply as a way to save the money their families would otherwise spend on bread.

So far, we have seen that marketwomen have a general sense of their daily or weekly incomes as measured by the money or food taken home. Sellers also reckon their earnings by calculating the potential income from a quantity of a particular product and keeping track of how long it takes to sell out. For example, if a seller buys a seventy-five-kilo sack of sweet potatoes at the official wholesale price of S/.9 per kilo and sells at the official retail price of S/.11 per kilo, her earnings on the sack will be S/.150. The important question for her, then, is how long it takes her to sell all the sweet potatoes. It makes a considerable difference to her whether she sells out in two days or five. A number of sellers explained to me that, while they do not know exactly how much they make daily, they do know *por producto,* or by the product. Accordingly, when I spoke to one woman about her earnings, she said she was not sure but pointed to a pile of carrots and said she would make S/.50 or S/.60 on them. Similarly, another woman indicated the size of her earnings by pointing to a bag of *ají,* saying she would have S/.40 or S/.50 when they were sold.

While marketers pay attention to particular products and how well they are selling, they rarely attempt any precise calculations of their total earnings. However, some sellers have an interesting way of keeping track of earnings. They have cloth purses with four or five pockets sewn inside, and in each pocket they place a small piece of a product they are selling. Then, they keep earnings for that product in the same pocket. These purses, usually embellished with machine-stitched designs, are made by women in Huaraz and sold in the market. Their use is considered "traditional," and some "modern" marketers reject them in favor of factory-produced coin purses in which earnings are not divided by product. For the most part, however, sellers toss money into a pile in their stalls as they sell or tie it up in a handkerchief.

In determining her earnings *por producto*, a seller can also compare present sales with business in the past. Most sellers remember that in previous years their goods moved much faster. For example, a woman who sells pork told me that she earns S/.100 for each roast pig she sells; but, whereas she used to sell one a day, it now takes her three or four days to sell a single pig (furthermore, the price is so high now that she can only afford to buy one at a time, while before she could buy several). Similarly, a poultry seller commented that a year ago she sold eighty chickens in a day, and now she only sells thirty or forty.

Marketers know what they can expect to earn when they are selling at fixed prices by the kilo. Some foodstuffs, however, are sold by bunches or units, and sellers sometimes find that they have to increase the size of their units in order to win customers, meaning a decrease in their earnings. For example, women who sell bunches of alfalfa for S/.5 find that they are forced to compete with each other by adding to their bunches to get customers, thus earning less. A woman selling parsley told me she is losing money since customers will not buy a bunch for S/.5 unless extra is thrown in. While it is Andean custom to give a little extra, known as *llapa*, these marketers selling by the unit are particularly vulnerable to pressure from urban customers to increase their portions, thereby reducing their earnings.

Consumers often believe that petty traders benefit as prices rise. This is not so under present conditions of underdevelopment in Peru, and, in fact, their business often declines with increased prices. The official prices of basic foodstuffs enforced by the military government allowed retailers only a few soles per kilo sold, and this did not, as a rule, increase as prices went up. On the contrary, if the wholesale price of an item increased two soles, the retail price generally went up by two soles as well. For example, one week potatoes rose in price from S/.10 per kilo to retailers and S/.12 to consumers to S/.13 per kilo to retailers and S/.15 to consumers. For the retailer, this meant she must pay more to obtain the same quantity of goods, and though her investment was greater her earnings were not. Furthermore, rising prices resulted in reduced consumption for some items, meaning lower sales and earnings for marketers. Poultry, for example, went up in price several times while I carried out field-work, from S/.110 to S/.120 to S/.130 per kilo over a few months. The sellers' earnings remained steady to S/.30 per kilo (not subtracting their expenses), but as consumers began buying less chicken their sales declined noticeably.

Although I have emphasized the low earnings of marketers, the difficulty they have in maintaining their income at a steady level, and their apparent lack of attention to total earnings, this should not be taken to suggest that petty retailers lack "business sense" or that they do not think through strategies for economic survival. On the contrary, sellers discuss the economic principles underlying their work and demonstrate an impressive ability to get by under difficult conditions. While petty traders often have no alternative but to sell as retailers, since they lack capital, they point to the advantages of selling this way. In comparison with selling at wholesale prices, selling retail allows them to charge a little more on the small quantity they sell. They show an awareness that they are substituting labor for capital, spending long hours selling as a strategy for earning the most on their stock. They also recognize the importance of carrying a variety of goods, since as small marketers they depend on a steady clientele of a few shoppers who look for an assortment of products. This also acts as a hedge against a single product spoiling or not selling well.

Many street sellers work without scales, and instead of selling by weight they sell by some accepted measure—cup, can, plateful, pile—or by the unit. These sellers see themselves as filling an important niche in the market, for, as they say, many people prefer to buy by the measure rather than by the kilo. This way shoppers who can afford only two or three soles' worth of an item may purchase it. Women who sell this way often buy from retailers themselves, by the kilo rather than by the sack, and then sell to consumers in even smaller quantities.

Sellers consider carefully the merits of trading in one item rather than another and weigh the risks involved in selling various goods. The women who sell foodstuffs, who make up the majority in the markets, recognize the risk taken in selling perishable items but often do not have the means to sell other goods. Sellers of *raspadillas*, a flavored ice snack, describe the uncertainties of their trade, noting that on sunny days more people want a cool refreshment but the ice melts fast, while on cloudy days the ice lasts but few customers come around. Other women, who sell such items as clothing or kitchen supplies, appreciate nonperishability as a major advantage in their trade. However, even these sellers must often be aware of the changing marketability of their goods, as for example sellers of shoes, who want to unload cloth and leather shoes before the rainy season, when plastic shoes are in demand.

The retailers I knew in Huaraz had different degrees of skills in selling. Some had a remarkable ability to calculate prices quickly in their heads, while others relied upon a book of multiplication tables. I was occasionally asked to work out an addition or multiplication problem, but a number of marketers could have offered the same service. Lack of arithmetic and reading skills (for price lists) clearly held back some sellers, but others seemed to make up for having little or no schooling with their years of experience.

Petty marketers, then, reveal a good deal of business sense and an ability to make a living creatively in the markets, often under difficult conditions. Their selling strategies, however, rarely suggest the kinds of entrepreneurial principles that are commonly associated with marketers. These principles were only articulated to me by informants (mainly men) who sold on a larger scale, primarily wholesalers.

A number of wholesalers explained the importance of keeping their capital working. This is why they prefer to sell wholesale rather than retail; they see a fast return on their investment, they lose less in overhead expenses, and there is less risk of losing perishable items. When wholesalers have sold as much of their stock as possible to retailers, they must often stay in the market selling to the public until their product is gone. Although they may earn a little more on their stock this way, they find it tedious and a waste of time since their capital is static. They want to sell fast and go out to buy again quickly, to keep their capital working. In contrast to retailers, who often attach relatively little value to their time, wholesalers value time highly. (Retailers want to sell fast enough to maintain a living income, but wholesalers want to sell much more rapidly because their mode of livelihood depends on the quick turnover of large quantities of goods.)

Enterprising wholesalers also described the best conditions for marketing. They contrasted the producers' favorable return in times of abundance with their own success in times of scarcity, when prices rise. One man, however, outlined some risks involved. He offered the example that when he comes from Piura to Huaraz with lemons and others come from Lima with lemons that are cheaper, he has to lower his prices even though he paid more; still, he may buy during an abundance in Piura and find a scarcity in Huaraz, allowing him to charge more. He noted that prices are in accordance with the marketplace (*la plaza*), adding, "It's the merchant's law" (*Es la ley del comerciante*).

Retailers, as was mentioned, generally prefer a diversified stock to attract customers and reduce risk. Wholesalers have several different strategies in this regard. Many specialize in a particular item, like the seller of lemons discussed above, in order to know the market for that item as well as possible, gaining an advantage in the plaza. These sellers know the best sources of supply, develop useful connections, and willingly take the chance that they may be unlucky with their single item and have to take a loss. Other wholesalers choose to diversify, saying that under present economic conditions a person cannot depend on only one enterprise but needs to engage in several.

Marketers and Social Mobility

Research in Huaraz has suggested that petty traders do not, on the whole, accumulate capital and evolve into large-scale retailers or wholesalers. Some large-scale marketers say they built up their businesses *poco a poco* (little by little) in the marketplace, but I have insufficient information about them to say whether these are sellers with exceptional talents or whether they had outside assistance. Two sisters who work together as wholesalers told me they began as retailers selling herbs until their business grew to the point where they could turn to wholesale trade. Their husbands are truck drivers, and probably offered assistance, if only in the form of transportation (as a number of truck driver husbands do for their marketer wives). The few similar cases suggest that individual mobility may occasionally be possible in the marketplace, though it is unusual.

My follow-up interviews in 1982, 1984, and 1987 revealed only a few individuals whose enterprises had expanded since my first visit to Huaraz. These were generally special cases. For example, Toribia and Pedro, who sold cosmetics as *ambulantes* when I knew them in 1977, had clearly met with some success. They had acquired impressive glass display cases, which were filled with merchandise (now, inexpensive jewelry in addition to toiletries and cosmetics), and they were located in an area covering four stalls in Mercado Central. Moreover, they recently acquired a photocopier, which is stationed at the post office, where their employee serves customers. While Toribia and Pedro were obviously proud of the growth of their business, they were more reluctant to be interviewed than most of my friends in the market. Some sellers suggested to me that the

This woman was unusually successful in expanding her business.

couple deals in contraband goods, avoiding taxes by buying products that come through Chile. This would not be uncommon and could explain their success. Víctor, the largest and most successful seller of fruit drinks in Mercado Central, has also seen the expansion of his business. When I returned to Huaraz, Víctor's wife was running the fruit-drink stand, while he himself worked up to sixteen hours a day in his new restaurant, Eight Flavors, named after his popular market enterprise. In Víctor's case, his wife's assistance and his earlier prosperity, along with his unusually high level of education, may account for the measure of success he has had recently. These examples are exceptional, however, and not typical experiences of those marketers I reinterviewed.

If a few individuals make their way up the marketplace hierarchy, do individuals move from marketplace employment to higher status commerce as shopkeepers? To investigate this question, I conducted brief interviews with shopkeepers along three city blocks of Huaraz. I chose blocks along important commercial streets in different areas of downtown Huaraz: a block along Jirón Ancash bordering on Mercado Central, a centrally located block along Avenida Raimondi, and a block along Avenida Centenario in the older commercial district. I took a census of merchants on these streets not only to discover how many were former marketers but also to find out how women's participation as shopkeepers compares with their participation as marketers.

Table 4 provides a summary of the number of merchants included in my census and the distribution of shopkeepers, or owners (*dueños*), by sex. While the majority of stores I counted could be called family businesses, most people I spoke to indicated whether the *dueño* was male, female, or a couple. In some cases this was not entirely clear, as, for example, when several women who obviously had responsibility for stores insisted the businesses belonged to their husbands or when a man told me that his wife was an equal partner because under law wives own half the business. Since I wanted to determine who actually controls the shops, that is, who spends time working there and makes the daily decisions concerning buying and selling, I sometimes needed to interpret such comments cautiously.

The three streets surveyed differ somewhat in terms of the kinds of store represented. Jirón Ancash includes, in the main, stores selling clothing, shoes, hats, and fabric and receives a slightly higher spillover business from the market. Raimondi and Centenario have a higher middle-class traffic and include hardware and appliance stores, bookstores, grocery stores, and restaurants in addition to some clothing stores.

On the basis of these data, it is possible to draw a few tentative conclusions. Overall, the composition of shopkeepers by sex differs from that in the marketplace. Of the thirty-four shops in the census, only four are run independently by women. In contrast, twelve shops are operated by men and eighteen are operated by husbands and wives together.

My questioning revealed that none of the women working in these shops are former marketers, while two of the twelve men working independently and four of the eighteen men working with their wives had earlier experience in the marketplace. Among the four independent women, two presently operate clothing stores on Jirón Ancash; one is a former housewife (*en casa*, or at home) and the other is a seamstress who acquired her own shop, where she makes and sells her clothing along with an assistant. The other two women who work independently operate restaurants, and they include a former maid whose husband, a barber, gave her the capital to open a restaurant on Centenario and a woman who operates a restaurant on Raimondi (I spoke to her employee since she was absent and did not learn much about her background).

The woman who formerly devoted herself to homemaking de-

Table 4
Shopkeepers on Three City Blocks by Sex

Street	Male	Female	Male-Female Couple	Total
Ancash	5	2	7	**14**
Raimondi	6	1	5	**12**
Centenario	1	1	6	**8**
Total	12	4	18	**34**

Source: 1977 survey by Florence Babb.

scribed how she opened her clothing store just six months before. Her store, located in her house on Jirón Ancash, consists of a large front room, which she previously rented to others. She began with the help of her husband, who is a carpenter (and makes guitars, which are also for sale in her store), and now has S/.6,000 capital. She buys clothes made by *campesinos* on credit, paying them when they return a week or two later. She described how present economic conditions make it necessary for women to work and how few opportunities exist for women in Huaraz. In her own case, supporting nine children through school has required that she and her husband both contribute to family income.

Of the six male shopkeepers who had marketing experience, four were *ambulantes* selling clothing who eventually acquired their own shops to continue the same business (one man only sold on the street temporarily, when the earthquake destroyed his store). Several of these shopkeepers asserted that, although having a shop is more respectable then selling on the street, the latter often attracts more customers. One man who runs a store with his wife simply began selling from their front room when selling was declared illegal along Avenida Raimondi; they have found that their expenses are up and sales are down since leaving the street. The other two men with marketing backgrounds include a former retail grocer, who now has a clothing shop, and a jeweler, who used to sell on the streets and now has a shop. The majority of male shopkeepers, however, had such previous experiences as working in family-owned stores, being apprenticed or employed in other stores, or working as artisans (e.g., tailor, baker) or as independent business agents (e.g., selling trucks, managing a brother's shoe store).

Two young men working on Raimondi, one operating the largest bookstore in the city and the other operating a moderately success-ful restaurant, recently opened their businesses. Their description of how they entered commerce illustrates the entrepreneurial outlook characteristic of male shopkeepers, which is quite distinct from the outlook of petty traders (particularly women). The bookstore owner left engineering school to open his store in 1974. Now he has four employees and says business is good. When I asked him how he managed to begin his business, he answered with a knowing smile that "after the earthquake everything was easy" since so little was left of the city. The opportunism of this shopkeeper contrasts with the alleged opportunism of *campesinos* who came to the city after the earthquake. The second young man opened his restaurant in 1975 after graduating from high school, where he had business train-ing. He was able to begin with a capital of only S/.1,000 since his restaurant is in his father's house and he has no rent to pay. From a small operation with only two tables, the restaurant has grown and now has seven tables, a refrigerator, a kitchen, and a cook and as-sistant. He attributes his success to the determination he has felt since boyhood to become somebody important (*llegar a ser grande*). He aspires, "like any man" (*como todo hombre*), to become the most successful restaurant owner in the city.

While those in petty commerce in the marketplace are feeling the serious effects of national economic problems, some of the shop-keepers discussed here are growing wealthier and expanding busi-ness. Three of the eighteen couples included in the census have re-cently opened a second establishment next door to their first (two couples with grocery stores opened restaurants, and a couple with a shoe store opened an electrical appliance store). Several shopkeepers talk of setting up branch stores to pass on to their children (and at least one man has done this as owner of a chain of hardware stores in Huaraz and elsewhere in the Callejón). These entrepreneurs main-tain that present conditions make it imperative to go beyond one family store.

This discussion of shopkeepers in Huaraz has indicated that only a few among the city's petty bourgeois have any background in the marketplace or in street vending; that women's participation as shop-keepers is much lower than men's, particularly when compared with their relative participation as marketers; and that shopkeepers often espouse the entrepreneurial views found lacking among marketers.

A thorough examination of the question of social mobility among marketers would require a consideration of whether market sellers, in significant numbers, leave their work altogether for other areas of employment. Those marketers who left marketing during the years between my visits to Huaraz were sometimes difficult to locate. The few I found had transferred to other tertiary-sector jobs, sometimes working in a bakery or as a domestic servant. While several preferred the location, hours, or conditions of their new work to those of marketing, the work would not be regarded as having higher status.

Given the paucity of employment opportunities, especially for women, and the weight of household responsibilities, sometimes a desirable move "upward" for marketwomen is to leave the income-generating work force and devote full attention to their domestic work. The dominant middle-class preference in Peru for women to stay at home defines such a move out of the marketplace and into the home as a move upward. This implies women's dependence on men, however, and assumes that women may be defined by the income-earning potential of the men in their families—which we may question as a standard of mobility among women.

Although social and economic differentiation is evident among marketers—with a few meeting success and a larger number experiencing difficulties—marketing is rarely a channel of upward mobility in Huaraz, at least under the present circumstances. However, if the question of mobility is extended to include marketers' families, some change may be taking place. The next chapter considers to what extent the children of marketwomen may be finding increased employment opportunities as a consequence of their mothers' efforts to support them through school.

The Productive Activity of Marketers

So far in this chapter we have considered the mechanics of marketing without examining very closely the content of the work of marketers. Buying and selling are of course essential features of marketing, but what occurs between the actual transfers of goods and money is also very important. Here we will discuss the productive role marketers play as they prepare items for sale to consumers. In my view, the physical transport, bulking and bulk-breaking, and other aspects of readying products for sale, which are generally considered distributive functions, as well as the creation, transformation, and finishing of products for sale, often referred to as processing, should be recognized as productive work—adding value to goods for sale.

Whether marketers transport the stocks they sell across the country or across the city, they are involved in some part of the process of bringing goods to the consumer. Actual transportation of the products may be provided by others, but marketers oversee their passage and ensure their safe arrival at the marketplace. This step in the process of bringing goods from producer to consumer is obviously essential, but it is often taken for granted.

Once goods are in the hands of marketers and until they are sold, a number of tasks may need to be performed. Bulking and bulk-breaking are important services carried out by marketers. Wholesalers often engage in both the aggregation of goods from various sources, large and small producers alike, and the distribution of goods in small quantities, such as by the crate or sack, to retailers. And retailers, in their turn, direct time and energy to breaking bulk as they prepare goods for sale in the quantities desired by customers, by the kilo, bunch, or plateful. For some marketers, like the sellers of staples, breaking bulk is a major part of their work. These sellers purchase such goods as rice, sugar, noodles, flour, and salt in heavy sacks, and while many of their goods are weighed and packaged on the spot as requested by customers, suitable quantities are frequently placed in plastic bags in advance. Several women described this work as time-consuming, difficult, and even unhealthful as it requires handling heavy sacks. Indeed, as I spoke with these women, they were often busy measuring and bagging items for sale.

Other related activities of marketers include sorting, cleaning, preserving, storing, and generally looking after the goods they have for sale. Sellers of perishable goods must pay close attention to the condition of their products and do all they can to protect them from the harmful effects of mistreatment, the sun, heat, and cold. Some food items, especially meat, must be preserved overnight through refrigeration. Storage is a problem faced by all marketers, and those without a secure place to leave unsold goods in the markets must take them home to ensure their safety.

Marketers' work also includes transforming (i.e., value-creating) aspects. Our analysis, however, need not treat as separate categories the caretaking tasks discussed above and the more creative tasks described below, since all these activities are part of the total production process that goods undergo as the cycle of production, distribution, and consumption is completed. In the case of the numerous vegetable and fruit sellers, caretaking operations often extend to innovative ways of transforming products into more desirable forms for consumption. When I began research in the Huaraz markets I was surprised at just how much of the sellers' time is devoted to working with their products. Many marketers were so busy with their goods, in fact, that selling appeared to be an interruption to the real work at hand.

After sellers bring fresh produce to their stalls, they begin to ready it for sale. This usually means removing goods from sacks and sorting through them to examine their quality and pick out any bad items. They arrange the goods carefully on their tables, often cleaning and shining them at the same time. This may be all that is necessary for some kinds of produce, but others demand more attention. Cauliflower trunks are removed, the outer skins of onions are peeled, and so on before these items are ready for sale.

For many marketwomen, the preparation of goods does not end here. A large number of women provide the extra service of cutting up a variety of vegetables to be sold in small packets for soup. The packets are not sold by weight but by the unit, say, S/.5 for a small paper bagful. Sellers claim that they earn no more money this way and that customers benefit because they can buy a small quantity of mixed vegetables at low cost. Actually, I ascertained that in terms of price per kilo consumers do pay more this way, but for the poorest shoppers the advantage is in paying less on a daily basis. Sellers do the extra work of preparing packets in order to win customers, who include those too poor to buy in larger quantity as well as others who buy packets to save time in cooking the family meal. Most women who sell prepared vegetables make up packets in the marketplace while they sell, but some do it at home. One woman described her work schedule, which begins at 6:00 A.M. when she buys four kilos of carrots, five kilos of squash, eight kilos of cabbage, and three kilos of tomatoes. These vegetables are put aside until after she finishes the morning's selling (of previously prepared packets), when she takes them home to prepare for the next day. She says it takes most of the afternoon, from 2:00 P.M. to 6:00 P.M., to prepare packets, but it is worth the effort because she sells faster that way.

Some marketwomen, like Elena, have special agreements to prepare vegetables for individual clients. As has been noted, she peels six kilos of potatoes and varying quantities of carrots and onions for her market neighbor each day. Peeling these vegetables takes up a good part of her time in the market, and she often says, "Until I die I'll be peeling."

Other marketers specialize in selling particular vegetable-derived products, which they prepare at home. Two such products are *tocush* and *chocho*. *Tocush* is made by allowing corn or potatoes to ferment, a process that involves around six weeks of waiting and watching to see that the product does not spoil. *Chocho* is made by boiling dry *chocho* beans (lupines) in water for three or four days until the bitterness leaves them and then adding onion, tomatoes, peppers, lemons, and coriander to the cooked beans.

Some marketers specialize in the preparation of condiments. They buy the ingredients, *ají*, garlic, and herbs, in the market and generally prepare the condiments at home since it requires more time than they have while selling. The ingredients must be ground with a mortar and pestle, a tiring process that may take several hours; the product is sold both as a dry powder for cooking and moistened with water for immediate consumption with meals. One woman keeps a second mortar and pestle at her stall in order to do part of the work while she sells. Her neighbor helps by peeling garlic for her, receiving S/.1 for each bunch she peels. Still, she says that when she runs out every four days or so she must work all afternoon at home to replenish her supply.

Grains are converted by some women into *mote* or flour. *Mote* is a hominy-like product made from corn, barley, or wheat, which is boiled in water (with some ash added to remove the tough exterior of barley or wheat). The product must be cooked for several hours, sometimes overnight, but if it boils beyond the point of peeling the ash may give it a bad flavor. Some sellers buy wheat, barley, corn, and beans to have them ground into flour. This normally requires several days in order to clean the grains, sort through them, and take them to a mill.

Sellers of meals and snacks are, not surprisingly, among the busiest in the marketplace. In Mercado Central, restaurant operators generally prepare a day ahead but still arrive as early as 4:30 or 5:00 A.M. to be ready to serve breakfast to people arriving from the countryside around 6:00 A.M. Mealtimes are often hectic, and cleaning up and preparing for the next day keep these marketers at work longer hours than most other sellers. When Carmen's assistant left her, she was barely able to manage. Justina, also of Mercado Central, has a smaller restaurant and works alone, but she has her hands full with the preparation of chicken stew each day; she brings a live chicken to her stall and butchers it herself in order to save money on the price of poultry.

The preparation of some snacks is also time-consuming. Rosa spends three hours every morning making *mazamorra*, the cornstarch pudding that consists of squash, sugar, flour, cinnamon, and a paste made of toasted corn. Then, for the next three hours, she sells the confection. *Ambulantes* sometimes sell *tamales*, another snack requiring two or three hours of preparation. First corn is peeled by boiling it in a mixture of water and ash, and then it is ground. In the meantime, condiments are prepared, eggs are hard boiled, and meat is fried with onions. The ingredients are mixed along with a few olives, and portions are wrapped in leaves to protect them while they cook in a pot of boiling water. *Raspadillas,* the flavored ice snack sold on *triciclo* carts, involve the preparation of *jarabe,* a syrup of boiled-down sugar and flavoring. This syrup is poured over ice to make *raspadillas* or mixed with water to sell as a drink (*fresco*).

Considerable time is put into the preparation of some drinks sold in the markets. Those who prepare *emolientes,* the hot syrupy drinks sold nights and sometimes early mornings along the streets, need to allow several hours daily to assemble and cook the ingredients and to collect the wood they need to burn to keep the drinks hot as they sell. Others sell hot fruit juices early in the morning and must rise by 4:00 A.M. to boil fruit, quinoa, sugar, and water to have it ready by 6:00 A.M.

Cold fruit juices are generally squeezed and blended on the spot while customers wait in the markets. In contrast, the traditional Peruvian corn beer, *chicha,* requires several hours of work, and then it must be allowed to ferment for at least a week. Several times a week owners of *chicherías,* bars serving *chicha,* combine corn, fruit (apples, bananas, oranges, or whatever is on hand), sugar, and water. The mixture is left in large ceramic containers with some sediment from an earlier batch until it is ready for consumption.

The preparation of meat for sale also involves considerable work behind the scenes. As noted, most women who sell beef have men helping them who go into the countryside to find cattle to lead to the slaughterhouse. The meat is delivered to the market on the following day, and the men are usually on hand to help butcher it, although some women do it alone. The work of butchering is difficult, requiring the use of large cleavers and blocks and muscle. As women sell the meat, they continue to cut it up for customers, and if any remains at the end of the day they must see that it is refrigerated to keep it fresh.

Like marketwomen who sell beef, those selling pork often have men who help them by going after animals and having them slaughtered, but many of these women also work alone. Some buy the animals in the market after they have been slaughtered and sell the unprocessed meat. Other women, however, buy animals live, take them to the slaughterhouse (or even slaughter the animals themselves), and then return home with the meat to prepare smoked, salted pork for the market. Gabriela, from Mercado Central, described the work involved. She buys animals from people she knows who raise them in their household corrals in Huaraz. When they notify her that there are pigs for sale, she buys one or two and cares for them at her home until she is ready to slaughter them, which she does herself. Preparation of the hams takes one to two weeks, and every day she works on hams at different stages in the process. For about three days, the meat is boiled and soaked in a mixture of *ají*, garlic, saltpetre, and salt and then hung and smoked for three or more days. Hams used to be cured for a month, producing a better result, but now people do not have the resources to buy as many pigs and need to sell the hams sooner. Gabriela works in the market from 7:00 A.M. to 2:00 P.M. every day and returns home to work on her hams. She also sells sausages (*salchichas*), which take one hour to prepare before selling. All the work of preparing her pork is felt to be worthwhile since the price of fresh pork is S/.100 per kilo in the market, while hams sell for S/.160 per kilo.

The poultry sellers also have much work to do before coming to the markets. They buy live chickens every few days from suppliers, care for them at home, feed them and give them water, until it is time to prepare them for sale. Each morning a certain number of chickens are killed and dressed. This begins as early as 2:00 A.M. or 3:00 A.M., depending on whether the seller has help, in order to begin selling by 6:00 A.M. The chickens are cut up at the time of sale. If any poultry remains after the second day, it must be refrigerated overnight to preserve it.

The focus in this discussion of the work performed by marketers has been on sellers of foodstuffs since they make up the large majority of women in petty commerce and also because so much of their work is "hidden," or not generally recognized. Nevertheless, conversations with other sellers reveal the considerable productive activity that is involved in nearly all the products they sell. For example, sellers of live baby chicks, who bring crates containing the animals from the coast, devote time and energy to ensure their healthy arrival in Huaraz and to care for them while they are there. Artisans who knit sweaters and weave ponchos do some of their work as they sell, but one must see them after they leave their market stalls and return to their workshops to appreciate the long hours they spend getting their goods ready for sale; after selling from 8:00 A.M. to 2:00 P.M., they work until 8:00 P.M. in their workshops producing clothing. One women who knits hats told me it takes her a half day of continuous work, in the market or at home, to produce a hat that sells for S/.80 (the yarn she buys is expensive and the cost cuts into her earnings considerably). And another woman, a seamstress, ex-

A seller of prepared fruit drinks in Mercado Central.

plained that she spends far more time making clothes at her home than selling them in the market.

This enumeration of the productive activities of marketers illustrates the importance of going beyond an analysis of marketers as the sellers of goods to a consideration of the actual content of the work marketers do. Such consideration reveals that marketers are not simply exchanging a sum of money for a product that they will later exchange for a larger sum but that they are adding value to their products through their own labor. The traditional view of petty marketers as nonproductive or exploitative intermediaries is clearly in error—they are productive workers.

Theoretical Frameworks for Conceptualizing Marketers' Work

Having examined some central aspects of the work that marketers do, let us now consider the best way to conceptualize their work. How marketers' work is understood is particularly important since it shapes our understanding of their position in society.

Researchers who have investigated the situation of urban marketers and street vendors in the cities of underdeveloped countries have taken three different approaches, discussed in more general terms in Chapter 3. While two of them have certain deficiencies, the third offers insights useful for the analysis of the Huaraz situation.

The first approach employed by students of urban marketing makes no qualitative differentiation between the economic sphere in which marketers participate and the larger capitalist economy.[2] Rather, a continuum is suggested by the often-used terms "small scale" and "large scale." Marketers are viewed as operating in small-scale enterprises but as having at least the potential for increasing the scale of their activities. The assumption behind this approach is that the same economic principles and motivations condition the work of petty marketers and large entrepreneurs. While this may sometimes be true, a number of recent studies suggest that these are exceptional cases.[3] If we are to understand the place of petty marketers in underdeveloped economies, this conceptual framework based on quantitative criteria does not appear to help us account for the unique features of the urban poor who are engaged in marketing.

A second approach is based on the concept of informal and formal sectors in Third World cities. This approach goes beyond the earlier notion of traditional and modern sectors but shares some of the same problems based on a similar view of dual economies. During the 1970s, a number of researchers emphasized the divergence of the informal and formal economic sectors.[4] In contrast to the capital-intensive, wage-earning formal sector, the informal sector is characterized by self-employment, easy entry, reliance on indigenous resources, and labor-intensive technology. Advocates of the informal-formal sector approach have contributed importantly to our understanding of economic activities among the urban poor, but the dualist thinking of some has obscured the significant interlinkages between the sectors. These interlinkages serve to maintain dependency and may explain the inability of most petty marketers to expand. Thus, to the extent that the concepts of the informal and formal sectors prove useful in the present study, they should be understood to be descriptive of interconnected sectors of the economy.[5]

A third approach to this problem, the one that I favor, has been proposed during the last few years by several researchers, but as yet few anthropologists have considered its advantages. These researchers use the concept of petty commodity production to locate the place of petty producers and traders at the margins of capitalist economies but integrated with them. Fundamental to this view is the notion that petty commodity production represents a subordinate form of production coexisting with the dominant capitalist mode. As originally discussed by Marx ([1867] 1967:761–762), simple, or petty, commodity production is characterized by the individual ownership of the means of production by independent producers. Furthermore, these independent producers are primarily engaged in household provisioning rather than profit making.[6]

Although first conceptualized as a transitional stage, the petty commodity production form has been found flourishing, rather than diminishing, in a number of Third World cities (e.g., Gerry 1978, 1979; Scott 1979; Long and Richardson 1978).[7] The persistence of petty production and trade is attributed to the distorted process of capitalist development in Third World countries, which have been historically subordinated in the world economy. Because of this process of underdevelopment, these countries have been unable to draw large numbers into the wage labor force, and the majority of the urban poor are finding employment in petty manufacturing and trading and the services.

The petty commodity production analysis has been undertaken in recent studies of producer-sellers, both rural agriculturalists and artisans (e.g., Cook 1976*b*, on stoneworkers) and urban artisans and other producers of goods and services (e.g., Gerry 1979, on furniture makers, leatherworkers, tailors, and mechanics). In my view, this same analysis, which has thrown light on the situation of petty producer-sellers and petty manufacturers, can appropriately and usefully illuminate the case of petty marketers like those in Huaraz. If it is agreed that there is no important separation between manufacturing and commerce and that the work of marketers is an extension of the productive work that (often) begins in other hands, then the petty commodity analysis is suitable here.

The petty commodity analysis avoids the main pitfalls of the first two conceptual approaches mentioned by recognizing the distinct features of the petty production and commerce sector and by, furthermore, demonstrating that this sector is conditioned by, and conditions, the larger society. For the Huaraz case, this third approach places the work of marketers in the total production process, provides a framework in which the productive component of marketing itself is revealed, and suggests a view of petty marketers as household provisioners rather than petty entrepreneurs, all of which appears consistent with what has been said of Huaraz marketers.

Nevertheless, as an analytical tool and not a description, the petty commodity form does not fit perfectly the Huaraz situation. Basic to the petty commodity analysis is the notion of the independence of producer-sellers, that is, of their self-employment. Huaraz marketers display many features of self-employment; for example, they have control of the times they begin and stop selling, the days and hours they work, the products they sell, and so on. Furthermore, most marketers consider themselves self-employed and value the advantages this offers. However, those petty retailers who told me on occasion that their work only supports the wholesalers may have a point. Since most marketwomen lack capital, they are completely dependent on the wholesalers who offer them goods on credit. In a sense, these retailers may be regarded as commission sellers since, once their goods are sold, they turn over to the wholesalers the earnings on the goods minus the margin they retain as a "commission." (Of course they are generally held responsible for paying the wholesaler whether they sell all the goods or not.)

Scott (1979), using data from Lima, has called attention to the various subordinated forms that "self-employment" actually takes among the urban poor. She shows convincingly that what may appear at first to be self-employment is often a disguised form of wage labor. Calling for a closer examination of the social relations of production, she demonstrates that, in the case of Lima, such arrangements as outwork, piecework, and commission selling are common in petty production and commerce.

In Huaraz, too, the degree of autonomy that workers have in the labor process varies. In addition to the widespread dependence of retailers on wholesalers for credit, other forms of dependency are operating. Some marketers, like clothing sellers, hold contracts with coastal manufacturers, by whom they are basically employed, to sell goods and turn over earnings. Others are hired by local producers of ice cream, cookies, and so on by the day or the week. In these cases, the formal and informal economic sectors are interconnected.

Among informal marketers themselves we may also discover socioeconomic differentiation. As mentioned, a small number of marketers hire assistants, either on a regular basis or occasionally on a piecework basis. Examples of those working for wages are Víctor's full-time employees, the assistants regularly hired by Carmen and other restaurant operators, and the woman who is paid by the bunch to peel garlic for her neighbor. In addition, garment makers and other artisans are sometimes employed by marketers as outworkers; often these workers are hidden from view, since they are supplied with materials to work at home on items that will later be sold by their employers.

Yet, while Víctor may gradually be entering the ranks of Huaraz's petty bourgeoisie and Carmen may be taking her place as a successful restaurant operator in Mercado Central, the woman who hires another to peel garlic is not significantly higher than her employee in social status. While each of these marketers employs wage labor, not all of them contribute to a process of capital accumulation. Thus, as we examine the careers of individual marketers, we see the contradictory aspects of petty commodity production and commerce—and the uneven development from independent seller to wage laborer or petty bourgeois employer.

In general, my research in Huaraz suggests that a transition is occurring from relatively autonomous marketing to more dependent forms of commerce. During my return visits to the city, I observed changes. Not only had the total number of marketers and street vendors increased substantially but also my interviews indicated that a significantly greater number of commission sellers and waged employees were among them. Particularly striking were the expanded number of *ambulantes* selling ice cream, candy, prepared drinks, and the like from carts on the streets, by day and night; a large number, if not the majority, of these sellers are wage workers, hired by absent employers. While further research is necessary to document this process of subordination to the wage form, or proletarianization, in the marketplace, the trend appears clear.

Many writers have noted the tendency in capitalist societies for capital to undermine independent producers. For example, Harry Braverman (1974:412) points to the "transformation from self-employment to capitalist employment, from simple commodity production to capitalist production, from relations between persons to relations between things, from a society of scattered producers to a society of corporate capitalism." Here Braverman follows Marx's view that the capitalist mode of production would subordinate and ultimately destroy all forms of work that do not contribute directly to capital accumulation.

It might be argued that, in the contemporary situation of underdeveloped Third World countries, petty commodity production has persisted because it has continued to contribute to the accumulation of capital and because it is a channel for relieving extremely high unemployment. Yet researchers have also found evidence of the transition from self-employment to wage employment in the cities of some Third World countries (e.g., Gerry 1979; Scott 1979). The proper stance at this time would appear to be a willingness to recognize both persistence and change where they are demonstrated in the employment structure in urbanizing, but underdeveloped, economies.

What we learn in the future regarding this question will add to our understanding not only of the work that people like the Huaraz marketers do but also of their social class position. At present their class status is somewhat ambiguous. Whether as "independent" sellers or as incipient commercial proletarians, the majority of petty marketers in Huaraz are poor, and in this respect there is no striking contrast among them. Marketers who view themselves as the marginal self-employed often see wage labor as more respectable and desirable, but the forms that wage-employment takes in the markets are not what they have in mind. To the degree that proletarianization is occurring, it may mean little change in the livelihood of the impoverished marketers. Still, if more marketers come to view themselves as exploited by the large wholesalers and capitalists with whom they have business relations, a significant change will have occurred in the development of class consciousness.

Six	*Marketwomen, Family, and Society*

MARKETWOMEN HAVE BEEN considered in their role as workers in petty commerce in Huaraz, but how do their work lives integrate with their social lives? Here we begin with an overview of some aspects of growing up female in Huaraz, noting the increasing responsibilities in and out of the home that come with womanhood. The life career of one marketwoman is presented to illustrate the strength necessary for dealing with daily and lifelong difficulties. Then, generational change is considered to compare the opportunities mature marketwomen have had with those of their daughters who are now approaching adulthood. Finally, the place of marketwomen's labor force participation in the family and society is examined in terms of interconnected modes of production in Peru. More than in preceding chapters, we will keep women's lives in central focus as we assess their place in the family, economy, and society.[1]

Becoming a Woman in Huaraz

Births are generally welcomed in Huaraz, and there seems to be no strong preference for children of one sex over the other. Most women have a friend or relative with the skills of a midwife, or *partera*, to help them; but others, like Elena, deliver their children "into the hands of their husbands." While middle-class women go to the Belén Hospital in Huaraz to give birth, few poor women do. The expense is too great (S/.100 per day in the past and, surely, much higher now), and women feel the care given there is not the best for mother or child. The hospital food, they say, is suitable for well persons but not for women giving birth; this means the family must prepare *caldos* (heavy broths) and other appropriate foods and carry them to the hospital. Furthermore, doctors are often condescending toward poor women and their families, making the hospital stay that much more unpleasant.

After giving birth, a woman reduces her schedule for a month or so; when she resumes her normal routine her baby accompanies her, often tied in a shawl on her back. Because most babies are breast fed mothers generally prefer to keep their babies with them, although there are *cunas* (nurseries) for infants in Huaraz. Infants are given a great deal of attention and affection by parents, older siblings, and other relatives. The rate of infant mortality is high as a result of infections and childhood diseases, and parents are particularly cautious in looking after their youngest children. In many families children have died, and when asked how many children they have, some women respond by giving the number of births they have had, not just the number of their surviving offspring.

At several times in the life cycle of their children, parents select godparents, or *padrinos*, to act as their sponsors. The relationship this establishes between the parents and the *padrinos*, who call each other *compadres*, as well as the relationship between *padrinos* and their godchildren are important throughout the Andes (and Latin America) for the ties of ritual kinship that are formed. The first occasion when these ties of *compadrazgo* are created is baptism.[2] A male (*padrino*) and female (*madrina*) sponsor are traditionally chosen at the time of birth or soon after, but often children are three or older before they are baptized. Sometimes the expense of a fiesta is prohibitive, and the baptism is put off indefinitely. (Before I left Huaraz in 1977, I agreed to serve as a baptismal sponsor for Elena's four-year-old daughter on my next visit to Peru; the daughter, Pilar, was nine when I returned to fulfill the promise.) *Padrinos* are expected to provide the baptismal clothing for the children and to take them to the church service. As they leave the church, the *padrinos* throw candy or coins to the children attending the service.

Sometime during the first few years of life comes the *corte de pelo*, or first haircutting ceremony. This may be immediately after the baptism or at a later time. On this occasion another set of *padrinos* are selected, and they are responsible for providing ribbons used to tie the child's hair in the ceremony as well as for making a generous contribution of food and money. Each person attending the family's fiesta, beginning with the *padrinos*, trims a lock of the child's hair, which has been tied up in a piece of ribbon. The lock is offered, along with a gift of some money, to the parents. A fiesta follows, with eating, drinking, and dancing.

During these early years, children are treated with indulgence by their parents, but they are also given responsibilities and expected to begin learning the skills that will be important in adult life. The socialization of boys and girls begins to take different directions when they are three or four years old. Little girls are encouraged to learn the tasks appropriate to their sex earlier than boys are expected to learn the skills appropriate to theirs. Girls of four or five sometimes have a corner of the household where they set up a small kitchen and playhouse area. Pilar had a tiny wood-burning hearth, where she was occasionally allowed to cook a small portion of what Elena had on her own fire, perhaps a single potato or a few noodles. The child used her own blow pipe to keep the fire going and watched the tiny clay pot (a replica of her mother's) as the food cooked. Elena needed only to glance from her own kitchen to check Pilar's progress. Other children often build small fires outdoors without adult supervision and appear to understand well how to control them, as I noted in watching children in the Nicrupampa *campamento.*

Pilar and her friends did not have many toys, but they were quite inventive in devising playthings out of materials that came their way. For example, Pilar's cherished doll was given a bed made from a tissue box I discarded and a sleeping bag (like mine) from a plastic bag of the right size.

Pilar also had a number of toys made by her mother and older sister that were replicas of the articles Elena used in marketing. This was somewhat puzzling to me, since Elena did not wish her daughters to become marketers; but mother and child were clearly delighted to have matching baskets, scales, coin purses, and shawls for carrying goods and "baby" on the back. Though she might not use her marketing skills as an adult, Pilar already had a talent for selling bread in the family store, and she could be trusted on errands to purchase small items from stores in the neighborhood.

Young children of both sexes often accompany their mothers and older sisters to the Quillcay River when they do their laundry. The children play on the grass and in the water and climb the rocks along the riverbank. Part of the play of girls, however, may include washing a few items of clothing. Some take along a small pail, a piece of soap, and dolls' clothes, while others just help their mothers wash the family's clothes.

Although young girls appear to be undergoing socialization for adult work roles at an earlier age than boys and boys have more time for sports and other activities with friends, children of both sexes carry out certain tasks in the family. Both boys and girls help with some of the lighter farming tasks, weeding and helping to harvest the family fields. And children are often delegated the special task of leading sheep to pasture; from the age of around five they may do this alone and save their mothers the time and trouble. Both boys and girls may be sent with pails to fetch water, and they may be asked to run other errands.

Moreover, although sex-role training begins fairly early in life, girls are not taught to be submissive or dependent but rather self-reliant. One time, when I was out walking with Pilar, she explained to me that she had fallen down earlier in the day but that she had not cried because she is "macho." I questioned her about the meaning of macho, and she told me it means to be brave like the family's sheep. Later, when I related the story to her eighteen-year-old sister, Teresa, she laughed and said Pilar did not yet understand that macho is used to describe male animals and men. Pilar and Teresa both know, however, that women in their society must be strong.

Children begin school when they are around six, and the goal of most parents in Huaraz is to see them continue through secondary school. Primary education is mandatory, and most children today complete five years, though some parents, particularly rural migrants, never send their children to school. A shortage of space in the city schools has meant that children must attend in split sessions. Generally, the primary schoolchildren attend mornings, and secondary students attend school in the afternoons. Schoolchildren wear a standard uniform, used throughout Peru, of gray slacks and white shirts for boys and gray jumpers and white blouses for girls. They are proud of their uniforms and keep them clean. Boys and girls both wear black laced shoes, which they dust off and polish to a shine almost daily before leaving for school. Children also highly value the notebooks and pencils their parents buy for them. The expenses of uniforms, books, and school supplies are prohibitive for some families, however.

Despite parents' proud assertions that girls today receive an education equal to that of boys, there still seems to be a stronger commitment to the education of sons. Whereas boys are encouraged to devote themselves to their studies while their parents make sacrifices, girls are expected to lend considerable help at home while they are in school. Daughters often look after younger children, prepare the noon meal, wash the family clothes, and perform other tasks; they may even need to leave school if their mothers require their assistance. This was true for Teresa, who left school for a year after Pilar was born because Elena could not manage without her full-time help. This would never have been asked of her brother Guillermo, who, though he is only a year older, completed two years of teacher preparation at the normal school before Teresa had a chance to graduate from high school. Daughters in general must or-

A marketer and her daughter.

ganize going to school and doing schoolwork around their domestic responsibilities, while boys are released from most household obligations during their school years.

Two rites of passage associated with the Roman Catholic church, first communion and confirmation, are celebrated by some families during their sons' and daughters' late childhood. As in the celebration of baptism and the first haircutting, these events require the selection of additional *padrinos,* who sponsor fiestas and may offer such gifts as clothing, a rosary, or a prayer book to their *ahijados* (godchildren). Many families, however, do not mark these events with ritual celebration. (Furthermore, since the earthquake, the number of Protestant evangelists in Huaraz has increased, and this has influenced the conversion of some Huaracinos.)

During adolescence young men and women are supervised by their parents, are required to be home at an early hour in the evening, and are generally expected to behave with self-restraint. Not surprisingly, however, the enforcement of family rules differs significantly for sons and daughters. Daughters are watched carefully and kept close to home, and they often have many restrictions on the activities in which they may participate; sons are allowed far more freedom, and if they overstep the rules occasionally the attitude is

"*Qué diablos*" (What the devil). Part of the difference in the treatment of sons and daughters may stem from a greater concern for the physical safety of daughters, but there is also a greater tolerance of intractability in sons.

In their late teens, young women and men approach the age of marriage. Not many acceptable forms of socializing exist for young people of the nonelite classes; formal dating is not practiced, and they rely instead on opportunities for group interaction at local fiestas, school gatherings, and parties. Women and men of the same barrio may steal moments together on the streets, and those who live in the valley uplands sometimes manage to slip away to a nearby field. Middle-class couples in Huaraz more often engage in dating—going to movies, restaurants, and bars—or they belong to various organizations, such as folk dance clubs. The urban poor have far fewer opportunities for courtship as a result of both economic and social constraints.

Despite the constraints, of course, women and men become acquainted, form romantic attachments, and eventually decide to marry. There are notable exceptions, individuals who choose not to marry or who decide after unhappy relationships to remain single, but most people marry. Marriage for women is common after age eighteen and into the early twenties, and men typically marry several years later. By tradition, a man proposes and then seeks the approval of the woman's parents.

Properly speaking, marriage is recognized after a civil ceremony and a religious ceremony, but many couples do not have both ceremonies, and some have neither, before they set up a household. Whether formally married or not, women and men usually refer to their mates as *esposo[a]* (husband or wife). Some, however, clarify the fact that they live together without a formal contract through the term *compañero[a]*. Most couples look forward to the religious ceremony and the accompanying fiesta, which is sponsored for them by newly selected *padrinos*, but if they simply move in together their union is still recognized and respected.

Most couples prefer to set up new households if this is possible, but a number of families include at least one son or daughter who brought a mate to live with the parents. This may be when a parent is alone, old, or ill or when a couple has no alternative residence.

The property that women and men bring to their marital alliance often includes a bit of land or, sometimes, a family home. These may be passed on to individuals by parents, or they may be promised as an inheritance after the parents' deaths. Inheritance is said to favor sons and daughters equally, but parents are also able to reward a favorite child. Informants explained that, if one child has been particularly helpful to the parents, looking after them as they grow old, he or she may receive a more generous portion of the property to be divided. It is my impression that sons may be more often favored in this way, but I have insufficient evidence to demonstrate this. Of course, poor families often have little or no significant property to divide (some people lost both fields and homes in the earthquake and now rent their living quarters). Land and housing property may be purchased, but the present economic conditions of the poor usually preclude this.

Children, as stated earlier, are generally welcomed in marriages. Indeed, pregnancy is sometimes the precipitating factor in a couple's decision to marry. In such cases, there may be some initial distress over the unanticipated pregnancy, but an overriding fondness for children frequently convinces the young woman's parents, her young man (*novio*), and, most important, the young woman herself that a child is cause for celebration. Children not only delight their families but also may be counted on for help in their parents' old age.

The joy of parenthood notwithstanding, women who have had several children are often concerned about the size of their families. A few children provide the security they desire, but more can drain family resources and mean more work for the women who raise them. One woman told me her ideal would be to have just two children. "Why more?" she asked. Others feel four or even five is reasonable but consider more to be undesirable. Juana, of Mercado Central, who has eight children, told me on several occasions that women in Peru "just have children like animals," meaning that they have no control over reproduction and have numerous offspring. Such concern is common, and many women, and men, too, asked me how people in the United States manage to keep their family size small. Condoms are available in Huaraz, but I do not know how many couples are aware of their use, for people revealed a good deal of ignorance regarding contraception. Some had heard of injections or of various natural remedies to prevent conception, but many seemed to feel that avoiding their husbands (sleeping apart or taking a child into the couple's bed) was the safest alternative.

Women are the primary caretakers for children, and they are held responsible for seeing that their children are well fed and clothed, at least to the best of their ability. While I heard of a number of families that had been abandoned by the husband-father, I heard of none in which a mother had abandoned her children. Mothers are expected to discipline their children as well as to indulge them, but when fathers are on hand they have responsibilities in this area, too. In many families fathers are considered stricter than mothers, and although mothers make the day-to-day decisions regarding discipline, fathers may have the final word on major disciplinary matters. In some families I knew in Huaraz, children attempted to receive permission to do things from their mothers before their fathers were consulted, for they knew their fathers would say no.

In addition to the rearing of children, there are a number of areas in which wives and husbands must try to come to an agreement. On the basis of observing married couples in their homes, I would say that husbands and wives seem to have fairly cooperative relationships, but since I did not witness some areas of family life, I relied on the reports of informants. Women told me that when a man and a woman understand and get along with each other (*se entienden*) there is harmony but that often there is a lack of understanding. For example, women say that men are sometimes domineering, and they complain of problems with drunkenness, jealousy, and laziness. Tomasa, who began selling chicken when her husband became jealous of her work as a schoolteacher, told me that her husband is a good man who shares work and decision making in the home. When I commented that it was strange that he ordered her to leave the job she enjoyed, she said: "Ah, helping around the house is one thing, but jealousy is another. When it's a matter of jealousy, there is nothing to be done." She added that women are not jealous the way men are.

Some women spoke of the periodic anger and violent rage of husbands, especially when they are drunk. Sometimes husbands beat their wives following jealous accusations or disputes over household matters. Some women leave such husbands, but those who stay have little recourse. Women who turn to the police may expect little help, for the police are likely to side with the husbands ("they beat their own wives," one woman pointed out).

Women consider the behavior of their husbands to be beyond their control. Some men, they say, are considerate and helpful, while others are not. A woman may only hope to be graced with a kind husband. A number of women, in fact, do count themselves lucky that their husbands are reasonable men who do not make excessive demands. The comments of such women revealed a respect and deep affection for their husbands.

A word frequently used in referring to the position of the man in the family is *mandar,* which means "to lead." Although women carry important responsibilities in the family, men are said to lead, to be the chief decision makers. Nevertheless, in the household, authority is generally delegated to the person who carries out particular tasks. Accordingly, the husband makes most of the decisions regarding both his own fields and those of his wife because he does more of the agricultural work. Since a man prepares the land and sows the family fields, he makes most of the production decisions. When it comes to cultivation, however, his wife is primarily responsible, and he does not usually involve himself in her work. Both sexes participate in harvesting and have a say in the disposition of the product.

While a man may be the *jefe* (boss) in the fields, a woman is the *jefe* in the kitchen. Most men know enough about food preparation to look after themselves when necessary, but women are almost solely responsible for seeing that meals are on the table under ordinary circumstances. Food preparation takes a good deal of time and effort. In part, this is due to the conditions of urban poverty. Kitchens are simple affairs, sometimes a corner of a single-room dwelling or an area only partly enclosed behind a family's living quarters. Food is generally cooked over wood-burning fires or small kerosene stoves, sometimes both. The only other facilities most families have are a work space and sometimes a cabinet for storing a few pots and leftover foods. Many poor families have no running water, and only the rich have refrigerators. This means that women must purchase their food fresh in the market each day and haul water from the river. Many women also must collect the wood they use to cook. Cooking itself is time-consuming, and women often call on the assistance of daughters. The major meal of the day may consist of a soup and a stew of vegetables with a bit of meat or fish served with potatoes, rice, or noodles. Bread nearly always accompanies the meal, and if the family can afford it they may have some fruit. To clean up after the meal, women boil water and pour it over the eating and cooking utensils, with or without benefit of soap.

In some households I visited, women remained apart from the rest of the family as they ate their meal. These women served the others at a table or sitting around a room and then stayed near their hearths, squatting close to their pots as they ate. In other families, like Elena's, women brought food to the table and joined the others to eat there. Elena's husband, Renato, and son Guillermo sometimes helped to bring food to the table and to clear, and they commented on the good quality of the meal.

Women of the household must also look after the family's animals. As noted, women are usually responsible for seeing that sheep are pastured, but they also may have chickens, pigs, rabbits, and guinea pigs to care for. These animals are usually in a small corral adjoining the household, in a courtyard, or even in the living quarters. Women with sheep may spin the wool and use it to make clothing for the family.

Added to all this work, of course, is the responsibility of child care. A woman's attention must often be divided as she carries out tasks and keeps an eye on the children. Women with both younger and older children are grateful that the schools' split sessions allow older siblings to look after their preschool sisters and brothers. This particular feature of the schools in Huaraz probably frees many women to market who might otherwise find it difficult. Older daughters may be depended on to supervise the younger children in the morning and to begin preparation of the noon meal in their mothers' absence.

For women, marketing has the advantage of being somewhat adaptable to their schedules at home. A woman can devote more or less time to marketing as she wishes. Unlike other household responsibilities, however, child care is one that cannot simply wait for later attention. Consequently, women without the help of older daughters are faced with the problem of ensuring their children's well-being while they market. This is a widespread concern and one on which many women commented.

Marketing is probably the single occupation in which women engage beyond the household in Peru that allows them to watch over their children as they work. In the Huaraz markets, however, this has not always been true. During several periods over the last half century, children have been prohibited in the markets. One of the oldest women I interviewed remembers that, when she began marketing fifty years ago, sellers were not allowed to bring their children to the markets. Women who were determined to sell and also to bring their infants with them had to hide the children, often in produce crates. If market inspectors discovered the children, the women could be thrown out or fined. This prohibition was apparently overturned when a new market administration took office.

Women who began marketing around twenty-five years ago remember that in those days, too, children were prohibited. This seems to have continued until the time of the earthquake. Women recall the period as a repressive one for marketers, when even hats were prohibited. This was no doubt a reaction to the pressure from middle-class consumers to "clean up the markets," bringing them into line with their notions of cleanliness and respectability. At one point, a woman president of the major market union successfully petitioned for funds to construct a *cuna* to serve marketwomen, but it was never built. Some marketwomen took their children to public centers, but mothers who were nursing infants or who found the

centers unsuitable for other reasons continued to find ways of clan-
destinely bringing their babies to the markets. Once they arrived at
their stalls, they would place their infants under their tables or in
other inconspicuous spots. A number of women told me that they
brought all their children to market this way and that they were
rarely caught.

Today, children are permitted in the markets, though there is talk
of prohibiting them once again (the market officials, however, seem
aware of the futility of trying to keep children away). A government-
supported day care center is now located in the Huarupampa barrio,
where children may be left at 7:00 A.M. and picked up by 4:00 P.M.
This center is said to offer good care, food, and medical attention for
children at a nominal cost. With these improvements, some women
say that combining child care responsibilities with marketing is no
trouble. Others, however, maintain that small children pose special
problems for marketers, particularly for those without sufficient
space in the markets to accommodate their children and those who
need to travel long distances. Some women only begin marketing
after their children reach school age because of these problems.

As children grow older, the job of caring for them becomes lighter,
and the children eventually come to help their mothers (and fathers)
in many ways. Nevertheless, the rest of a woman's productive life is
generally spent in an effort to balance the work she does in the
household with that she does outside it. What has been described is
a bare outline of the wide range of tasks marketwomen perform in
Huaraz. In practice, a woman may have many other responsibilities
as part of the unpaid and paid work that maintains her family.

Men among the urban poor in Huaraz also work very hard to
provide for their families. Those with fields and large animals to
care for take primary responsibility for this work. Most men seek
income-generating work in and around the city in such areas as construction, agricultural day labor, local businesses and government
organizations (e.g., SINAMOS and ORDEZA), and petty production
and commerce. Although they work hard and often provide a larger
income than their marketer wives, men generally have a narrower
range of work activities, and they have some leisure time once they
return home.

This difference in the work of women and men was mentioned
spontaneously by a number of informants, both female and male. It
was also noted in response to the final question on the questionnaire
I administered, which asked whether in the families of Huaraz the
work of men and women is worth the same. Nearly all these informants pointed to the double work load of women, who work

both outside and inside the home. They often made a distinction between paid and unpaid work, and many said that in the purely economic sense men's work is worth more since they earn more. But these same people added that women work more and their contribution to the family is greater. Informants conveyed the sense of women's "double day" with remarkable clarity, as the comments below illustrate.

> Men have one single job, while women have two: outside the house and in the house. Women work more.

> A woman's work is worth more. A man works awhile and that's it, but a woman just keeps on working. Although a man's work is difficult, a woman works more. [Here she enumerated the types of work women do in the house.]

> Men's work is worth more. It earns more. For example, a mason earns more. When a woman works, she earns little. With the little we sell we can't make much. . . . At home the woman works more. The man just works at one job, while the woman has many [she lists sweeping, washing, cooking, etc.].

> The work of men is worth more; they earn more. Men have regular wages and earn decent salaries. Women in commerce earn one day, lose the next. But women work more. Men have a single job, while women have two, in and out of the house. Women have lots of different jobs in the house: washing, cooking, ironing, sweeping, cleaning.

> What a woman earns isn't enough [*no alcanza*]. A man has a regular income. But a woman works more. When she gets back from work outside, she returns to work at home. A man has one job, a woman, two.

> The work of women could be said to be worth more. It's more sacrificing. A man has a single job, but a woman has much to do in the house. In the economic sense? Men's work is worth more.

Only the last comment is that of a man, but other men voiced an opinion on the matter. One afternoon's interviewing produced interesting contrasts in the responses of marketwomen and their husbands to the final question in my questionnaire. I went to the home of María (of Mercado Central) in Nicrupampa, where I interviewed her and her husband as well as her daughter Delia (also a marketer) and Delia's husband. Each interview was conducted out of hearing of other family members. Their responses follow.

MARÍA: Men's work is worth more. They work more and earn more—in my family and in general. Equality? Yes, men and women should earn the same and have the same opportunities.

MARÍA'S HUSBAND: It appears false, but the *señora* works more than the man. A man goes to work, returns, and that's it. The *señora* has a permanent job—the children, and one thing and another. Equality? Men and women should help each other and be equals in and out of the house.

DELIA: The work of men is worth more than the work of women. They earn more. Of course, they should be equals.

DELIA'S HUSBAND: Women work more than men. They really work without rest. It depends on the family; sometimes the man contributes more, sometimes the woman. Men and women should be equal, but women aren't capable of doing some of the work men do. In the sense of intelligence, women are brighter [*más pensadoras*] than men. It is because women have less education that they have fewer opportunities and do certain types of work.

Clear in all four responses to the question by these family members is the recognition that social conditions determine the relative worth of men's and women's work. In this set of responses, it is interesting that the women value men's work more highly, and the men judge women to be the harder workers. While this pattern was not the same for all couples interviewed, it occurred in enough cases to suggest the mutual respect wives and husbands have for each other's work, which they view as complementary in the family.

The intentional ambiguity of my question confused some people who did not know whether to respond in terms of economic or social worth. The brief response of a number of informants who said simply that the worth of men's and women's work is "the same" may suggest a challenge to the question itself—since it assumes a ranking of worth. Perhaps most people view the work of both sexes as essential and do not perceive a hierarchical difference in the way the question implied. Nevertheless, the main point to be made here is that the double work load of women is recognized by both sexes.

A Marketer's Life

During my first period of field research in Huaraz, the seventy-four-year-old secretary of the press and propaganda for the principal market union, Carolina Sánchez, spoke to me often about her long and interesting life. She left out many details (adding some when I returned to the city) but made up for this by offering her views on life as a marketer and as a woman in Huaraz.

I knew Carolina through the market union, where she was one of the first to befriend me. Later, through talking with her casually on the street where she sold, I grew closer to her and learned more about her personal life. With great generosity, Carolina took an interest in me, calling me her *nieta* (granddaughter) and asking to be called *abuelita* (grandmother). She invited me to her home and shared her thoughts as well as her food, and when I left she gave me a memorable *despedida* (good-bye party) with the traditional dish of *cuy* (guinea pig). First, however, I knew Carolina as a small old woman, recognizable by her single remaining front tooth, who had apparently boundless energy in herding marketers to union meetings and keeping them in line once they were there. She was an outspoken woman, who was not always taken seriously by everyone around her. Another union member said to me that Carolina "talks just to hear herself speak." Others would agree, but Carolina's spirit seemed indomitable, and she was undeterred by such criticisms.

Carolina has sold for many years along the street that faces the Frigorífico outside Mercado Central, where she sits on the ground with her back against the market building. She does a small business in dried *ají*, maize, barley, and wheat, which she spreads before her on her shawl. She sells only modest quantities carried from her home each day.

When Carolina first invited me to her home, she led me to a one-room "apartment"—part of a row of connected living quarters. Her home is in downtown Huaraz, only a five-minute walk from the market, but the poverty of her surroundings suggests a great distance from the modern houses built for the middle class since the earthquake. The street where she lives is a poor one, unpaved and dusty, though it is only a stone's throw from the respectable Avenida Fitzcarrald.

Inside, Carolina's home is small but very well organized to make the best use of available space. Her furniture, a bed and several chairs, takes up one side of the room. On the opposite side, in one corner, she has her kerosene stove, a pail, some pots, plates, and a few more cooking items. Other household goods are hooked to the

A marketwoman's life can be long and hard.

walls or placed neatly against them. Baskets, bags, and the stock she brings home find a corner and do not require much space. The guinea pigs that share the room with Carolina scurry around the floor.

The circumstances of Carolina's life are among the most unfortunate of the marketwomen I knew in Huaraz, but she is also one of the proudest and strongest women I met. She spoke about her life in fragments, preferring the present to the past, leaving me to piece together the parts.

Carolina remembers her childhood in Huaraz, when she lived in the outskirts of the city with her parents and her two brothers. Her family had fields to work in, but her mother also dedicated herself to marketing. As a young girl, Carolina went along with her mother when she took burros to the coast and purchased products to sell in the Huaraz marketplace. Thus, when Carolina says she has traded all her life, she is not exaggerating.

Carolina was not sent to school as her brothers were. Her mother was often ill, and Carolina stayed home to help with household responsibilities. Besides, in those days it was believed that girls should not be sent to school, for at school they would only look for husbands.

When she married at twenty-two, Carolina began selling independently in the market. From that time to the present she has worked steadily as a small retailer of agricultural goods. Her husband works in the manufacture of adobe bricks, obtaining employment when it is available. He no longer lives with Carolina, however, having left her for another woman before the earthquake. About their separation, she commented that she was a good wife, yet her husband grew tired of her after many years of marriage. She views this as characteristic of many marriages, saying, "When a woman is good, her husband leaves her; when a man is good, his wife leaves him." Her husband drank and would not help her in her work; although she found being alone difficult at first, she now finds it more peaceful (*más tranquilo*).

The great misfortune of Carolina's life lies in the experience she has had with her children. She had thirteen children, and only one is living today. As she put it, "God must have wanted to carry my children away so they would not suffer." The remaining daughter lives next door to her, but she and Carolina broke off their relationship some time ago. According to Carolina, her daughter was not properly dutiful and cutting ties with her was a matter of self-respect. This has left her, despite the fact that she has a couple of grandchildren, without the security of any certain support for the time when she can no longer carry out her work as a marketer.

Carolina does have brothers and *compadres* who may help her. At present, she gives seed and fertilizer to her *compadres*, who work the fields belonging to her and share the product. She can continue to draw on that source of support, but it is not adequate to meet all her needs. The land that she and her brothers jointly own amounts to under a hectare, and the production has been poor. Her brothers are in commerce; one of them, her older brother, is in Lima. He has appealed to her to come live with him and his family, saying, "Who will take care of you?" Carolina told me this with tears in her eyes, showing gratitude for her brother's kindness but a preference for remaining independent in Huaraz.

In her mid-seventies, Carolina is remarkably active. When I first visited her at home, she proudly showed me a framed diploma on her wall bearing the title Certificado de Paternidad y Maternidad Responsable (certificate of responsible fatherhood and motherhood). She explained that she earned this certificate recently, after attending a two-week course that met for two hours nightly in the city. The course was intended to teach parents the fundamentals of raising children, with talks by social workers and other "experts," and those attending took an exam at the end before they received their awards.

For a woman of her age and experience, taking such a course means that her life's work has been recognized as important. Besides her own experience as a mother, Carolina has the skills of a midwife. She speaks with confidence of how she learned by watching other midwives and then for many years assisted women in childbirth. She gauged the due dates for births, calculating nine months and nine days for a normal pregnancy and monitoring the woman's pulse. At the time of the birth, she prepared special foods and stayed with the mother for two days—services that hospitals do not offer. Carolina's pride in having a diploma must derive in part from the recognition of her responsibility in the birthing and rearing of children.

Carolina has been secretary of the press and propaganda in the market union since she was elected before the earthquake. According to her, her main responsibility is to get people to meetings, and although at one point she was denounced (she did not say why, but probably because of her outspokenness), she has stayed in office because no one else can fill the job so well. She is a loyal member of the union leadership (the junta) and expresses great confidence in the union's ability to win concessions from the mayor and the Provincial Council.

About the present situation for marketers, her views reveal a combination of revolutionary and religious fervor. Compared to the past, when marketers were more unified and conditions were not so bad, she sees the present as a critical time. She asks, "How can we provide for ourselves when we don't sell enough to live?" She talks about the rising prices of basic foodstuffs and concludes, "For this reason, I just want to die." Still, she has "faith in the Virgin" and goes to bed at night and gets up in the morning grateful for her help. The Virgin helps her through the day as she sells, she says, and gives her hope.

Carolina recalls earlier, more militant days in the markets and feels that the marketers today are not well organized. But she declares herself ready to fight against the conditions that oppress poor marketers. She states firmly that she is not afraid of dying and that "if they kill me, they kill me, or maybe I will kill them with my rock and my stick [*con mi piedra y mi palo*]." She believes that a revolt against local authorities will be necessary, but she also sees a need for change at the national level, where repressive price controls are instituted.

Like many other marketwomen, Carolina has not been to school, but, she says, her ideas come from her life. She has not needed formal education to learn about the particular condition of being poor and being a woman in Huaraz; her long experience has taught her that "women must be strong," and her own life testifies to this.[3]

Mothers and Daughters: Marketing and Generational Change

One of my earliest discoveries in talking to marketwomen in Huaraz was that a large portion of them are first-generation marketers. My expectation that nearly all the women would have learned to market from their mothers was unmet, and I found instead that a considerable number of the mothers of marketwomen worked at home, *en casa*, or *en la chacra* (in the fields). More of the marketers native to Huaraz learned to market from their mothers than did their rural counterparts, but in general I was struck by the lack of continuity from the previous generation to the present.

I began asking marketwomen whether they hoped or expected that their daughters would later engage in marketing. With some notable exceptions to be discussed below, the consensus was an emphatic no. This led me to question whether the marketwomen I was studying are to be the only generation in their families to engage in marketing. The rapid influx of rural people to the city appears to indicate that an ever-ready supply of new marketers is at hand and could replace townswomen as they retire from the market. If a change of this kind is occurring in the composition of the market population (and if it is more than the aftermath of the earthquake), then some form of mobility is suggested from one generation to the next.

The opportunity to go to school is the one outstanding advantage most daughters of marketwomen are given that their mothers were not. While nearly all girls in Huaraz go to school today, at least through primary school, the marketwomen I talked to told me of numerous obstacles that had stood in the way of schooling for them. When they were young, most marketwomen were expected to stay home and help their mothers in the fields and the pastures, while their brothers were sent to school. It was believed that a woman need only know how to sign her name and that if she knew how to write more she would "write love letters." Sons were encouraged to have an education in order to improve their chances of finding work and, in the case of rural people, to become fluent in Spanish and be able to "defend themselves" against townspeople. Although women rarely express anger over the conditions that prevented them from going to school, some criticized the society, their parents, or even themselves for their low educational achievement. For example, one woman complained that women were not concerned to get ahead or to work outside the house. Others, however, located the problem in external conditions that prevented women from getting and making use of an education, specifically in male privilege and discrimination against women.

In comparison with their own experience, most marketwomen view their daughters' career options as almost unlimited. Their faith in education is strong, and they believe that by going to school their daughters will be prepared to enter areas of employment that were closed to them. When asked whether their daughters would be marketers or, if not, what they would do, women's responses were varied. The majority said their daughters would surely not market but do something else, something better (*algo regular*). A good number expressed hope that their daughters would become professionals, which is a broad category including teachers, nurses, doctors, office employees, and the like. Others, perhaps less optimistic but also expressing a belief in equal opportunity, simply said that their daughters' futures would depend on their abilities, their intelligence, and their interests and that they would find employment accordingly.

The decision of the national government in 1977 to provide funding for a university in Huaraz lent encouragement to many parents in the city who formerly could not afford to send their children to college in Lima or other cities on the coast. On my survey questionnaire, a question that asked for reactions to the new university received responses that were nearly unanimous in their enthusiasm. Marketwomen who had never been to school themselves judged the promise of a university to be tremendously important for their children.

As mentioned before, the announcement that the university was to be built was met with celebration in Huaraz. On the evening of May 25, a speech making the announcement was broadcast on the Huaraz radio station, and people listened eagerly. At the appointed hour, Elena's thirteen-year-old son, Manuel, and about ten of his cousins and friends crowded into the room I occupied to play my radio and tape the speech on my recorder. Clearly, they understood it as a historical event. The following day, schoolchildren had a holiday and all commercial operations, including the markets, closed early in recognition of the importance of the new university. Students, workers, and marketers as well as the local bourgeoisie gathered in the street for a speech by the mayor, a parade, and music and dancing.

However, some marketwomen were not convinced that the university was the answer to their problems. Some were even doubtful about whether the plans would materialize; after a century of struggle for the university, they said they would reserve comment until the opening of the school. Others pointed out that having a university in Huaraz would attract more people to the already crowded city. Still others noted that those with more wealth or from a higher social class would have the privilege of being the first to enroll. A particularly critical informant raised a serious objection to the university, saying: "When there is no work, what good is a university? It will be worse. There is no work, no industry here."

In some ways, the university was more a symbol of the opportunities that Huaracinos wanted for their children than the realization of those opportunities. Some people believed that specialization in such areas as archaeology and nursing would be possible, though there was no official promise of these programs. Instead, the university was opened in 1978 with programs in mining and agricultural engineering. A year later civil engineering was included, and the following year programs were added in food industry engineering and environmental engineering. By 1980 auxiliary courses were offered in the social sciences and humanities and in theater, music, art, and sports, apart from the major programs.

Although women made up about 30 percent of students by 1980, the real opportunities that the university has opened for women appear to be quite limited. Many women, as well as men, had looked forward to training for the tourism industry, which is growing in the region. However, instead of the academic program they had hoped for, a "research center" for tourism was created. The dubious explanation for this decision was that the largely female graduates of other programs in tourism were an unstable labor force, with the result that few entered the industry or were available as university instructors (Universidad Nacional de Ancash 1980). Whatever the reasons, the areas of specialization offered at the university provide training for male-dominated fields. Thus, it is unlikely that women will enter the university in large numbers until such time as more programs are added. For now, the normal school in Huaraz seems a better choice for women, since teaching is a career that has long accepted them.

The daughters of marketwomen themselves have various outlooks on their futures. Some of them are genuinely confused by the alternatives they see available to them. Elena's daughter Teresa often confided in me about her plans for the future. These ranged widely from a serious consideration of entering a convent in Lima, a desire to study tourism at the Huaraz university, and an interest in the military (particularly in a parachutist division) to a curiosity about the field of anthropology. Although Teresa does not have a very clear idea of what she wants to do, she knows she would like to see other parts of Peru and be on her own for a while. At the same time, she is loyal to her family and will no doubt defer to her mother's wishes by staying near the family. Furthermore, Teresa has had such an important role in raising Pilar that she feels compelled to stay to look after her. But Teresa would not consider, at least at this time, a career in petty commerce or manufacturing. She worked during her school vacation for a small dressmaking enterprise run by a relative, but she viewed this as only temporary and resented it when her brother called her an *obrera* (worker).

Other daughters of marketwomen discussed their aspirations with me. The eighteen-year-old daughter of Juana has a part-time job in a bookstore, and after work she sometimes comes to help Juana close up her stall. When I asked her if she would ever consider working as a marketer, she scornfully insisted she would not. This was a common response given even by daughters who regularly assist their mothers in the market. Yet Juana's daughter has a sister, a year older, who works as an *ambulante* to support her child.

Like Juana's older daughter, a number of young women who have been to school and would prefer other types of employment turn eventually to the marketing profession of their mothers. The nineteen-year-old Frigorífico employee who sells fish in Mercado Nicrupampa has completed secondary school and would like very much to leave Huaraz to study medicine. This is impossible, however, for as the oldest in a poor family of nine children she must stay to contribute to the family income. She has looked for office work but has found no alternative to marketing. Another young woman, a fifteen-year-old in her first year of secondary school, substitutes for her mother during her school vacation. As she was selling vegetables outside Mercado Central one day, she explained that when she has finished school she will "just sell." When asked if she would like to do something different, she said no. Asked about what her friends would do after completing school, she said that some would leave Huaraz to find work elsewhere, while the ones who stayed would probably work as marketers or maids. She said she felt she could earn a living income in the marketplace. A few daughters who plan to sell after they finish their studies told me they expect to work on a larger scale than their mothers (interestingly, marketers' sons who presently attend school and sell express more confidence than daughters in either expanding their enterprise or leaving the market for professional employment after completing school).

The experiences of daughters like those described above, educated young women who take up marketing, are not rare in Huaraz. Women have so few employment options in Huaraz that many young women who want to find work in the "modern" sector need to consider relocating to other cities (though it is by no means certain they will have better luck since they may be discriminated against as highlanders, or *serranas*, in the coastal cities). Those who stay in Huaraz, as one young woman pointed out, may find that only the "traditional" sector jobs, such as marketing and domestic service, are open to them.

Marketwomen generally encourage their daughters to prepare for employment outside the market, but I discovered that in a number of cases one daughter in a family is expected to take over her mother's marketing when she is old enough. Women say these daughters will enable them "to rest," that is, to retire from the market. Consequently, it is not uncommon to find families in which one daughter is an apprenticed marketer while her sisters and brothers are trained for teaching or professional careers.

To the extent that the daughters of marketwomen find alternatives in Huaraz to marketing, what do they do? As mentioned already, staying home with household work is often considered preferable to outside employment for women, at least to such marginal employment as marketing. A marketwoman is satisfied to be able to say that her married daughter is *en casa;* this indicates that the daughter's husband can support the family, that the daughter's life is less difficult than her mother's, and that she is more "respectable." Daughters who seek work in the paid labor force face competition for the few available positions; but some find employment in such areas as office work in local government and wage work in Huaraz stores, restaurants, and hotels. These jobs are considered more respectable than self-employment in petty commerce.

Despite the advantages of a stable income from "modern" sector employment or the security of a marriage in which the husband can support his wife and children, such alternatives are not necessarily in every respect preferable to women's traditional work in marketing. Employment in petty commerce has been described throughout this study as at best providing a marginal livelihood, but it has several features that offer marketwomen a measure of self-respect and autonomy. The long history of marketing as a predominantly female

A schoolgirl sells candy part time in the streets.

occupation that is essential to the family and to society continues to give marketers a sense of the importance of the work they do. Furthermore, insofar as they are self-employed (or at least have some of the characteristics of the self-employed), they have a greater degree of control over the work they do than most wageworkers have. This degree of autonomy is particularly important for them as women, for it offers the economic independence that women *en casa* lack and that women in wage work generally find greatly reduced. Significantly, their daughters at home and in the paid labor force are typically in positions dependent on or subordinate to men—which suggests that, rather than leading to women's equality with men in the work force and in society, such "respectable" alternatives may lead to further inequality.

The position of women relative to men may not necessarily improve with an improvement in the material conditions of women's lives if their autonomy decreases. Nevertheless, many marketwomen would forfeit autonomy to relieve some of the hardship in their lives and their daughters' lives. Not surprisingly, marketers invest less in their businesses than in their children's education, since they view this as their only hope of seeing their sons and daughters move out of poverty. Marketwomen who have struggled against difficult conditions in their own lives are particularly gratified to send their daughters through school, helping them to *superarse,* to get ahead and overcome oppressive conditions.

Family, Society, and Modes of Production

We have seen that almost all marketwomen and their families in Huaraz must depend on several different sources of livelihood in order to "get by." Some women are fortunate enough to have husbands who find local employment, while others living alone, like Carolina, depend on the occasional help of other relatives to work their shared landholdings. These familial strategies for economic diversification have implications at the national level as well. While participation in several modes of production—both noncapitalist and capitalist—may be the family's resourceful way of coping with poverty, it is also a feature of the Andean social formation, which helps maintain Peru's capitalist economy by permitting greater exploitation of Andean people.

Three types of economic activity generally available to the urban poor in Huaraz have been discussed: subsistence agriculture and unpaid household labor, petty commodity production and commerce, and wage labor. Each of these activities, representing three modes of production (among which wage labor and the capitalist mode are dominant), is by itself generally inadequate to support a family.[4] Enough has been said about the poor earnings of marketers to demonstrate that few families survive on this income source alone. A word may be said about subsistence work and wage labor, however, as sources of family livelihood.

The landholdings of the poor in Huaraz are very small in size. Those lucky enough to have any land have *minifundios,* plots of land below subsistence size. Thus, while a large number of the families have fields, only in exceptional cases do they have as much as one hectare. Indeed, when I asked people how many hectares they had, most laughed and said they have no hectares, just tiny plots. Of the twenty-seven people who responded to my survey questionnaire, only two couples had a hectare while the other couples and individuals who responded in terms of hectares averaged just a quarter hectare. The others said they had small parcels or no land at all, and in one case a woman measured her land in square meters. For all these people, their fields are important sources of family foodstuffs but far from sufficient to meet household needs.

Housework, of course, must be performed in every household.

Unlike middle-class Peruvians who employ cheap domestic help, the poor of Huaraz are their own household labor, and this labor usually falls to women. Housework is an activity that often goes unrecognized in studies of local economies, but the discussion of women's work earlier in this chapter makes clear how much labor takes place at home. In addition to the work women carry out in the household, they are required to enter the marketplace as consumers, using shrewd judgment to stretch family resources and provide for the family. Since housework itself results in no income, housewives are dependent on other family resources in order to purchase food in the marketplace.

Unskilled or semiskilled wage labor around Huaraz—generally available to men—includes employment in construction, carpentry, occasional agricultural work, and the like. Such work results in earnings of around seventy to eighty soles (or about one U.S. dollar in 1977) daily, and a meal is sometimes included. Some jobs, particularly those requiring more skills, pay better, but the husbands of marketers are usually at the lowest pay levels and in positions with the least security. The instability and low pay of wage employment in Huaraz are often cited by marketwomen to explain why their commerce is so important to the family.

Thus, many families engage in all three modes of production—subsistence farming and household labor, petty commodity production and commerce, and the capitalist mode of production. The articulation of these modes at the household level is explained by the inadequacy of any one of them alone to provide a family livelihood under present conditions in Peru and the consequent need to diversify.

We may refer to the familiar example of Elena's family to see how a household economic strategy works in practice. Subsistence activities based in the household and on four small plots of land are the first source of sustenance for Elena's family. These are complemented by Elena's earnings as a marketer and by Renato's piecework income as a tailor. The daily sale of bread from the front room of their home provides another small but regular source of livelihood. In addition, Elena occasionally knits an article for sale or takes some flowers from the fields to market in order to earn a little more. And during their school vacations, the older children sometimes contribute to the household income through work in petty manufacturing and commerce (e.g., Teresa's work sewing). Furthermore, the investment that Elena and Renato have made in their children's education has begun to pay off. Guillermo is ready to obtain employment as a schoolteacher, and Teresa will soon be ready to seek work. Their parents will be able to count on at least some assistance from the children in the years to come.

While multiple sources of family livelihood are essential to most households in Huaraz, the increasing reliance on commerce as a source of income is noteworthy. City planners now estimate that a majority of Huaraz households participate in commercial activity. This corresponds to a brief survey of twenty households conducted in the barrio Nicrupampa, which found that thirteen households included members who are currently engaged in some type of commerce. In this neighborhood, involvement in commerce ranged broadly from selling goods in front room stores, producing and selling items as artisans, and working as transport agents to participating as marketers and street vendors.[5]

Household diversification may be viewed at the family level as a strategy for coping with poverty and for spreading the risk of failure in any endeavor, but it should also be viewed at the broader level as a response to economic underdevelopment in Andean Peru. If families participate in several modes of production out of economic need, this has the effect at the regional and national levels of keeping down the cost of reproducing, or maintaining, the labor force because none of the forms of livelihood need provide all that is necessary to support a worker. As long as poor families manage to "get by" despite below-subsistence landholdings, wages, and market earnings, the national economy is bolstered and higher levels of surplus are extracted from an already impoverished sector; landholdings continue to shrink, wages are kept low, and price controls on foodstuffs reduce the real earnings of marketers.

The Peruvian situation is similar to that in other Third World countries in which noncapitalist modes of production have persisted within capitalist social formations. Critical analysts (e.g., Oxaal, Barnett, and Booth 1975; Deere 1976; Foster-Carter 1978) have argued that, under the terms of contemporary dependent capitalism and underdevelopment, surplus is extracted from noncapitalist sectors to dominant capitalist sectors, contributing importantly to the accumulation of capital. Consequently, capitalism is subsidized by the hard work of families like those in Huaraz that practice economic diversification as a strategy for survival.

Seven *Social Relations and Politics of Marketwomen*

GIVEN THE DIFFICULT circumstances of most Huaraz marketers' lives and work, how do these women respond? Do they find ways of joining forces to lend each other support and to collectively express their dissatisfaction? Have they been active participants in the city's market unions? What role have they played in local- and national-level protests in recent years? These are a few of the questions we need to ask in order to discuss marketwomen as social and political actors.

The Social Relations of Marketers

The visitor to the Huaraz markets receives an impression of friendly cooperation among the sellers. Indeed, most of the time personal interactions are smooth, and disagreements rarely evolve into larger conflicts. Marketers often come to each other's assistance, though competition and conflict find expression on occasion. The fundamental differences that do exist among marketers appear to be based on their position in the Andean social structure.

The setting of prices, the basis for competition in marketplaces in many parts of the world, was effectively out of the hands of sellers of basic foodstuffs during most of the decade of the 1970s. In 1974, the Ministry of Food began establishing food prices, and these were enforced by officials in the local markets.[1] Consequently, the Huaraz markets were not characterized by much haggling or bargaining over the prices of goods (though conflicts did occasionally arise, as described below). Marketers' efforts to increase business instead took the form of trying to win loyal customers, and this rarely created problems among themselves. On the contrary, marketers often helped each other in surprising ways, recognizing the common difficulties they faced. "We all suffer," they told me, referring to the everyday struggle they all wage to get by.

Sellers help one another in many ways.[2] Elena, for example, who devotes time every day to preparing vegetables for sale to a woman at a nearby market restaurant, is often assisted by María, who helps her finish the job faster. Isabel, as mentioned earlier, is given considerable help at the small restaurant by her father-in-law, Señor Eduardo. One day, when I requested a *cafe con leche* (coffee with milk), she said she could provide it. Actually, she got the drink from her father-in-law in the next restaurant stall. She explained that they often help each other this way; she gave him the money I paid her and later returned the glass. That same day, she gave him a plate of *caldo* for a customer, and they made change for each other occasionally. This way, Señor Eduardo and Isabel help each other to satisfy their customers.

Marketers who work near one another often have a special cooperative relationship. All sellers must leave their spots from time to time, and most have a neighbor they can depend on to watch over their stock and tend to customers. This is usually for short periods of time, but if a marketer must leave Huaraz for a few days or is sick, her neighbor may agree to take charge of her affairs for the time she is gone. For example, one woman left for three days, and her neighbor took her stock back and forth to the street where they sell and sold the goods to customers. This way the perishable goods were not lost, and the absent marketer did not lose income. In another case, a woman's neighbor was particularly helpful in looking after the first woman's infant, who slept in the neighbor's stand; in return the woman did a number of small favors for the neighbor.

Another form of cooperation among sellers is the sharing of information. This may be information concerning the availability of products for sale, current prices issued by the Ministry of Food, or the actions of the Provincial Council and officials regarding the marketplace. When the council announced a rise in market fees, word circulated rapidly and sellers formulated strategies for action. And, whenever a representative of the PIP, the most feared officials, was identified in the markets, sellers speedily alerted their neighbors.

Beyond the cooperation revealed in the working relations of marketers, strong friendships frequently exist. Women are often affectionate, especially when they work daily in the same area together, and express interest and concern about one another's lives outside the market. "We are *compañeras* (close friends)," they say. The strongest bonds generally appear among retailers. Nevertheless, the associations of wholesalers with retailers and retailers with their

customers are often marked by expressions of friendship and cooperation. Huaraz retailers frequently seek out wholesalers they know,
people in whom they have a certain degree of confidence. The retailer generally expects that she will be offered goods on credit and
that the goods will be of satisfactory quality. In turn, the wholesaler
expects to be able to collect the price of the goods on schedule, usually after three to five days. Disagreements may arise, but it is in the
interest of wholesalers and retailers to resolve them in a friendly
manner.

Retailers sometimes have similar relationships with the shoppers
who buy from them regularly. For example, most sellers I asked in
Mercado Central said they extend credit to at least a few favored
customers. Some, like Elena, cannot afford to do this for many customers because they need the daily income, but she gives credit to
two or three people. One of them, a young girl, comes almost every
day to shop for her mother, who has ten children at home. Because
Elena is a family friend and sympathizes with their economic hardship, she allows them a few days to pay her. Blanca, a fruit and vegetable seller who does a fairly good business and whose husband
makes a comfortable salary, can extend credit to more customers.
This may explain, in turn, the large number of people who buy from
her. Some people, such as schoolteachers who are paid on a monthly
basis, rely on the few marketers like Blanca who can afford to wait to
be paid at the end of the month.

Strong market relationships are sometimes based on family
ties, but as far as I could determine they are rarely linked to ties of
compadrazgo, the ritual kinship of co-parenthood. This system, in
which adults sponsor a child (e.g., in baptism or marriage, as described earlier) or an object, is common in the Andes and serves to
define rights and obligations among the adults concerned. While *comadres* (co-mothers) might do business together, they make no special effort to establish such relations for the purpose of widening
their range of customers. Indeed, sellers were often explicit in telling me that, while they often know the people with whom they do
business, they are generally acquaintances (*conocidos*) rather than
friends (*amigos*). Possibly, increasing urbanization and the growing
number of marketers have lessened the importance of these ties; I
have no conclusive evidence but only the impression that all of the
ritual surrounding market activity, including market fiestas and the
sponsorship of new stalls, is diminishing.

Although many sellers emphasize the friendship and warm relationships in the marketplace, others claim that competition and
envy characterize social relations. Most often, marketers who are

not well acquainted make accusations of unfair competition, but even neighbors occasionally quarrel. This is not too surprising given the demands of the work marketers do and the serious effects of poverty in recent times.

Marketers compete at certain points in their work: when they are attempting to establish themselves in the market, when they are buying goods to sell in the market, and when they are selling to customers. Although sellers disagree over how hard it is to acquire a selling place, some suggest that the people who find desirable stalls use aggressive tactics to do so. A woman in Mercado Centenario told me that, when new stalls were built in Mercado Central, the most aggressive women got them; she added that she prefers the Centenario market because it is calmer. In a couple of instances in La Parada, I observed *ambulantes* who were competing for space in the streets, each claiming the area as her own.

With the expanding number of sellers, it is increasingly difficult for them to locate sufficient stock for their stalls. Whenever I arrived in the marketplace in time to observe the transactions of wholesalers and retailers, which begin as early as 3:00 A.M., I was impressed by how eagerly sellers approached trucks as they arrived. Before a truck carrying produce from the countryside has even reached its destination in the market, a crowd of sellers may be seen running after it. Women, sometimes thirty-five or forty of them, crowd in to be among the first to see what the truck contains, and those who are boldest in pressing close and grasping the back of the truck have the clear advantage. I noted that Elena, despite her quiet temperament, was often among the most successful in chasing after trucks. While she appeared to be good-natured, I saw one day that she could be aggressive. A truck arrived outside Mercado Central and offered to take a few marketers to a house in the city where visiting merchants were selling potatoes and onions. Elena argued with one of her neighbors from Mercado Central, Julia, over which of them would fit in the cab of the truck. Julia was pushed out and only managed to climb in the back as the truck was pulling away. Elena later explained that they fought to ride in the truck because they knew there was only a small quantity of goods to buy at the house. Interestingly, Elena also bought for her sister-in-law, María, on this trip, and almost the entire contents of the three sacks she kept for herself were bought by a seller from Carhuaz within minutes after she arrived at her stall.

Another response of sellers to the increasing difficulties of locating foodstuffs is to compete in their transactions with wholesalers. Although most prices are controlled, some retailers offer to pay a little more in order to enhance their stock. I recorded cases of business agreements between wholesalers and retailers that were broken when other retailers offered to pay more. Most sellers, however, look down on this type of behavior.

Just as retailers will sometimes be willing to pay more to wholesalers in order to pick up the pace of business, they are also willing occasionally to lower prices to consumers. *Ambulantes*, in particular, are known for this practice, and one *ambulante* told me that as a group they are especially competitive in trying to sell cheap and fast.

As noted, sellers direct considerable energy toward building a loyal clientele, particularly sellers with permanent stalls, who need to attract customers to their stationary spots. While this is not as a rule the basis for competition between sellers, it sometimes generates hostility among market neighbors. On several occasions, I observed conflicts as they developed. Once, the only time I saw a public confrontation between my friends in Mercado Central, Blanca accused Graciela of taking away a customer. The customer stood by as the two fruit and vegetable sellers shouted across the stalls at each other. Blanca was the more abusive in her insults, calling Graciela an ambitious woman and telling her not to meddle with her clients. I later learned that the two had had a similar argument once before but had gotten over it and remain friendly most of the time.

Some hostilities, however, are not so quick to mend. I learned of one feuding relationship when it was brought to the floor at a meeting of the market union, and I followed it for several weeks afterward. Two women with adjacent restaurant stands outside Mercado Central began fighting for what they called personal reasons but ones that revealed competitive jealousy. One of the women claimed that the husband of the other passed her stand hurling insults at her. She has responded since then with episodes of fighting with her neighbor (once, throwing stones and pulling hair). The other woman denied this explanation of the problem and accused the first woman of being a prostitute and of robbing her. The first woman began working at her stand before her neighbor and has a corner spot from which she can easily attract customers from the street. The fact that she actively calls people over to her stand makes me suspect that the friction between the two women is business related, at least in part.

Clearly, conflicts can develop among neighbors who sell the same items in the same market areas. Generally, marketers say that sellers of similar items are not competitive. Artisans told me that as a group they are not competitive, and restaurant operators said there is no competition among them. They may be denying some of the problems that sellers of like economic standing and commercial activity have in the markets, but for the most part conflicts are expressed among groups more fundamentally opposed to one another. Accordingly, local fish sellers assert that independent vendors and employees of the Frigorífico do not compete, but that the fish sellers who come from Chimbote with refrigerated trucks are highly competitive.

The principal conflicts in the markets emerge around differences between sellers of urban origin, the Huaracinos, and sellers of rural origin, the *campesinos* or people of the Callejón (which in the city refers to non-Huaracinos in the valley). Sometimes references are made to the indoor marketers versus street sellers or registered sellers versus *ambulantes*, and although these distinctions are not strictly identified with the urban-rural distinction, people usually have this division in mind.

The Huaracinos, chiefly including sellers in Mercado Central and the sellers in nearby streets, who identify with this market, and sellers in Mercado Centenario recall earlier days when fewer sellers meant better business and friendlier relationships. They attribute many of their present problems to the rapid entry of newcomers from the countryside (*el campo*), exaggerating (and fabricating) characteristics of rural marketers to show they are undeserving of whatever success they may have. The *campesinos*, they say, only learned to sell after the earthquake, and now they have overrun the marketplace and are putting long-experienced sellers out of business. Some insist that *campesinos* work out of greed rather than economic necessity (*por vicio*, or as a vice, one woman told me) and can afford houses and fields. Furthermore, they point out, while most urban sellers pay to be registered and receive a license, rural street sellers do not pay these fees and even avoid paying the daily fee by hiding when officials come around. Urban marketers appeal to middle-class sentiments when they criticize street sellers for working under unhygienic conditions on the ground, not using aprons or setting up tables. And they emphasize that, if *ambulantes* sell a little cheaper, it is because the quality of their goods is inferior.

Rural sellers do not remain silent when confronted with these charges. Instead, they are adamant in insisting on their right to make a living in the market and in denying that they are greedy intruders. If the conditions in which they work are simple, they say, this attests to their poverty. They do not have the privileges of indoor marketers, who have stalls and storage space, water and latrines. Furthermore, they point out, Huaraz has always needed to depend on *campesinos* to provide urban consumers with food, and urban marketers ought to remain mindful of this. One rural seller expressed the feelings of many *campesinos* when she was forced from the place where she was sitting in La Parada by another seller: "In Huaraz we can't sell. They throw us out of the place. This way, I don't feel like bringing my goods here again. If it weren't for the Callejón, Huaraz would die. Huaraz doesn't have anything. There's no water. And there are no vegetables. If we didn't come, Huaraz would die. And then they treat us with scorn!"

Many urban sellers and customers recognize the importance of the Callejón and the wholesalers and retailers who come with products of the region. Sellers say, sometimes grudgingly and sometimes in solidarity, that they are all struggling to get by and times are hard for everyone. Middle-class customers take out their worries about rising food prices on rural marketers, but I observed at least one shopper come to the defense of a *campesina* seller (out of self-interest as well, no doubt). On this occasion, a seller from the Callejón was selling wholesale and retail, and a retailer wanted to pay S/.15 rather than S/.16 per kilo for lettuce. A shopper, hearing their dispute, told the retailer, "For one sol you are not going to lose anything." Others in the area agreed and pointed out the additional expenses that *campesinos* pay in transport. They supported the woman, saying: "The Callejón de Huaylas is what maintains Huaraz with vegetables and many things. In Huaraz there is nothing. They [the *campesinos*] are the ones who sell and who supply the Huaraz market. And if we treat them badly, they are not going to want to sell here another day."

The kinds of conflicts that I observed and the views I heard expressed by Huaracinos and people of the Callejón in the marketplace reflect their position in Andean society. The historical relationship of *mestizos* and *campesinos*, that is, of a dominant town group and a subordinate country group, continues to manifest itself, though in changing forms. In the present urban setting, one place where these inequalities surface is in the marketplace, where *mestizos* attempt to get the better of *campesinos* in their commercial relationships. In market commerce the poorest sector of the urban population is represented, but while urban sellers are sometimes as impoverished as rural sellers, they still have some of the privileges of *mestizos*— knowledge of Spanish, sometimes literacy, and the "superior" urban way of life—to draw on.

The division that exists between urban and rural sellers in the markets may nonetheless be a consequence of the poverty they share, which weakens the unity that might develop among them. The sellers themselves sometimes attempt to overcome their differences, as the market interchanges described above reveal. Another example illustrating divisiveness and unity among sellers concerns a discussion about meat sellers and their soaring prices. One vegetable seller complained that, while the prices of her goods were tightly controlled, meat sellers charged what they liked; but other marketers rose to the defense of the meat sellers and pointed out that they do not control the prices and are not happy about rising prices either, since their business declines. On another occasion Víctor, of Mercado Central, argued persuasively at a union meeting that the Provincial Council deliberately tries to divide sellers by charging different fees, giving fines selectively, and controlling some marketers more strictly than others.

If small marketers agree on anything, it is that the big wholesalers dominate market commerce. When petty traders say, "We are the slaves of the wholesalers," they are not referring to all wholesalers who make a living as intermediaries but only the most powerful ones. The feeling of shared powerlessness unites urban and rural sellers, who see they have much in common in their relationship with the few large wholesalers who benefit from disproportionate control in the Huaraz markets. Retailers sometimes compare their impoverished condition with that of wholesalers who can buy homes and cars. Many note that some wholesalers cannot be trusted because they sell food that is spoiling or they cheat on the weight. Furthermore, some add that wholesalers have more freedom from official control, which allows them to raise their prices above the established rates.

Many small traders told me, "We just work for the wholesalers" or "Sometimes we just sell for the wholesalers." Their earnings are so low that it often seems as though they are working only to keep the wholesalers in business. These marketers' analysis of their situation is perhaps correct, for, essentially, they are working as commission sellers for the wholesalers; they buy on credit and earn a small amount above what they must pay the wholesaler. This increment, I suggested earlier, may usefully be viewed as payment for their work selling for the wholesalers.

The Market Unions

Almost all sellers in the Huaraz markets are aware that there are unions (or *sindicatos*), but only a minority attend meetings regularly. Many think that the unions do not act effectively in their interests or that the membership fees and dues are prohibitive. Others believe the unions are important; but they are not members and only attend meetings when issues affecting them are to be raised, since their work in the market and at home demands most of their time.

The principal union of marketers is the Sindicato de Trabajadores de Mercados y Anexos de Huaraz (Union of Workers of the Markets and Annexes of Huaraz). This union is affiliated with the CTRP (Central de Trabajadores de la Revolución Peruana, or Confederation of Workers of the Peruvian Revolution), a labor organization originally sponsored by the military government as an alternative to party-affiliated labor unions. In 1977, the union's 230 dues-paying members were drawn primarily from the downtown sellers of produce and prepared food.

Another important market union in Huaraz, composed largely of clothing sellers but also of other sellers from La Parada and the streets outside the Mercado Central building, is known as the Sindicato de Minoristas y Vendedores (Union of Retailers and Sellers). Many members of this union are *ambulantes,* and they often identify their union with the activity outside Mercado Central (and they associate the union mentioned above with the interior of Mercado Central, though this distinction is not currently accurate). This union, which has been in existence since the 1960s, is affiliated with the CGTP (Confederación General de Trabajadores de Perú, or General Confederation of Peruvian Workers), the labor union federation connected with the Communist party in Peru. They hold meetings approximately once a month or when there are problems. About 200 members pay S/.100 to join and S/.15 monthly. Some members say the union is helpful in offering aid to members who are sick or have special difficulties, but others are dissatisfied with the union, saying that it does little for them. They point out that the union did not take any action concerning an announced rise in market fees. One woman who sells clothing along Jirón Ancash emphasized her unhappiness with the union by recounting an incident that took place several years ago. Union members had received permission from the mayor to construct twenty *kioskos* (booths with doors, for the sale and storage of goods) along the street. They built the *kioskos,* but when ORDEZA (the government organization for the reconstruction of the earthquake-damaged area) presented some obstacles to the marketers' using the booths, the union's secretary general was the first to leave his *kiosko.* He offered no protest, and the others were forced to do the same.

The meat sellers have their own union, and the thirty-one beef sellers in Mercado Central and Mercado Centenario are recognized as members. The Sindicato de Carniceros (Meat Sellers' Union) charges sellers to become members; some years ago it cost S/.2,000, reflecting the higher economic status of these sellers, but there are no monthly dues. One woman maintained that the union acts in the sellers' interest by trying to bring down the price of meat. Another woman, however, said that the union does nothing—has not protested rising market fees and does not help when sellers are fined or have other problems. This same woman complained that at their monthly meetings men dominate and women remain silent, and she was surprised when I described the active participation of women at meetings of the principal market union.

Among other downtown sellers, the independent fish sellers belong to the principal union, while the employees of Frigorífico are unorganized. The twenty-eight pork sellers are not unionized, but they are discussing whether to organize separately or join the meat sellers' union. Also, the men with *triciclos* have their own union of marketplace transporters.

Sellers in Mercado Centenario were forming their own union, but their efforts to be recognized failed, and they ended their attempt to organize.[3] Their junta consisted of six or seven women and three men (including the president, a man selling staple groceries). Marketers paid S/.15 each week in dues but after a while decided they did not want to pay any longer, and later the union disbanded. According to some sellers, the union wasted the money on paintings for the market and a Christ figure for the chapel. While they were organizing, the sellers put pressure on the Provincial Council to send more wholesalers and sellers to their market, but little attention was paid to their request, and now they feel they have no power in the matter at all. A number of sellers expressed regret that their efforts to unionize did not succeed.

The principal market union, the Sindicato de Trabajadores de Mercados, was founded in 1965, and many members recall that in its early years the union was more active and had greater member participation. They had a hall, where they held meetings, and even a day care center, where they could leave their children. Early members remember that there was enthusiasm in those days and marketers united around political and social issues.

Several marketers recall the support that their union gave during the struggle for the university in 1968. At that time, the marketers participated in a demonstration for the university and in a general strike in Huaraz. About a year later, union members participated in another protest over rising market fees and the cost of living, and two of their leaders were arrested. They considered the outcome a success when the projected increases in prices and fees were lowered (daily fees were to be raised from S/.0.20 to S/.2 but instead were raised to S/.1). One woman remembered proudly: "All rose up together because we were united. And we won."

Others remembered that union members used to join together to contribute money when relatives of members died or to celebrate during holidays. The past was not all harmony, however, and one woman who has long been active in the union described a time when a split among union members almost occurred. A *campesino*, Ignacio Colonia, was attempting to form a separate union of *campesino* sellers, she recalled. In response, the two largest market unions in Huaraz, the Sindicato de Trabajadores de Mercados and the Sindicato de Minoristas y Vendedores, acted together with the aid of the CTRP to prevent the formation of the union. One day, a wholesaler's truck stopped where some *campesinos* were selling instead of the usual area where Huaracinos sold. The Huaracinos complained to an inspector in the police department, and they were encouraged to use force to prevent trucks from stopping near the *campesinos*. They had a confrontation in the marketplace but did not need to use force. The *campesinos* became fearful, and Colonia escaped out of Huaraz. Thereafter, trucks came to the accustomed locations.

In contrast to the present union leadership, some past juntas have been led by women. Several women presidents are remembered fondly, and a past vice-president, Juana, of Mercado Central, continues to be a respected seller in the marketplace. Juana is disappointed that women no longer lead the union because, she says, the men have no enthusiasm. When I asked why fewer women are involved now, she explained that most women have children to care for, life is especially difficult now (referring to the economic crisis), and many sellers today are *campesinos* who just sell and leave, without participating in union activities. She says that she did good things helping sellers as vice-president but could not continue to be so active in the union when she had more children.

In 1977 there were nine men and five women in the union junta, with men holding all the top leadership positions. This represented a decline in women's participation since the 1975–76 junta of five men and nine women with women in important positions, including that of vice-president. The succeeding junta was generally considered weak, and there was much talk about making changes in it before the end of the 1977–78 term. Beginning in 1975, the president, or secretary general, of the junta had been a man named Vicente Figueroa. He and several other men were union leaders and under them were two women active in the junta. Beatriz León, the secretary of defense, had the responsibility of speaking on behalf of union members and of seeing that their problems were heard by the leadership. Carolina Sánchez, the seventy-four-year-old secretary of the press and propaganda whose life was described in the previous chapter, served primarily to inform members of the time and place of meetings and to see that they attended. While both women played a kind of advocacy role for their constituency, they also acted as disciplinarians, herding sellers to meetings, telling them to keep quiet, and standing guard to see that nobody left early. Other members of the junta often did not fulfill their responsibilities and did not attend meetings.

Figueroa came under heavy criticism, and many union members were inactive because they opposed his leadership. A number of women who sold vegetables and fruits expressed their feelings by saying that Figueroa was in *otro negocio*, another business, and he did not understand their problems. Figueroa sells *mercería:* knives and kitchen supplies, needles and threads, scissors, combs, and other household items outside Mercado Central, near the corner of Raimondi. His merchandise suggests a level of capital investment well beyond the means of most of the people that he represented in the union. In addition to his insensitivity to many of the concerns of the people in the union, a number of members felt that he treated them in a disrespectful and patronizing manner. Furthermore, many considered Figueroa to be ineffective and conciliatory in his negotiations with local authorities on issues facing the union.

The women in the junta discussed their feelings about Figueroa with me. Beatriz, the secretary of defense, expressed her annoyance with the secretary general, saying he treated members badly, even contemptuously. She noted that, while the term of leadership was generally two years, the dissatisfaction with Figueroa made it likely that a change would come sooner. Carolina was somewhat more optimistic about Figueroa, finding him enthusiastic and capable of doing good things for the union. Still, in speaking of the improvements she had seen in him during his term, she noted that when he was elected he knew nothing of unionism and was just beginning to learn. "Although he leaves much to be desired," she offered, "he was worse before."

When I met Figueroa one day in the market and told him of my interest in attending union meetings, he invited me to one that Saturday afternoon. I was accompanied by Tomás Camino to that and subsequent meetings, and we were warmly received. In what follows, I will describe the proceedings of three union meetings I attended, focusing on the issues that were raised and how they

Despite the male leadership of the unions, marketwomen play active roles.

were treated by the male-dominated leadership and the female-dominated rank and file.

The meeting that first Saturday afternoon was held, for lack of a meeting hall, in a child care center then in a bad state of repair. The gathering was not called to order until almost an hour late, and I had the opportunity to observe as people slowly entered. I was most surprised to find that the majority of marketers present were women and predominantly *campesinas*. Altogether, about fifty women and five men came and sat on rows of benches. Most of those attending appeared to be over thirty, and some were quite old. In addition, the members of the junta present were Figueroa, three other men, Beatriz, and Carolina—the men sitting at the front of the room and the women surveying the assembly from the side. Before the meeting started, people could be heard discussing the rising prices in the markets and the low attendance at this meeting.

After attendance was finally taken and the meeting came to order, several issues were raised and discussion followed, more in Quechua than in Spanish. The major item on the agenda, which explains the high proportion of *campesinas* in attendance, was a report by Figueroa concerning a meeting he had had with the city's inspector of hygiene. During that meeting it was agreed that sellers of pre-pared food who sat along the riverbank in La Parada must move to an area between Mercado Central and the Frigorífico. According to the inspector, their conditions were unhygienic since they prepared food on the ground without tables and they had no facilities to clean their serving implements properly. Figueroa had complied with the in-spector's wishes by providing a list of names of women selling food by the river in order to expedite their move to the new area, where stands were under construction.

The women at the meeting who were involved in this decision had anticipated such an announcement, but they would not accept it. There was a tremendous uproar, and the women concerned all agreed that none should move. Figueroa weakened in the face of their protest and lamely threatened that, if they did not at least ac-quire tables, chairs, clean tablecloths, and napkins at their usual lo-cation, they would be fined, and the union would do nothing for them. (In the weeks that followed this meeting, few women com-plied, and many explained that they could not afford such improve-ments, especially since they would have to pay porters to carry their tables and chairs to and from the market every day. The women also resisted moving because they knew their business would decline sharply if they left La Parada, where many people from the Callejón come to eat while in the city.)

After this heated discussion, the junta attempted to go on to the next item on the agenda, which was to register union members. Their request for S/.50 and two photographs from those wishing to become members was met with great impatience. Women began to rise out of their seats, arguing that the junta leaders paid no atten-tion to their problems, and several tried to leave. One woman was calmed down, and at Beatriz's urging she spoke to the group about the difficulty she and other sellers in La Parada were having in gain-ing access to the storage area they were accustomed to renting. She proposed that a committee be formed to investigate the problem. Following this, two women loudly began to discuss their difficulties as neighbors selling outside Mercado Central (their relationship was described earlier in this chapter). Figueroa appealed to them to stop fighting, but when they did not he said he would have to notify the police or suspend them from working for three days if they continued.

By this time, people were on their feet and the assembly had moved to the other side of the room. Many people slipped out the door, until only the junta members and a few sellers remained. Figueroa told us apologetically that the meeting was over. At this meeting and others, the women were confident, outspoken, and resolute in maintaining their position on the issues raised. Figueroa, however, revealed himself to be more interested in satisfying local authorities than in acting in the interest of his constituency.

The next meeting of this union was called with some sense of urgency for a Friday afternoon two weeks later. For several weeks, word had been circulating among marketers that the annual registration fees and the daily fees collected by the Provincial Council were to rise significantly. The vegetable and fruit sellers, for example, believed that their annual fee would rise from S/.50 to S/.500. All marketers were alarmed by the talk of increasing fees, and this meeting was to inform them of the mayor's plans on the matter and to decide on their own course of action.

This time, the group met outdoors since the building they had used before was occupied. The issue to be discussed drew a larger number and a wider variety of people than the previous meeting; eighty or ninety marketers, including about a dozen men, attended, and urban sellers seemed to outnumber rural sellers. In addition to the junta members present, a representative of the CTRP had been invited because of the serious nature of this meeting. As people sat talking on the grass before the meeting was called to order, it was clear to me, although their conversation was in Quechua, that the topic was the rising fees.

After people had settled down and the representative was introduced, the meeting began. Figueroa came to the point, announcing that the mayor planned to raise annual and daily fees by 100 percent and that the marketers must decide whether this was acceptable. He encouraged the group to consider a compromise and accept a slight increase in fees. The women in the group immediately shouted him down, saying they would not pay a centavo more than the last year. Figueroa lost his composure and the CTRP representative took over the meeting.

The representative said that if they were determined not to pay more they had better show unity, since fewer than one hundred sellers came to this meeting and they should expect resistance from others who did not come. He asked what they would do if the mayor refused to listen to them, and the women present shouted in unison, "*¡No vendemos! ¡Una huelga pues!*" (We won't sell! A strike then!). All were in agreement that neither the registration nor the daily fees should go up a single centavo. They argued that with their small earnings they could not possibly afford any increase. The representative suggested that they present their position to the mayor and get his response, to which they agreed.

Following this, several issues related to the proposed increase in fees led to disagreement between sellers from inside Mercado Central and sellers working outside that market. There had been a certain power struggle between these two groups in the union. Until the end of Víctor's term as president (when Figueroa was elected), the union leadership came from Mercado Central. When Figueroa assumed office, many former members became inactive, and they expressed the hope that when a new junta was elected its officers would once again come from inside their market. The tension between the groups was felt during the rest of the meeting, though few members from Mercado Central were present.

At this point in the meeting, after the group agreed to protest a rise in fees, several people said they thought that sellers inside Mercado Central ought to pay higher registration fees than sellers outside since they had water, latrines, storage space, and other advantages. Those from inside the market quickly argued that they pay for those services on a daily basis, and the issue was dropped.

Then those present were informed that Víctor and others in Mercado Central had been collecting donations in their market for the preparation of a document to be sent to the mayor protesting the increase in market fees. This independent act, undertaken apart from the union, was seen by those at the meeting as divisive, and they left the meeting in agreement that Víctor should be denounced publicly as an agitator and a traitor to the union.

The next union meeting was postponed several times as the mayor's response to the union's petition was delayed. When it was held on a Saturday two months later, about seventy-five people (at least seventeen of them men, including junta members) gathered in the courtyard of a boarding house. Figueroa announced that he had good news from the mayor's office, and he asked another man in the junta to read the mayor's response.

The mayor stated that the registration fees would increase by 100 percent, but that, until the Provincial Council and the Ministry of Food studied the matter further, the daily fees would remain at their present level. In addition, a number of promises were made to the marketers, including the building of more latrines, the continued availability of storage space in La Parada, and the agreement that some wholesalers would be told to stop in the area of the Frigorífico. Discussion did not follow this presentation, which I thought indicated acquiescence, but in the days to come I heard women say they were still opposed to any increases.

After the mayor's response was read, a number of sellers from Mercado Central arrived at the meeting, including Señor Eduardo, Víctor, Blanca, and Juana. Señor Eduardo spoke to the group, saying that he, not Víctor, organized the Mercado Central protest. He asked to read the document they sent to the mayor, and this was reluctantly allowed. The document was a formal appeal, emphasizing the serious consequences that any increase in fees would have for marketers, especially for the women with children who make up the majority of sellers.

At first, most of those present remained critical of the action of the Mercado Central sellers, and they argued that these sellers come to meetings only when their own interests are at stake. Víctor interrupted, however, and convinced many of them of the sincerity of their act. He explained that they felt compelled to protest to the mayor since many of them were already being pressured to pay increased fees, and they believed that their document would give additional support to any action the union might take. He concluded with an eloquent plea for unity, saying the marketers must not allow the mayor and his Provincial Council to divide them. The meeting soon came to a close, with Figueroa expressing hope that the differences between the sellers inside and outside Mercado Central might be resolved.

Despite the male-dominated organization of the union, the militance of the women often exerts pressure on an otherwise complacent leadership to take action. Although the issues discussed at these meetings were not settled when I left Huaraz in 1977—and similar problems arose over the next few years—many women were clearly determined to fight against the enforcement of what they felt were unjust market regulations.

Huaraz Marketwomen and National Politics

Finding that Huaraz marketers, particularly the poorest women, and their families were often outspoken in their views regarding local issues, I was interested to see what stance they would adopt during the two national strikes that were called while I was in Peru in 1977. The first was a teachers' strike, set for July 5. This twenty-four-hour work stoppage was called by the radical teachers' union, SUTEP (Union of Peruvian Education Workers), as a protest against extremely low wages, recent layoffs, and the arrest of teachers active within the union. At the time of the strike I was in Lima, where the action was most effective, but I talked with Huaracinos both before and after the strike to get their reactions.

Among the marketers I spoke to, many of whom have children in school, there was generally strong support for the teachers. Teachers are highly respected in Huaraz, but nationally they rank very low on the pay scale of professional employees. The marketers regard teachers as underpaid, and some, whose children are teachers or in training at the normal school, are particularly sympathetic to their situation. Several weeks before the strike, the PIP detained several normal school students and even a few secondary school students who were known to be supporters of SUTEP, and this angered Huaracinos. By late June extra police had been called into Huaraz to control the situation. In addition, it was said that SINAMOS was encouraging parents to oppose the teachers in their demands for higher salaries.

Nevertheless, many parents remained supportive. On July 5 in Huaraz the teachers went to their schools under threat of reprisals for striking, while many parents kept their younger children home. At midday, the striking teachers and a number of secondary school students who were active in organizing the protest led a march, which grew in strength as they went from school to school. Along the way, the police followed, using sticks and tear gas in the schools. By this time parents, outraged at this treatment by the police, were arriving at the schools and taking their children home. The march ended at the Plaza de la Soledad, where the police confronted the teachers and students, wounding some and taking others in for questioning. Many mothers, like Elena, were doubly angered on this occasion by the government's repression of teachers and by its brutality toward their children.

Just two weeks later, July 19, 1977, the communist CGTP led a national work stoppage, the first of several general strikes in the country during this period. Again, marketers and their families in Huaraz expressed fairly strong support, although many did not view their participation in the strike as important to its success nationwide (and some were not aware of the strike or knew little about it). Everywhere, in the days leading up to the general strike, people discussed the economic crisis. As uprisings and strikes were reported around the country, they talked of how long cities had been "shut down." By July 17, reports appeared that little was passing in or out of Lima. Marketers in Huaraz anticipated few trucks of goods arriving in La Parada, and they tried to stock up. Students had a week left before their annual vacation time, but the schools dismissed them early, before the strike, supposedly because of possible violence but undoubtedly to prevent students from organizing to support the strike.

In the marketplace the day before the strike, those I spoke to said they hoped the strike would be effective, and they discussed the worsening economic conditions that prompted it. There was talk that the markets might be shut down as they were during demonstrations for the university. Some planned to come in as usual or for a little while to sell some goods, and still others planned to stay away. The strike had been declared illegal by the government, and that night the minister of the interior addressed the nation, threatening reprisals against striking workers.

July 19 came and activity in Huaraz was slow but by no means at a standstill. The markets were open, though police stood guard at the entrances as they did at street corners throughout the city. Inside Mercado Central business appeared normal; and outside, Figueroa, head of the market union, explained a bit apologetically that their union central, the CTRP, had not sent word for them to strike. In contrast, the Jirón Ancash, where many clothing sellers set up, was nearly abandoned, as were some streets of La Parada where *ambulantes* come to sell. The clothing sellers, whose union is affiliated with the CGTP, were striking, while many *ambulantes* from outside the city may have felt that it would be better to stay away. The Centenario and Nicrupampa markets were slightly less active than usual. And walking through the major commercial streets of downtown Huaraz, I estimated that about 20 percent of the stores were closed.

In the days following the general strike, people talked about it. Although the Lima papers reported little on events in the capital, word spread in Huaraz that support was strong there—as was police repression, causing a number of deaths. One marketwoman spoke for others when she commented on the relatively low level of support shown for the strike in Huaraz, saying, "Only we marketers went to work, because we aren't united and the union is in favor of the government."

In contrast to this woman's critical assessment of the role of small marketers in the strike, a shopkeeper who closed his store for the strike described his participation in different terms. As the owner of a fairly successful store of musical instruments, electrical appliances, and other "luxury" goods and a member of the local Camara de Comercio (Chamber of Commerce), he claimed to have stayed away from work because he believed "a general strike should be general." Although shopkeepers made independent decisions about whether to support the strike, he believed that people must unite to make such actions effective. He eloquently compared the unity of working people to a machine, all parts functioning together. I suspected, however, that the man may have acted more out of fear than support for the strike (there had been rumors of possible looting and open confrontations).

For several weeks after the teachers' strike and the general strike, I had occasion to ask people for their views on the national situation and on the role of Huaraz in the growing opposition to the government. Informal conversations as well as formal interviewing on these questions (see Appendix) revealed a strong feeling that things were very wrong in the country. Many marketers and their families expressed a willingness to take personal risks in order to support a movement for change, yet they were not convinced that poor Huaracinos could be effective. Accordingly, the comments of those who made the most radical statements sometimes closed on a note of resignation.

Huaraz marketwomen, we have seen, are frequently vocal in expressing their strong dissatisfaction with the conditions of their lives and work. Their wide-ranging criticism is directed to the practices of unscrupulous wholesalers, to the increasingly restrictive measures of local officials, on up to the level of national policy makers. While marketers occasionally reveal a sense of hopelessness or resignation, they are rarely complacent. Instead, the women are refusing to quietly endure their worsening economic situation.

The solidarity and resistance of marketwomen can be seen on a daily basis. Street vendors who help each other evade fee collectors, sellers who assist one another prepare goods for sale and alert their neighbors to changing price policies, all demonstrate a cooperative base of support among these working women. Being marginalized in the society and economy has not prevented these women from developing a consciousness of their collective contribution as marketers and of the political potential they represent.

Eight   *Economic Crisis and the Campaign against Marketers*

THE ECONOMIC CRISIS confronting Peru since the mid-1970s has been marked by the government's increased difficulty in keeping food prices at a tolerable level. In an apparent effort to turn attention away from its own responsibility in the crisis, the government launched a campaign against petty marketers and street vendors, among whom a large majority are poor women. While it has served middle-class interests to hold small marketers responsible for soaring food costs, closer examination shows that both high prices and the growth of petty commerce are responses to more fundamental economic problems of dependent capitalism in Peru. The Peruvian case may be understood in the more general context of the situation confronting many Third World countries in which economic underdevelopment is accompanied by an expanding informal sector.

Of course, much can be said about the irrationality of the present system of marketing in Peru. Ninety-nine percent of retail activity is in the hands of small, independent sellers (Esculies Larrabure, Rubio Correa, and Gonzales del Castillo 1977:181), and we may imagine a situation in which economic planning might result in far smoother functioning of distribution.[1] Certainly, many marketers would be delighted to leave their market stalls and places in the streets were employment alternatives open to them. But to expect the state, in its present form, to successfully reform the system through curtailing petty trade overlooks certain critical factors. First, the strategy ignores the role of the Peruvian government itself in generating and perpetuating the current economic crisis—and it never considers the broader international context of the crisis and the implications for Peru's food prices. Second, this view neglects some important features of the work of marketers within the present structure of underdevelopment in Peru, such as their capacity to keep down prices, their productive contribution to the process of bringing goods to consumers, as well as their self-sufficiency, which acts to offset the level of unemployment. If small-scale marketers provide essential services in Peru and if petty commerce offers employment—however marginal—to members of society who might otherwise be unemployed, why, then, has the Peruvian government taken actions that appear to jeopardize the livelihood of marketers?

In what follows, I discuss the relationship of small marketers to rising food prices, counterposing the government policy position with my own view. Developments in Huaraz over the last decade are then presented to illustrate the way that national policy directives from Lima have resulted in tightening control of commerce at the local level. Finally, some new initiatives for managing the informal sector at both the national and local levels are considered.

Marketers and Food Prices: Two Views

As Oscar Esculies Larrabure, Marcial Rubio Correa, and Verónica Gonzales del Castillo (1977 : 9) point out: "Much has been written in the last few years concerning the commercialization of agricultural products in Peru, pleading for the injured rights of the consumer in some cases and for the legitimate interests of the producer in others. But the almost invariable factor in the various inquiries has been the facile *blaming of the intermediary, presumed responsible for the majority of problems inherent in this process that concerns everybody: the provisioning of food"* (my emphasis).

Under pressure from middle-class and working-class consumers (and international interests as well), the Peruvian government has directed considerable attention to controlling food prices since the early 1970s. Much less attention has gone to the problem of unemployment and underemployment, which Peru's least powerful constituencies face. Lack of employment opportunities is most dramatic in Lima, but in provincial cities with little industry, like Huaraz, the level of unemployment is also high. Furthermore, unemployment is a special problem for women, who have even fewer alternatives than do men (Bunster and Chaney 1985; Mercado 1978). The problem would be still more severe except that a growing segment of the population is counted among the self-employed—a large number in petty commerce. In a limited but important way, small-scale marketers reduce the national employment problem by sustaining themselves during a time of economic hardship. Just the same, the government has pointed the finger at commercial intermediaries as a group, holding them responsible—as the preceding quotation suggests—for the troubles Peru has in providing its people with food at affordable prices.

From the vantage point of urban consumers and their representatives in government, the number of marketers engaged in the distribution process directly corresponds to the ultimate cost of food. Small retailers, who make up the last link in the chain of intermediaries, are often singled out for attack since they are the most numerous and the most visible to consumers. These small marketers are viewed as providing an inessential service, bringing goods to urban neighborhoods in very small quantities. Their impoverished and sometimes unhygienic working conditions are frequently viewed with alarm at the same time that these marketers are considered social parasites. Middle-class Peruvians bemoan the proliferation of the urban poor, many of them recent migrants to the cities who have taken up residence in squatter settlements, or *pueblos jovenes,* and who seek work wherever they can find it. Though they clearly earn little in their retailing endeavors, to the urban consumer their very presence represents an increment in the price paid for primary foods.

This popularly held view of marketers and *ambulantes* in Peru is shared by some writers who have considered the problem. For example, the work of Esculies Larrabure, Rubeo Correa, and Gonzales del Castillo (1977), is sensitive to the socioeconomic forces that propel marketers to their work and recognizes the essential nature of the work they do; yet the authors conclude that the reform of the marketing system in Peru must begin with the elimination of much of the wholesale and retail network and tighter control of the rest. This position overlooks the role of the Peruvian government in maintaining the present economic structure, the grave unemployment problem that would result from the proposed reform, and the positive contribution that marketers make under conditions of national underdevelopment.

When Peru's economic troubles deepened in the mid-seventies, the nation turned to international lending agencies for assistance. As the country became more entrenched in debt over the next few years, the IMF imposed severe conditions for the granting of further loans. Peru's compliance with these conditions has been largely responsible for the high cost of living relative to the low pay scale of working people in the country. Added to this, the government's concern for development in the capital-intensive formal sector has meant the neglect of the labor-intensive informal sector in which petty marketers participate. To the degree that the state has entered into the affairs of the informal sector, it has generally done so in the interests of urban consumers and the national and international elite. In controlling the prices of staple foods, the Ministry of Food set bounds on the "profits" marketers make. In the case of small retailers, earnings rarely are enough to support a family, much less reinvest in business.[2] But, by working for so little reward, marketers are in effect helping to keep prices at a more tolerable level.

This study has shown that, to appreciate the contribution that marketers make, it is essential to assess the work they do within the framework of the total production process. The work of bringing goods to the consumer is necessary to the realization of the products' value as the final step in the production process, just as it is an indispensable social service. Moreover, the work of marketers generally goes beyond the physical transport of materials from one place to another to include, at the least, the safeguarding, cleaning, sorting, preserving, measuring, weighing, and packaging of goods. Many do even more, adding value to the goods they sell by transforming raw food to cooked food, unprocessed grains to flour, fresh pork to smoked ham, whole vegetables to chopped vegetables in packets for soup, and so on. All these activities should be regarded as productive work for which the consumer pays the marketers, and this must be figured into any plans for curtailing retail trade.

Furthermore, the importance of marketers' self-sufficiency during a period of high unemployment has been noted. Their resourcefulness in making a living has the double advantage to the government of quelling dissent—to a degree—and keeping on hand a ready supply of workers who would enter the wage-labor force when called on. It is in this context that we must view the role of marketers in Peru and their relationship to present economic problems.

In arguing that the analysis must encompass the wider national and international situation, which conditions the activity of marketers, the food supply, and food prices, I challenge the position taken by the government and encouraged in the media, which portrays marketers as cunning social parasites. Other researchers (e.g., Lele 1971 : 1; Bucklin 1972 : 5; Clark 1988), writing about marketing in developed and underdeveloped economies, have noted the unwarranted antipathy of the public and the state toward market intermediaries, who are often regarded as antisocial villains. In India, for example, this is traced to consumer and governmental ignorance of the fundamental importance of distribution to the total production process in society and to the mistaken assumption that traditional markets cannot be successful channels for trade (Lele 1975 : 100–101).

The research of Kelly Harrison et al. (1974) on market systems in three Latin American countries has also emphasized the need to understand marketers as providers of socially useful services and as productive members of society. They offer the case of Bolivia (ibid.: 23–24), where policy makers attempted without success to eliminate "unproductive" intermediaries.[3] Such interventions, they note (ibid.: 90), are sometimes the efforts of political leaders to create a show of concern for consumers at the expense of marketers. This broad study concludes that, contrary to popular opinion, when the labor of marketers is assessed at the minimum wage level, there is little or no return on their capital (ibid.: 42).

My observations are similar. In Huaraz, daily earnings of as little as forty to fifty cents—or about half the wage for day laborers—were common in 1977, and by the 1980s marketers were reporting even lower incomes. Growing inflation brings increasing pressure on family budgets to meet such basic expenses as food, electricity, school and medical needs, and, in some cases, rent and water bills. We have seen that marketers rarely earn enough to support themselves and their families, and most only manage to get by with other household resources.

The Threat to Marketers: The Case of Huaraz

In 1977, the Year of Austerity was declared in response to the economic and political demands exacted by the IMF in exchange for emergency loans. That year saw rapidly rising food and fuel costs—conditions that have grown steadily worse—and increasing control over the labor force. Here, I describe the growing regulation of petty traders by the Peruvian government, the response of the marketers, and the resulting implications for our understanding of the economic crisis in the country. I go on to discuss how marketers have met this threat to their livelihood.

Marketers throughout Peru are regulated, taxed, and supervised through a number of mechanisms.[4] As noted before, the wholesale and retail prices of basic foodstuffs were officially controlled in Peru during this period, and when marketers failed to comply with biweekly changes in prices issued by the Ministry of Food, they could be heavily fined. Fines were also given by the inspectors of hygiene and weights and measures for large and small violations. The authorities have the power to remove sellers from the markets if they cannot pay the fees and fines issued to them. Small retailers maintained—and I think they are correct—that they must pay a disproportionate share of such fees and fines, while larger violators, usually wholesalers, are less often apprehended and penalized.

These mechanisms for the control of marketers already make it difficult for many impoverished sellers to carry on their trade, but in recent years government control of marketing has increased. In a national campaign against the broad category of commercial intermediaries, the government has portrayed itself as the champion of urban consumers. As early as 1974, the program known as *De la chacra a la olla* (From the field to the cooking pot) was launched in Lima with the announced goal of bringing goods directly from producers to consumers on a periodic basis (Shoemaker 1981:215–216). The efforts, while short-lived, were repeated in subsequent years. The effects of this campaign, which was in evidence through the mid-eighties, have been strongest in Lima, but they are felt in cities like Huaraz as well.

In 1977, an increasing number of articles began to appear in the Lima newspapers on the topic of producers' and wholesalers' markets being established to bring goods more cheaply to consumers. The Lima dailies *La Prensa, El Comercio,* and *Expreso,* all of which were government controlled, invariably contained reports of actions taken for consumers and, often, against marketers. For example, on July 1 the *Expreso* ran the headline "Wholesalers' Stronghold Falls." Inside the issue no fewer than three articles were devoted to the government's decision to open several of Lima's wholesale markets to the public on a limited basis. The lead article was entitled "Starting Today: Food at Prices below Official Rates" and was accompanied by one bearing a title denouncing intermediaries, "They Buy Sweet Potatoes for Two Soles . . . and Sell Them for Twelve!" Finally, a third article addressed housewives, "Prefect to Housewives: You Too Are to Blame for Speculation!" This last article rebuked shoppers for not denouncing marketers they knew to be conducting illegal activities (*Expreso,* July 1, 1977:3). These articles and many others around this time implied that marketers, both wholesalers and retailers, had an undifferentiated responsibility for current high prices and the scarcity of certain items.

Two days after *Expreso* celebrated the direct sale of goods from wholesalers to the public, *La Prensa* (July 3, 1977) published an article declaring the effort a failure. But, instead of criticizing the plan's conception, *La Prensa* declared the sellers to be responsible due to their noncooperation.

Back in Huaraz, plans were underway for the Ancash Regional Fair to take place in the outskirts of the city in late July. The fair was to feature exhibits by artisans and, as a special attraction, to bring producers directly from their fields to sell agricultural goods to the public ("From the field to the cooking pot"). Despite the fanfare, however, the producers' market was only a small part of the fair; just

A local official clears sellers from the street.

one actual producer was included among the ten people selling food at booths. This man, a producer of wheat and barley, stated that producers preferred to sell quickly to wholesalers and get back to work. Others at the fair had been recruited from the Huaraz marketplace and were paid to participate in the event. One man who normally sold meat in a Huaraz market was hired by a nearby agricultural cooperative to represent their organization at the fair. He explained that the members of the cooperative preferred to leave the job of selling to the public to marketers. Indeed, the view that it was better to sell in large quantities to sure buyers rather than slowly to the public was expressed to me by many producers in the region.

The regional fair was not well attended, and those women who came to shop for food were critical of it. Some had to pay for transportation to and from the fair, and they were annoyed to have to pay an entry fee as well. When they arrived, they found few sellers, little selection, and long lines. Furthermore, primary foodstuffs were rationed; if a woman wanted to purchase more than three kilos of rice, for example, she needed to take her children along to receive extra portions. Several women felt that the saving of a sol or two was not worth the trouble of coming to the fair, and they spoke appreciatively of the marketplace, which better served their needs.

The producers' market at the fair did not have any significant impact in the city. After it was over, an official of the Ministry of Food apologized for the low participation of agricultural producers at the fair. Even so, the mayor of Huaraz expressed some interest in turning the fairgrounds into a permanent market for producers and artisans. This enterprising mayor also had a personal interest in building a supermarket in the city, though he lacked funds for such a project.

One marketer responded to the rumors of new markets and expressed a view shared by many others. He judged the notion of producers' markets to be a good idea for the public but a very bad one for wholesalers and retailers. He explained: "In the first place, for us marketers, it would mean marginalization. And second, what would we do, what work would we dedicate ourselves to? You could become a delinquent, a thief. The government has not thought this through carefully." This man went on to make the salient point that the idea of "from field to pot" was being implemented only in the area of food production, where the majority of people involved were weak, and not in the area of manufactured goods, where the truly powerful were. The government, he noted, cannot control the latter because they constitute the national bourgeoisie, who rule the country. He commented, moreover, that he could not see the advantage to agricultural producers in selling their own goods, since the goods must be divided among marketers in order to get them to the public while they are still fresh. If a producers' market were established, he said, he would try to buy out producers in the market, and, furthermore, marketers as a group would be certain to launch a protest. Another man, a former wholesaler now selling retail, agreed that marketers would not permit a producers' market to exist in the city. "The people would rise up," he said, and "the retailers would not accept it." He pointed to the high level of unemployment that would result if these markets were founded.

While marketers may be concerned about the future threat of new markets, which might eliminate their jobs, the few showcase producer and wholesaler markets in Peru had limited success through 1977. The producers and consumers interviewed regarded the work of small marketers as providing essential services. The continued reliance on petty marketers testified to the large amount of work these people do and suggested the difficulty in passing this on to other workers under present conditions.

Still, marketers were threatened by government actions in a more immediate way. While the Lima papers were unveiling a campaign against the abuses of large wholesalers and the proliferation of intermediaries, reports also revealed government efforts to apply greater control over one particular group of retailers, the *ambulantes*. In establishing regulations that would affect this group, the authorities were clearly responding to middle-class pressure to do something about the impoverished sellers who were crowding the streets, particularly in Lima. New legislation, based on studies of "the *ambulante* problem," was publicized, calling for zoning (i.e., containment), increased surveillance, and tighter control over the fee collection, price setting, and hygienic standards of these vendors. One article (*La Prensa*, August 6, 1977 : 10), titled "How to Eliminate the Factors That Maintain and Stimulate Ambulatory Commerce," revealed the government's intentions to close down some areas where *ambulantes* sold in Lima, move others and relocate the sellers, and direct propaganda to consumers "to orient their attitude toward ambulatory commerce." Such conditions naturally made it very difficult for many of the poorest vendors to carry on their work.

In Huaraz, similar measures were taken by the Provincial Council. In one action, a committee was formed to oversee the commerce of milk and sugar. This was designed to control the activities of the "bad merchants that exist in Huaraz" (*El Departamento*, August 11, 1977). In another decision, the inspector of hygiene determined that 85 percent of *ambulantes* selling bread in the city were doing so under unsanitary conditions. In order to combat this situation, the council agreed that any sellers not in possession of a health card would be issued heavy fines. Furthermore, fines were to be given to those without appropriate baskets and those who did not properly protect bread from dust, and price, quality, and weight were to be more stringently controlled.

While even the well-established marketers in Huaraz had difficulty paying their annual fees, poor *ambulantes* would be even less able to afford these fines. The action of the council to tighten these regulations must be viewed as a threat to *ambulantes'* way of making a living. Such action had the further effect of creating divisions among marketers, since one group, the *ambulantes*, was singled out for criticism.[5] Indeed, some permanent marketers shared the view of the council that *ambulantes* constituted a health hazard and ought to be controlled.

The Situation Since 1977

The government assault on sellers did not begin in 1977, nor was that year necessarily a turning point in national economic policy.[6] Jorge P. Osterling and Dennis Chávez (1979:196) comment on a campaign to evict sellers in Lima in 1969, and they point to the growing preoccupation of the city and national government with the expansion of commerce by *ambulantes* by 1975 (ibid.: 198). However, the new austerity measures in 1977 marked the introduction of increasingly harsh conditions for workers in petty commerce, and since then the situation of small marketers and street vendors in Peru has grown worse. While increased inflation and a repressive political climate affect the majority of Peruvians, marketers and, particularly, *ambulantes* have continued to be singled out for attack.

A 1978 article in the leftist journal *Marka* (July 27, 1978: 19–20) on the declining economic and health conditions of the poor in Peru noted that petty commerce was the activity to which most people were turning in an effort to overcome miserable lives. Consequently, this sector had expanded in an "extraordinary manner." Children were being pressed into service, as their families struggled to get by. Street vending had earlier been little known outside Lima, but at the time of the article the streets of provincial cities were crowded with sellers "in constant battle with municipal authorities." In Lima itself, another effort was mounted in 1978 to dislocate downtown vendors, with government agents backed by large business interests and the police, which affected the poorest sellers most (Osterling, de Althaus, and Morelli 1979: 23).

During the second half of the 1970s, the Peruvian government retreated from the nationalism of the Velasco years and returned to a policy of attracting and favoring foreign capital. Articles in *Marka* called attention to the influence of multinational businesses underlying Peru's "economic packages" of price hikes. Five multinational interests (among them Purina, Carnation, and Nestlé) were shown to control the price increases of bread, noodles, milk, and oil (*Marka*, January 4, 1979: 12–14). The seller of bread on the corner did not benefit from the rise in prices, the author noted, but the monopolies that controlled 60 percent of the bread industry in Peru did. Sellers of milk suffered similar effects; half of the milk sold in Lima is Leche Gloria, a subsidiary of Carnation, while the second-largest beneficiary of increased milk prices is its competitor, Perulac, a subsidiary of Nestlé. With the dominance of Leche Gloria over milk processing and distribution, producers throughout a wide region in Peru are obliged to sell to the corporation. When the government ended subsidies on basic foods, including milk, and raised official milk prices "to benefit producers," the producers saw only a 5 percent increase in prices obtained from milk sales, while the real beneficiaries were the processing industries—first among them Leche Gloria, whose profits rose 30 percent (*Marka*, September 14, 1978:

These ice cream sellers are linked to a large coastal enterprise.

11–12). One article concluded: "Imperialism has us caught by the stomach. There is no question. The government is preparing to offer bigger profits to its enterprises by means of the announced price rises. And it will cast the blame for the people's hunger on the bread seller on the corner and the marketwoman in the street" (*Marka*, January 4, 1979:14).

Marka's analysis of marketers as scapegoats points to the need to trace the pricing problem to its roots, to the national and international linkages. While Peru's government seeks a scapegoat for its troubles, it also finds the thousands of vendors that crowd the capital city's streets, selling everything from apples to men's socks, to be a national embarrassment. Apparently, the public display of so much poverty threatens the image the government would like to project to international visitors and to its own middle class. The vendors' presence might also challenge the notion that this impoverished group is so largely responsible for the economic crisis. Accordingly, before Belaúnde's inauguration in 1980, the government undertook a campaign to clear central Lima of *ambulantes* so that the city would have a better appearance for its dignified guests (Bourque and Warren 1981*a*: 193).

Summer 1981, however, marked the most serious government

campaign to rid Lima of its street vendors (*Peru Update,* June–July 1981:1–2). In April a mayor's committee announced that all downtown vendors were to be removed in mid-June to clearings on the outskirts of the city. This was met by a good deal of anger and resistance by the vendors, who knew that their marginal earnings would be further diminished on the tiny, square-meter plots assigned to them at the city's remote sites.[7]

The government, nonetheless, began its relocation program in June, requiring huge financial expense and the presence of the National Guard and tanks in the streets to ensure the successful removal of sellers (*Caretas,* June 8, 1981:23). Removal was only possible, however, with the use of force, numerous arrests, and a television and radio campaign that discouraged shoppers from buying goods in the streets. The secretary general of the Federación Departamental de Vendedores Ambulantes de Lima (FEDEVAL), the street vendors' association, projected dire consequences as increased poverty could only mean increased crime as people tried to survive (*Marka,* June 18, 1981:22). Meanwhile, the *New York Times* (September 20, 1981) hailed the removal of vendors a great success, as crime was reduced in Lima's fashionable downtown area and women "are beginning to wear simple jewelry again."

Some members of the political left in Lima, including the well-known Hugo Blanco, then a senator, joined forces with the vendors and FEDEVAL and marched alongside them at the time of the relocation. The occasion brought together thousands of men, women, and children in peaceful protest but ended in a violent confrontation by the National Guard (*El Comercio,* June 12, 1981). Blanco, who was injured during the march and hospitalized, commented a few days later on the situation of the vendors in an interview with *Marka* (June 18, 1981:21). He pointed to the contradictions of a capitalist government that has generated the *"ambulante* problem" and then tries to cover its responsibility by blaming the victims of its policies. Until the government comes up with real employment opportunities for the vendors, he predicted, we may expect their number to increase.

Similarly, the Peruvian writer Romeo Grompone (1981:98) traces the growth of petty commerce to the contradictory and uneven development of capitalism in Peru. He describes the process as one in which anterior, or preexisting, economic forms and social relations, such as petty commodity production and distribution, are challenged yet sometimes persist. Only in this context may we understand the present tensions surrounding the persistence of small-scale marketing in the country.

On my return to Peru in 1982, I had the opportunity to assess the effects of these national developments at the local level in Huaraz. Although the degree of overcrowding that I observed in Polvos Azules (one of the areas where Lima's *ambulantes* were relocated in 1981) was not matched in Huaraz, I did discover a significant increase in the density of sellers there. My census of the same markets and streets where I had counted sellers in 1977 produced a total of nearly 1,600 sellers in 1982, or a 33 percent increase over five years. As in Lima, the heaviest concentration was in the streets.

While the proportion of female and male sellers had remained almost the same, the number of children marketing had notably increased. Some children are always on hand to assist their parents in the market, but after interviewing a number of children it was my impression that more of them are working on their own now. Boys as young as eight selling newspapers or ice cream or shining shoes and eleven- or twelve-year-old girls selling drinks along major intersections at midnight are commonplace.

As noted, another of my observations on returning to Huaraz was the growing number of dependent sellers, that is, those working for others on commission or for wages. For example, interviews with sellers of *raspadillas* revealed that as many as half a dozen might be working for a single absentee employer. Vendors of packaged candy and cigarettes produced in coastal factories worked as commission sellers for distant firms whose products were distributed through local wholesalers. Small market restaurants hired assistants at low wages or sometimes simply in exchange for meals. Not surprisingly, this social differentiation in petty commerce has resulted in a disproportionate number of women and children subordinated to larger interests.[8]

Though Huaraz had at this time a leftist mayor, a member of the Izquierda Unida, his party was outnumbered on the Provincial Council by conservative forces, which undermined his government's effectiveness. This mayor issued a letter of strong protest to the national government, pointing to the policies of the minister of the economy, Manuel Ulloa, as the cause of rising transportation and food costs and calling for unified opposition to this recent economic aggression (*El Diario de Marka*, July 12, 1982:2). Yet in Huaraz small marketers were still under scrutiny as the source of economic difficulties. A study of street vendors was conducted by the Ministry of Commerce in Huaraz in 1982, but little change in policy seems to have been introduced. One may surmise that, rather than opening the way for reform, the study may have had the objective of further regulating sellers. Indeed, the municipal government was stepping up measures to control marketers. One group of *ambulantes* new to Huaraz, *campesina* herb sellers who traveled to the city once a week, were repeatedly forced to leave their selling places; many arrived early to sell and then left by midmorning, when market officials appeared on the scene. Marketers in general were treated with impatience, if not abuse, and local newspaper reports of "bad merchants" continued as before.

Marketers did not passively accept criticism, but their worsening conditions were accompanied by weak leadership in the major market union. Five years earlier, when the conciliatory union president was willing to accept the Provincial Council's proposed increases in market fees, angry women members pushed him to stand up to the mayor on the issue. In 1982, however, the young man who had recently assumed the presidency for lack of another literate and willing candidate appeared entirely ineffective as union leader. Participation in union meetings was falling off as members recognized his serious shortcomings and as more difficult economic circumstances made union activity a heavier burden for the several hundred registered members. Consequently, when a unified response to public criticism would have seemed appropriate, they were silent.

An effort to hold biweekly producers' fairs in Mercado Centenario met with little success around this time; while the local newspaper *El Huascarán* (May 1982 : 6) called the fairs a success, they were discontinued after just a few weeks. The Ancash regional fairs I attended in 1982 and 1984 attracted tourists and local people with time and money to spend on regional specialties but few food shoppers. As before, almost no producers were at the fair and only a few low-priced staples were for sale, despite the "field to the pot" rhetoric. And by the mid-eighties, there were still no supermarkets to compete with marketers in Huaraz, only a few grocery stores ("mini-markets") stocking luxury items for the local elite. The small-scale marketers continued to supply the city and surrounding area with food and other basic goods.

The lifting of price controls from all but a few foodstuffs under the Belaúnde presidency resulted in little apparent change in market conditions. The "free market" is far from free in a setting where impoverished sellers—many of them dependent sellers—proliferate, struggling to obtain enough sales to maintain their often minuscule operations. Inflation has greatly affected all prices in Peru since 1977, but marketers' earnings have remained at a very low level.

Government control and the domination of large business interests have taken new forms, but the nationwide assault on marketers has persisted. In Lima, *ambulantes* continue to march in peace-

*Young boys (and, occasionally, older rural women) sell
newspapers on the street.*

ful protest against government initiatives to relocate them to undesirable and even dangerous locations. They have been met vio-
lently by the National Guard, which shows little regard for women
with small children (*El Diario de Marka*, June 11, 1982:6; June 15,
1982:5). When Lima's mayor organized Committees for the Defense
of Consumers, the public was given the right to demand sellers'
identity cards and to oversee the setting of prices and weights and
measures. What is more, high school students were to form support
committees with their own responsibilities for "protecting consumer rights" (*El Comercio*, July 20, 1982:D12). One wonders how
many sons and daughters of marketers questioned whose rights they
were in fact protecting. This government strategy became more central to national policy, and for its 1983 economic program to "fight
inflation," policy makers created the Prices and Consumer Defense
Office (*Latin America Regional Reports: Andean Group*, December
17, 1982:8).[9]

By the mid-1980s, with Peru in a state of emergency arising
from the political hostilities between the government and Sendero
Luminoso, tensions throughout the country were mounting. Still,
the government made efforts to quell widespread dissatisfaction
about the deepening economic crisis by appealing to urban con-

sumers through the news media. The daily newspaper *El Comercio* carried a regular supplement on "Food in Lima" with a back page entitled "Defense of the Consumer." Here were featured the current prices charged by sellers in a number of districts around the capital city under the banner "Are You Paying a Fair Price?" Frequently, articles charged street vendors with aggravating the economic situation.

While the urban middle class received assurances of government concern, some poor and working-class residents in Lima's *pueblos jovenes* were taking matters into their own hands. *Comedores populares* (communal kitchens) had been organized since the late 1970s in some neighborhoods (CELATS 1983) and were attracting widespread attention. As many as one thousand kitchens were estimated to be operating by 1985, with groups of women purchasing and preparing food collectively in large quantities in order to provide nutritious meals to children, pregnant and breast-feeding women, and families of the unemployed. Not surprisingly, these self-help efforts were greeted enthusiastically by the press. Doubtless, the government viewed the communal kitchens as easing the problems of the poor without requiring change at the national level. The resourceful women who have organized these kitchens form part of the same social class from which the majority of marketers and street vendors come, yet marketers receive a negative response to their efforts to improve their life conditions.

A View to the Future

Peru's increasingly restrictive policy on the marketing of foodstuffs and other goods sold by small-scale marketers—though not the actual elimination of retail marketing—may be viewed as an attempt to generate sympathy for the government's handling of the economic crisis or at least to turn attention away from the source of the crisis. Keeping food prices at a tolerable level is of critical importance to the Peruvian government, yet this has been more and more difficult since austerity measures were introduced. In an attempt to appease middle-class and working-class consumers in the face of soaring food prices, the government has turned impoverished marketers into scapegoats who suffer doubly from rising prices, as sellers whose business is declining and as consumers themselves. National policy has had the effect of dividing consumers and marketers, largely women, obscuring even those problems they share in common. Marketers themselves are unequally affected by recent legis-

A sign announces the future construction of a new model market.

lation, with the poorest women bearing the brunt of repressive measures.

In his inaugural address in July 1985, President García championed the street vendor in Peru, promising help for his country's poor. Since then, however, the APRA government has introduced further regulation of marketers and street vendors and continued the use of citizen volunteers to aid in policing the markets. New controls on basic food prices are resulting in rising costs to consumers, and small-scale traders still take much of the blame. Three years into his term in office, García turned his attention to the country's grave political crisis, and his commitment to economic reform appeared to have waned.

Nevertheless, the "informal sector" has become one of the most important issues under discussion in Peru today, one that has received international attention. Hernando de Soto of Lima's Institute for Freedom and Democracy has predicted serious consequences for the future, when petty manufacture and commerce may expand to include three-quarters of the population (de Soto 1986; *El Comercio*, April 14, 1986: A6). In contrast to most analysts, however, de Soto recognizes the large contribution of "informals" to the national economy and he calls for an end to state regulation so that individuals may compete legally in a "freer market." Whether the middle class will become resigned to the almost inevitable growth of the informal sector and whether the state will tolerate deregulation remains to be seen. Up to now, de Soto's well-financed institute has had little influence on government policy making (*Latin America Regional Reports: Andean Group*, April 11, 1986:5–7), though this may change as a result of national and international pressure. A lifting of harsh regulations would ease conditions for petty producers and traders, but broader measures must ultimately be taken in the Peruvian political economy if a real improvement in their work situation is to occur.

During my most recent visit to Peru in 1987, I found that discussion of the informals (*los informales*) was not limited to Peru's major cities but was taking place in smaller cities like Huaraz as well. In many respects, this was consonant with earlier concerns about the growing number of *ambulantes* in the city. However, instead of efforts to eliminate or bypass small-scale sellers, the mayor and his advisors were calling for projects to investigate and, ostensibly, to improve the situation of informal sellers.

The municipal government authorized studies of the informal sector to be carried out by the university in Huaraz and by independent research groups. One survey commissioned by the mayor's office put the number of informal street sellers at over thirteen hundred, which appears to be a conservative figure. A research and consulting group known as Fenix administered questionnaires to four hundred informal sellers, a majority of whom expressed their willingness to move to new markets or pavilions once these were constructed and offered their views as to desirable locations. Still, the objective of city planners was to manage the situation, and while some sellers were persuaded of the beneficence of the city government, others were clearly doubtful. The director of Fenix himself expressed the view that the study's recommendations would only offer a stopgap to the real problem faced by informals, which he identified as the severe unemployment and underemployment currently experienced by Peruvians. In general, the proposals drawn from these studies have concerned ways to relocate street vendors to new markets in order to ease congestion in the downtown area, to improve the conditions of petty commerce by extending credit to informal sellers, and to make the city more appealing for the active tourist industry.

Although rumors had been circulating in Huaraz for at least five years concerning a new model market (*mercado modelo*) to be built in the city, the marketers I questioned had been skeptical. On my return to Huaraz in 1987, I learned that the national government had guaranteed funds for the project and that the mayor's office was moving forward with plans to construct a large new three-story market. This was to accommodate the sellers of Mercado Central, which was regarded as inadequate to meet the current needs of the growing city, as well as many of the informal sellers in the surrounding streets. Still, marketers questioned whether the market would be built, and many noted that with soaring inflation the promised financial support would be far too low.[10]

Given the uncertainty about the construction of the new market, I was surprised to learn that, two months after I left Huaraz, Mercado Central was destroyed. Without more detailed reports, I can only surmise that the city government decided to relocate residents living within the projected site of the new market, perhaps with the idea of moving them to the area where Mercado Central had stood. This would open the way for construction on the new site. Half a year after Mercado Central was torn down, however, the local newspaper *El Huascarán* (May 1988) expressed the view of many that, after waiting so long, city residents had despaired of having their new market. For now, by thrusting many more marketers into the streets, the planners seem to have aggravated the problem they are attempting to solve.

The campaign to bring goods directly "from the field to the cooking pot" seemed all but forgotten by 1987. Evidently, at both the national level and the local level in Huaraz, there was a growing acknowledgment that small-scale retailers and wholesalers are here to stay. This was apparent at the Ancash Regional Fair, which I attended for a fourth time that year; as in past years, there were a few food producers, but far more emphasis was placed on the craft specialties of artisans and on small restaurant-bars serving to tourists. Food sellers and buyers, as usual, were conducting their business in the city markets.

My census of marketers and street sellers in Huaraz that year showed that the total number had risen to nearly two thousand, with the largest increase among street vendors. Marketwomen told me, "There are more sellers than buyers now." Clearly, the problems of rapidly expanding petty commerce are of as much concern to sellers as to city officials and urban residents. Yet finding mutually satisfactory solutions to these problems, even for the short term, will present a challenge in Huaraz in the years ahead.

Nine   *Conceptualizing Marketwomen*

CONSIDERABLE RESEARCH HAS recently been devoted to the relationship of women, work, and the family in societies throughout the world.[1] Most of this research concentrates on the advanced capitalist societies, where interest has been directed to women's roles in the home as homemakers and to their participation in the paid work force as wage laborers. Somewhat less attention has been focused on these concerns in relation to the Third World, but the scholarship on the underdeveloped areas is fast expanding. Following the lead of research on Western women, studies of Third World women have emphasized family roles, household labor (including agricultural labor), and women's entry into the paid labor market. While these are important areas to investigate in the Third World, women's position in the growing urban informal sector has received little critical notice. African studies have paid attention to women's traditional importance in marketing, but the emphasis has only rarely been on the contemporary structure of underdevelopment. Latin American studies have produced significant analyses of women in domestic service, but only a few analyses of women in petty manufacture and trade have emerged.

Boserup's (1970) cross-cultural overview of women's economic role in the underdeveloped countries was the first to bring the situation of female informal workers to wide attention. Among the areas she examined were the condition of female rural migrants in towns in Asia, Africa, and Latin America and the limited employment opportunities they encounter. Boserup (ibid.: 87–99) notes substantial cross-cultural differences in the sexual division of labor in the marketplace, but she finds women generally concentrated in the sale of foodstuffs. She explains the persistence of female market trade in many areas by reference to the ability of small traders to compete successfully with large commercial establishments through maintaining low prices and profits. These observations are clearly relevant to the Peruvian case. In general, however, Boserup's comments on female marketing patterns in Latin America seem less relevant to Mesoamerica, the Caribbean, and the Andes, where women have a history of active trade; at least, the pattern she describes of increasing female participation in areas where the modern trade sector is replacing traditional trade is not evident in the Andes.

While Boserup's work locates women in the distributive trades and services, other researchers have analyzed these women's situation more closely. More recent scholarship has contributed toward a conceptualization of women in Third World urban economies by examining such critical problems as the reproductive and productive aspects of women's work, the implications for political consciousness, and why women, specifically, are marginalized in the poorest economic sectors.

The work of women in commerce and the services is often likened to housework, and the women themselves are often viewed as housewives whose economic role extends to the marketplace. The nature of work in these areas is frequently similar or even identical in content to the work women perform in their own homes. Housecleaning, laundering, sewing, and food preparation are all services that may be purchased on the market in Third World cities. Elizabeth Jelin (1980:139) discusses the work of independent female petty producers of merchandise (e.g., crafts, clothing, and food) in Salvador, Brazil, as commercialized housework. Similarly, in her study of women in the informal labor sector in Mexico City, Lourdes Arizpe (1977:36) describes the way in which poor women "press the system for payment of their domestic services," which are then offered to others on the market through domestic service and street selling. This view of women's paid work as an extension of their unpaid work at home is expressed by a number of others who have undertaken research in the Third World (Nash and Safa 1980:106; Vasques de Miranda 1977:274).

Yet others have cautioned that, while women's work in the labor force may resemble housework in many respects, to regard women's paid work as a mere extension of domestic work is incorrect (Beechey 1978:193). In this view, we must go beyond surface appearances to discover the relationship of women's work to capitalist production in the underdeveloped economies. Andean researchers Carmen Diana Deere and Magdalena León de Leal (1981:358–360) show, for example, that in areas where wage labor is incipient women's employment opportunities may extend from their work at home, but the diversity of women's productive activity reveals that it is not a simple reflection of their domestic role.

Both views bear on the case of Huaraz marketwomen. The content of market work shares much in common with housework, yet in many respects market work requires different skills and involves women in a fundamentally different relationship to the economy. The majority of marketers contribute their labor to the products they sell and thereby save the consumers the time they would spend in carrying out these tasks at home; foods are prepared or processed, clothing is sewn, and so on. Nevertheless, many skills necessary to sellers are not learned in the home and are not extensions of housework. Buying and selling must be learned from other marketers or from experience in the marketplace, as must transporting, bulking, bulk-breaking, and other types of market work. Furthermore, focusing on the resemblance of market work to domestic work diverts attention from the fact that housework and marketing form part of distinct modes of production; they are situated at different places in the social formation, and this has implications for women's views of themselves as workers and their opportunities for political mobilization. Huaraz marketwomen themselves do not speak of marketing as an extension of their role in the home but describe it in quite a different way, as a separate job that is essential for the earnings it provides.

Despite these reservations about viewing women's work in the labor force and in the home through the same conceptual lens, at another level of analysis the two forms of work do indeed have much in common: their similarity lies in their reproductive function in the capitalist economy and society (Edholm, Harris, and Young 1977). Just as housework is essential to the well-being and survival of the family, the distributive trades and service occupations maintain and nourish society. As collective caretakers, women in these occupations look after the needs of the people they serve on a daily basis. Over the longer term, they ensure the continuation of society from one generation to the next. Housewives through their subsistence work and marketers through the sale of their products and their services feed, clothe, and shelter society. Because of the vast amount of caretaking work these women do, their husbands and children are able to go off to work or school each day. Such a division of labor in the family, whereby women carry out "reproductive" work and free men for "productive" work (a distinction lacking clarity), thus serves the interest of the wider society.

A marketer carries produce to her selling place on the street.

Marianne Schmink (1977:157), writing about the labor force participation of Latin American women in commerce and the services, expresses this point well: "Many service occupations are in some sense reproductive functions which secure the maintenance of the capitalist system: they are functions which in earlier stages of historical development may have been performed within the walls of a firm or household but which become separate entities through the increasing division of labor in the work force. It is precisely these less visible aspects of production which are least understood in terms of their relation to the productive process and to the class structure. And it is into these ambiguous little niches that a large proportion of women in the labor force fall." The ambiguity of the socioeconomic position of marketwomen in Huaraz has been noted. Another ambiguous aspect of their situation is the apparent productive-reproductive dichotomy implied in the sexual division of labor. Lourdes Benería and Gita Sen (1981:292) have addressed this question and suggest that, where the wage labor system has not penetrated fully, the distinction between productive and reproductive activities is often artificial. Similarly, Janet M. Bujra (1982:20) has argued against polar categories, calling for attention to "interlocking productive and reproductive processes."[2] Based on my observations in Peru, this advice bears relevance for an analysis of small-scale marketers.

This book has contended that marketwomen's work can indeed be regarded as productive, that is, contributing directly to the accumulation of capital. The political and intellectual debates over what forms of work are productive and what forms unproductive have been wide ranging.[3] Here, the question is considered only as it applies to women in petty commerce and the services, generally, and to Huaraz marketwomen, in particular, in order to shed light on the labor process and social relations of production characteristic of marketers. A number of writers argue that women's work in this sector should not be regarded as productive in the technical sense since it "is often not directly connected to the production process" (Schmink 1977 : 168), that is, it often creates no new value and does not contribute to the growth of capital, although it may be socially necessary work. Others would go further and agree with Arizpe (1977 : 34), whose study of Mexican street sellers was mentioned earlier, that women in petty commerce "tend to offer an unnecessary service and to create their own demand." Those taking this position usually focus on women's role in the circulation of goods and services, sometimes disregarding the productive component of such work.

I have suggested that often no sharp line exists between work that produces goods and work that circulates them. Some scholars discussing productive and unproductive labor in the context of the advanced capitalist nations have held this view. Braverman (1974 : 410–423) points out that in the contemporary period there has been a tremendous expansion of employment (especially clerical) in the areas often called "unproductive." He shows that in modern capitalism these occupations "have lost many of the last characteristics which separated them from production workers," and that, despite certain remaining distinctions, "the two masses of labor are not otherwise in striking contrast and need not be counterposed to each other" (ibid. : 423).

This question has been addressed by those concerned with understanding the position of women in growing clerical, sales, and service occupations in industrial capitalist countries as well as by those interested in the position of women in the urban Third World. Jackie West (1978 : 248) considers the question for female white-collar workers in industrial capitalism and offers a useful examination of the changing class position of these women as their work is proletarianized. West's and others' efforts to contend with the present lack of clarity in the terminology and to bring to light the productive aspect of the sales and service occupations are linked closely to the problems faced by researchers analyzing commerce and the services in underdeveloped nations. Jelin (1977:131), in her study of domestic servants in Latin America, maintains that "it seems unjustified to equate 'industrial' with productive and 'service' with unproductive employment." And Glaura Vasques de Miranda (1977:268) describes the commerce in goods in which Brazilian women participate as a "productive activity." Unfortunately, the authors do not develop the point, leaving this to other analysts.

Throughout this study I have emphasized the productive aspect of marketwomen's work in Huaraz. Although ambiguities are present in the work role of the Huaraz marketers, they may be called productive in the strict sense of contributing to the accumulation of capital. If, on the one hand, we regard marketers as operating in the petty commodity mode of production, they are productive insofar as they add value to the goods they market through their own labor. If, on the other hand, we deem it appropriate to view some marketers as disguised wage laborers, they may again be understood as productive workers since their labor in the preparation and sale of goods to consumers allows the wholesalers (who in this view engage retailers as workers through the extension of credit) to operate on a larger scale and to see a faster, greater return on their capital. And if, finally, other marketers are engaged more directly as wage laborers, working for local enterprises or coastal firms, their relation to capital accumulation is readily apprehended.

My emphasis on the productive quality of the work of Huaraz marketers should in no way be taken to suggest that I view the present situation as a satisfactory arrangement for the exchange of goods and services. Nor do I think that marketwomen ought or would want to engage in such employment if they had real alternatives. Certainly, their productivity as informal sector workers is very low when compared to workers in the formal sector. Currently in Peru, however, indications are that the informal sector will continue to expand and that small-scale marketers and street vendors will remain central to the production and distribution process.

The recent discussion concerning productive and unproductive labor has in large part been generated by a desire to discover the political potential of various groups of workers in society. The view has generally been that only productive workers are in a position to develop a critical awareness of their situation in society and to seek to change it. Whether only productive laborers may be expected to mobilize in working-class struggles is not certain; in any event, it is essential to challenge the unjustified classification of so many workers in commerce and the services as unproductive and the related belief that their class consciousness will remain at a low level. This is all the more important because women so often fall into this category. Indeed, a male bias may underlie the notion that these workers are unlikely to mobilize.

Of course, the nature of some women's work in impoverished Third World economies makes it difficult for them to identify with working-class interests. This has been especially notable for the majority of Latin American women workers who acquire jobs as domestic servants. The isolation they experience in middle-class homes and their close association with their employers has made a strong identification with workers' issues unlikely (though some are beginning to organize). Other researchers, however, have found this characteristic of domestic servants to be shared by women in the tertiary sector generally. Schmink (1977: 175), for example, explains the lack of class consciousness among Venezuelan women in petty commerce and manufacturing in terms of their indirect relation to the production process, as self-employed and family workers. Moreover, she calls the idea that this sector is undergoing proletarianization "illusory" and concludes that these women are not likely to mobilize.

The situation of Huaraz marketwomen poses some significant contrasts to those described by other researchers. First, these marketers are in direct relationship with the production process and do create economic surplus, which is extracted through unequal terms of trade in the marketplace—where price controls have acted to the disadvantage of small marketers and relations with large wholesalers have been exploitative. At the societal level, surplus is transferred from the impoverished sector in which marketers work to the urban industrial sector, where both capitalists and workers benefit.

Furthermore, the working conditions experienced by marketers are very different from those characteristic of domestic servants and other service workers, whose jobs isolate them from other workers. Instead of identifying with those they serve, as isolated workers may, Huaraz marketwomen identify with other marketers. They are in constant interaction with other sellers in the market, and they have ample opportunity to discuss common problems and grievances. Unlike some women in the service occupations who do not easily recognize their exploitation—or if they do are reluctant to oppose it because of the immediacy of the human needs they serve—the

Huaraz marketers understand their exploitation to stem from dominant class interests, and many appear willing to use their collective force to challenge intolerable working conditions.

To refer to women's reproductive function in the economy and society is to describe the situation but not to explain it. To explain why it is precisely women who are marginalized in Third World economies we must consider the interlinkage of social class and gender. Clearly, as long as women occupy the lowest-ranking areas of employment and receive the lowest remuneration for their labor, a larger proportion of surplus value may be appropriated from them. Keeping women in this marginalized position, however, requires a supporting structure. In part, this support is offered by the dominant ideology in class societies, generally, and, in this case, Peruvian society, which maintains that women's contribution to family income is supplementary and not a major source of livelihood. This ideology may serve to justify the below-subsistence earnings of women, since they are not expected to provide full support for their families. In fact, the ideology may even allow for women's earnings to sink below the level necessary to reproduce their own labor power (Beechey 1978 : 185 – 186). Furthermore, if women's work outside the home resembles housework, which has been devalued under capitalism, that provides another rationale for their low earnings.

Women, consequently, form an eminently exploitable group. Class oppression is coupled with sexual oppression as dominant class interests maintain the ideology that permits the greater exploitation of women workers. In addition, however, male privilege accrues to men of the same social class as a result of the extra burden shouldered by women. Interviews with husbands of marketers in Huaraz revealed their recognition of the double load women bear and of the difficult working conditions in the marketplace. While men surely desire better life conditions for both their wives and themselves, they are also able to take advantage of somewhat greater work opportunities than women and to benefit from the care and services of wives at home. It may be in their immediate interests, then, to preserve women's secondary status—even though the social and economic marginalization of their wives and daughters can hardly be something they consciously desire.

Any conceptualization of Huaraz marketwomen must come to terms with the problems of their marginalized social class and sexual status. Here, I have pointed to some of these problems, but far more must be understood about women's place in the informal sector, generally, and about Peruvian marketers, specifically, before this conceptualization can be refined. Huaraz marketwomen themselves are aware of the double burden they carry as workers and as women and are developing a consciousness of their situation. Just how these women will come to terms with and struggle against the increasingly difficult conditions in their lives remains to be seen.

Appendix

Questionnaire for Marketwomen and Their Husbands

1. ¿De dónde es usted?
   [Where are you from?]

*2. ¿Cuánto tiempo está vendiendo en Huaraz? ¿Vende seguido? ¿Qué vende? ¿Al por menor o mayor?
   [How long have you been selling in Huaraz? Do you sell regularly? What do you sell? Retail or wholesale?]

3. ¿Cuántos años tiene usted?
   [How old are you?]

4. ¿Ha ido al colegio? (¿Hasta qué año?)
   [Did you go to school? (To what grade?)]

5. ¿Cuántos hijos tiene usted?
   [How many children do you have?]

6. ¿A qué trabajo se dedica su esposo(a)?
   [What does your husband (wife) do?]

7. ¿Tienen ustedes otras fuentes de ingresos aparte de su trabajo principal (hijos qué trabajan, etc.)?
   [Do you have other sources of family income aside from your principal work (children who work, etc.)?]

*8. ¿Vende usted el producto de sus chacras? ¿Compra otras cosas para vender?
   [Do you sell the product of your *chacras*? Do you buy other things to sell?]

9. ¿Cuántas hectáreas tienen ustedes para sembrar?
   [How many hectares do you have to plant?]

10. ¿Más o menos, cuánto gana usted diario o semanal en el mercado (otro sitio)? ¿Cuánto capital tiene usted?

[More or less, how much do you earn daily or weekly in the market (other work)? How much capital do you have?]

11. Los productos que se venden en el mercado pasan de los productores a los mayoristas y de éstos a los minoristas. ¿Quiénes ganan más, los productores, los mayoristas, o los minoristas?
[The products sold in the market pass from producers to wholesalers and then on to retailers. Who earns more, producers, wholesalers, or retailers?]

12. ¿Actualmente, que le parece a usted el costo de vida y la situación general de Perú? ¿Cree usted que el gobierno está haciendo lo mejor posible? (Si no, ¿Qué deberían hacer los Peruanos?)
[At present, what do you think about the cost of living and the general situation in Peru? Is the government doing the best thing possible? (If not, what should Peruvians do?)]

*13. ¿Es usted socia del sindicato de vendedores? ¿Qué le parecen sus actividades? ¿Sabe usted algo sobre la decisión del alcalde de aumentar la matrícula y las sisas y la respuesta del sindicato?
[Are you a member of the marketers' union? What do you think of its activities? Do you know anything about the decision of the mayor to raise the registration and daily fees and the response of the union?]

14. ¿Qué opina usted del paro de los maestros del Perú del 5 de julio?
[What do you think of the Peruvian teachers' strike of July 5?]

15. ¿Y, qué opina usted del paro general del 19 de julio?
[And what do you think of the general strike of July 19?]

16. ¿Qué le parece la nueva universidad de Ancash?
[What do you think of the new Ancash university?]

17. ¿Le gustaría a usted que todos los Peruanos sepan Quechua y que se enseñe Quechua en los colegios?
[Would you like for all Peruvians to know Quechua and for Quechua to be taught in the schools?]

18. ¿En la familia en Huaraz, el trabajo del hombre y el trabajo de la mujer valen igual, o no?
[In the family in Huaraz, is the work of men and the work of women worth the same or not?]

*Asked of marketwomen only.

Notes

1. Introduction

1. Throughout this book, the 1977 equivalent of S/.75 to the U.S. dollar will be used unless otherwise noted.

2. I am not entirely satisfied with the term "informal sector" for reasons that will be discussed in later chapters. Elsewhere in this study, I will refer as well to the "tertiary sector" to indicate the part of the economy that includes domestic servants (wageworkers and, thus, part of the "formal sector"), petty traders, and others who perform services. In general, the available terminology seems inadequate for describing marketers and their work.

2. The Peruvian Political Economy

1. The 1907 census enumerated the population by race, identifying the following: 3,740 *mestizo,* 2,285 white, 1,590 Indian, 8 black, and 23 "yellow." How these categories were determined is not clear.

2. In 1977, the local Huaraz government was in the process of renaming some old streets and naming new streets, as an official map was prepared to accurately represent the reconstructed city. Here I will use the old names of major streets, since they were in use during the principal period of fieldwork.

3. See Yauri Montero (1972) for a discussion of the incident.

4. The Universidad Nacional de Ancash "Santiago Antunez de Mayolo," created in 1977, opened for instruction in 1978.

5. No reliable data are available to me concerning the distribution of the Huaraz population by economic activity except what is based on my own observations and questioning of people I met in Huaraz.

6. The Peruvian sol was exchanged at the rate of S/.75 to the U.S. dollar until August 1977, late in the first period of fieldwork, when the sol was devalued to S/.77 to the U.S. dollar. Since that time devaluation has been dramatic.

7. For similar views of this period of Peru's history under military rule, see Cotler (1975), Bollinger (1980), and Latin American Working Group (1980).

8. Shoemaker (1981:203–233) has described intermediaries as the beneficiaries of price policy. Had he examined the situation of the abundant

small retailers in Peru, he might have qualified his remarks.

9. See Vandendries (1973) for a comparison of government policies on industrial and agricultural production and their consequences.

10. See Bode (1974) for more discussion of the aftermath of the earthquake in Huaraz.

3. Marketwomen and Theory

1. Mintz (1956, 1964, 1971, 1974) must be mentioned as a forerunner on the topic of marketing and its articulation with different modes of production within historically specific social formations. Though he does not distinguish petty commodity from capitalist production, Mintz makes clear the articulation between the sector in which marketers work, the subsistence agricultural sector, and the wage labor sector. Taking a wide view of the economy, Mintz demonstrates that, in societies with little capital where families participate in several economic sectors, peasant marketers keep down the cost of distribution of goods and services and, thus, are vital.

2. In the research on women in Latin American cities, domestic service is often emphasized as the eminently expandable employment opportunity to which women turn. Some revealing studies have focused on the experience of domestic servants (e.g., Smith 1971, 1973; Rutte García 1976; Jelin 1977; Rubbo and Taussig 1983). Less attention has been directed to women in petty commerce, however. In order to gain an understanding of women marketers and street vendors in Latin America, we will need the kind of serious research that has begun for domestic servants.

3. The information recorded about early markets in the Andes is much less abundant than that available for Mesoamerica. Whether this reflects a gap in the historical record or the relative insignificance of market trade in the Andean region cannot be assessed at this point.

4. Bromley (1975) offers an account of nineteenth-century developments in marketing activity in Ecuador, but to my knowledge nothing comparable has been written on Peruvian marketing.

5. Before conducting fieldwork in Peru, I, too, concluded on the basis of my reading that market activity was in decline (Babb 1976:35).

6. Case studies of rural migrants—*serranos,* or highlanders—reveal the complex organization of land invasions by squatters who establish *barriadas,* or *pueblos jovenes* (literally, young towns) (Mangin 1970a, 1970b, 1970c; Doughty 1970). Collier (1976) shows that permissive attitudes on the part of government toward the formation of squatter settlements are a response to the problem of housing the urban poor and a way of winning political support.

7. More attention has been directed to urban marketing in the cities of Peru's neighboring countries, and some of this research raises questions pertinent to urban Andean markets in general. Buechler (1978), in her study of women marketers in La Paz, Bolivia, examines the city markets as modern urban phenomena. Bromley (1978b) examines the organization and exploitation of street traders in Cali, Colombia, taking a critical view of the informal sector. Rusque-Alcaino and Bromley (1979) provide an occupational au-

tobiography of a Cali bottle buyer, revealing the precarious conditions under which he lives and works. Also from Cali, an official investigation of public markets (ILMA 1965) offers a wealth of information about the structure and internal workings of the city's markets. Finally, Tokman (1978) examines competition between small-scale and large-scale retailers in Santiago, Chile, and the success of small enterprises in meeting the needs of low-income consumers by reference to the linkage of the informal and formal sectors in the urban economy.

8. For a discussion of marketers, principally women, in Huancayo's weekly fair, see Stolmaker (1979).

9. In fact, the household has been, along with the community, a key unit of analysis in Andean studies. A problem with the focus on the household as the basic socioeconomic unit is precisely that it has tended to obscure relations of production that cut across various demographic units of analysis (Stein n.d.).

10. The first Spanish women in the Viceroyalty of Peru also played a significant role (Martín 1983), but this goes beyond the scope of the present discussion.

11. See, however, Prieto de Zegarra (1980) for an expansive overview of women in Peruvian history from early civilization through the end of the nineteenth century.

12. For another feminist contribution to our understanding of the feminine condition in Peru, see Andradi and Portugal (1978). These Peruvian journalists present interviews with thirteen women ranging from well-known political and cultural figures to a *campesina*, a housewife, and a prostitute.

13. But see, for example, testimonies of domestic workers collected by the Sindicato de Trabajadoras del Hogar (1982) and data on the occupational careers of prostitutes collected by Arnold (1977, 1978), both for the Andean city of Cuzco.

4. The Marketplace

1. Agüero León (n.d.: 19), however, writing in the early 1970s, remembers his childhood more than fifty years before when a school (Colegio Nacional de Mujeres) stood in the place where Mercado Mayorista was later built.

5. The Work of Marketwomen

1. Five years later, when the sol had devalued from S/.75 to S/.750 to the U.S. dollar, marketers' earnings had barely kept pace.

2. This approach to market studies is characteristic of formalists in economic anthropology (e.g., Tax 1953; Katzin 1960; Dewey 1962). However, other writers who insist that the question is one of scale also argue that the chances of small enterprises becoming large ones are very slight (e.g., Roberts 1975).

3. See, for example, Gerry (1978), Bromley (1978b), and Forman and Riegelhaupt (1970).

4. See Hart (1973) for a pioneer article. More recently, others have adopted, modified, and criticized the view (e.g., Arizpe 1977; Bromley 1978*a*, 1978*b*; Davies 1979; Long and Richardson 1978; Nelson 1979; Tokman 1978).

5. Acceptance of the informal-formal sector terminology has grown in the last few years, even among researchers persuaded of the validity of criticisms that have been raised. For example, in Portes and Walton (1981) and Safa (1982), the terms are used in a critical, dynamic way that draws attention to the interdependency of the economic sectors.

6. In emphasizing that these producers direct themselves toward household provisioning, or reproduction of subsistence requirements, I do not mean to suggest any underlying psychological basis for this. I would agree with Deere and de Janvry's (1979) criticism of the view that the simple reproduction of petty commodity producers is behaviorally motivated. As they point out, the inability to accumulate must be explained by reference to surplus extraction (e.g., unequal terms of trade and taxation through market fees).

7. While Ennew, Hirst, and Tribe's (1977 : 309) reading of Marx suggests that the concept of simple commodity production was constructed as an abstraction and not a historical stage, others would follow Mandel's (1970 : 68) reading, that petty commodity production is a transitional stage "between a society consciously governed by labour cooperation, and a society in which the complete dissolution of community ties leaves no room for anything but 'objective' laws, that is, laws which are blind, 'natural,' independent of men's will, as the regulators of economic activity."

6. Marketwomen, Family, and Society

1. A note on research methods is in order here. Since my research problem was designed to concentrate on marketwomen in the economy, I did not investigate some aspects of family and social life. Nevertheless, in conversations with marketers, they or I frequently brought up topics relating to these areas. Moreover, living with one family and visiting others made it possible for me to observe marketwomen at home as they worked and interacted with husbands and children.

In addition, halfway through my first period of fieldwork I drew up an open-ended question schedule (Appendix) designed for marketwomen and their husbands. The questionnaire included eighteen items; some of them asked for personal and occupational data, and others were designed to elicit views on several issues of national as well as local importance. I originally planned to compare the responses of women in marketing with those of their husbands engaged in subsistence agriculture, in order to learn something about the relation of work and consciousness as mediated by sex. I became interested in this question after reading Mintz (1964, 1971) on the conservatism of men in agriculture and the progressive orientation of women in marketing in the Caribbean. Mintz emphasizes that the different work activities of men and women require different skills and result in different temperamental responses.

For a variety of reasons this questionnaire was not taken to as many couples as I had intended. (There were seven couples in a total of nineteen female and eight male informants who responded.) Practical problems arose when I tried to arrange interviews with men from outside the markets and when informants responded with some reticence to formal interviews. The questionnaire data did reveal that the situation was more complex than I had anticipated. Few men were devoted solely to subsistence farming, and most men were as integrated in the market economy as their marketer wives. The strong differences in social and political consciousness that I had expected to discover between the sexes were not borne out in the data. Even so, the responses gathered from this sample of small marketers and their husbands offer significant data, which, along with material from my informal interviews, are presented in this and the next chapter.

2. See Mintz and Wolf (1950) for a discussion of *compadrazgo* in Latin America and Stein (1961) for a discussion of the institution in Hualcan, a community in the Callejón de Huaylas.

3. Some of the information offered by Carolina when I reinterviewed her in 1982 did not match earlier statements. For example, she told me she was eighty-three (aging nine years since 1977), though she noted that she was not sure of the year of her birth. Also, when asked how many children she had had, she said fifteen but then added that two pregnancies had resulted in stillbirths. Counting unsuccessful pregnancies and deceased children this way is not uncommon among women in Huaraz. More important to know about Carolina is that she continued to support herself as a marketer and to participate in union struggles until the time of her death in 1984. (For the reasons given in Chapter 1 and because this account was written while Carolina was still alive, I have kept her life history in the present tense.)

4. While some would disagree with my use of the "modes of production" terminology here, I use the concept advisedly. The persistence of non-capitalist forms is well known in the Andes, and I refer specifically to production for direct consumption (subsistence agriculture and domestic labor) and production characterized by an incomplete separation of producers from the means of production (petty commodity production and commerce) as two such modes of production. Of course, these modes must be understood as both subordinate to and in articulation with the dominant capitalist mode of production in Peru.

5. I am indebted to my research assistant, María Elena Mujica, for conducting this survey of households in Nicrupampa in 1987.

7. *Social Relations and Politics of Marketwomen*
1. With the end of military rule and the return of civilian government in 1980, price controls were lifted from many staple goods.

2. The extent to which this may be related to the Andean tradition of reciprocity is not clear, for cooperative relations characterize marketers in other areas of the world as well. See, however, Alberti and Mayer, eds. (1974), and Lehmann, ed. (1982), for articles on Peruvian reciprocity dating from pre-Hispanic Quechua culture to the contemporary period.

3. In 1982 renewed efforts were made to form a union, with little apparent success.

8. *Economic Crisis and the Campaign against Marketers*

1. Here, the word *independent* is used to distinguish these retailers from the 1 percent of workers employed by larger self-service retail establishments in Peru. See, however, Scott (1979) for a discussion of the subordination of "self-employed" workers to larger firms in Lima.

2. For a discussion of the constraints on small-scale manufacture and commerce in Third World areas, see, e.g., Schmitz (1982) and Moser (1977, 1980).

3. For a critical account of a similar effort in which these U.S. researchers were involved in Cali, Colombia, see Bromley (1981).

4. In other Third World cities, government policy has tightened control over the pricing and distribution of goods. Bromley (1978*b*) has examined the case of street sellers in Cali, Colombia, where official regulation contains and represses petty trade, and Gerry (1978) describes the situation of petty producer-sellers in Dakar, Senegal, where government intervention has benefited only a few and the majority have undergone worsening conditions. Jellinek (1977) offers an account of a Jakarta street trader who must constantly evade government "trader clearing campaigns." And Oliver-Smith (1974), whose fieldwork was carried out in the Peruvian town of Yungay, not far from Huaraz, points to the importance of official regulation of marketers through fee collection and fines as a means to generate public revenues.

5. Some divisions exist between permanent marketers and *ambulantes* anyway, due to their competition for sales and the regional differences among urban marketplace sellers and rural *ambulantes*. Even so, the two groups expressed a certain degree of solidarity stemming from their recognition of shared problems, and this may be undermined by the recent attacks on *ambulantes*.

6. Controversies over the role of marketers have arisen in other areas as well. The work of Mintz (1955) on Jamaican higglers became the focus of attention in a policy debate, reported in the pages of Kingston's *Daily Gleaner* in the 1950s (Mintz, personal communication). More recently, the stalls of street vendors in Kingston were cleared by bulldozers as part of a crackdown on petty traders, hailed by the *Daily Gleaner* as "a welcome change" (January 4, 1983). Other cases of tighter government control of marketers in response to public pressure are cited in note 4, above.

7. Osterling (n.d.) discusses the removal of *ambulantes* to one relocation site, Polvos Azules, as the government's weak response to the problem of rapid urban migration and high unemployment.

8. Zamalloa (1981), writing on the current situation of *ambulantes* in Lima, notes the large number of dependent sellers, working for wages or on consignment, and the fact that the majority of sellers are poor women.

9. In an interview around this time with José Matos Mar, director of Lima's Institute for Peruvian Studies, rising prices were attributed to the

commercial sector, and Matos Mar called for further efforts to bring goods directly from producers to consumers (*El Diario de Marka,* June 21, 1982 : 13). An unfortunate result of such a position is that it does not distinguish large from small commercial interests and fails to recognize the expansion of petty marketers as a consequence rather than a cause of the economic crisis.

10. A *mercado popular* (popular market) was also planned to allow wholesalers to conduct their transactions off the city streets.

9. Conceptualizing Marketwomen

1. This chapter title takes its inspiration from the article "Conceptualizing Women," by Edholm, Harris, and Young (1977). See that work for clarification of the concept of reproduction as it is used to theorize the situation of women and women's work. Here I will refer to the process of social reproduction, particularly as it concerns the regeneration of the labor force.

2. See also Mackintosh (1981 : 10), who notes that the concepts in question are not of the same order, with reproduction subsuming many productive activities.

3. I would agree with those critics (e.g., Fee 1976) of the debate over whether women's work, especially housework, is productive or unproductive who note that the discussion is often beside the point and does not contribute to an understanding of the relation of women's work to the wider economy. However, insofar as the issue has divided analysts of petty marketing, it is taken up here.

Glossary of Spanish and Quechua Terms

abarrotes: staple grocery items
abuelita: grandmother
ahijada: goddaughter
ahijados: godchildren
ají: chili pepper
alcalde: mayor
algo regular: something better
al por mayor: wholesale
al por menor: retail
ambulantes: itinerant sellers
amigos: friends
artículos de primera necesidad: articles of primary necessity
barriadas: squatter settlements
cafe con leche: coffee with milk
caldo[s]: heavy broth[s]
campamento: survivor camp
campesina[s]: rural woman [women]
campesino[s]: rural man [men] or person[s]
cargadores: porters
chacra[s]: small land parcel[s]
chicha: traditional Peruvian corn beer
chicherías: bars serving *chicha*
chocho: vegetable dish made from *chocho* beans
chocho beans: lupines
comadres: co-mothers (mothers and godmothers)
comedores populares: communal kitchens
como todo hombre: like any man
compadres: co-fathers or co-parents (parents and godparents)
compadrazgo: ritual kinship of co-parenthood (parents and godparents)
compañero[a]: male [female] companion; friend
conocidos: acquaintances
conquistadores: Spanish conquerors
con tragos: with a few drinks

contribución personal: head tax
corregidores: provincial representatives of the Spanish Crown
corte de pelo: first haircutting ceremony
cuna[s]: nursery[ies]
cuy: guinea pig
de la chacra a la olla: from the field to the cooking pot
despedida: good-bye party
dueños: owners
el campo: the countryside
emolientes: hot syrupy drinks
empleados: employees
en casa: at home
en la chacra: in the field
es la costumbre: it is the custom
es la ley del comerciante: it is the merchant's law
esposo[a]: husband [wife]
fastidioso: bothersome
fotonovelas: fiction with photographs in comic book format
fresco: flavored drink
gente baja: people of low moral character
gente decente: respectable people
hacendados: landowners
hacer algo: to do something
hacienda: large landed estate
huayno: popular Andean dance tune
ingreso: income, or fee, on goods brought into a region
jarabe: flavored syrup
jefe: boss
kiosko[s]: sales and storage booth[s]
kurakas: Indian chiefs
la plaza: marketplace
las alturas: the heights
latifundios: large landholdings
llapa (Quechua): a little extra
llegar a ser grande: to become someone important
lliklla[s] (Quechua): shawl[s]
lonche: before-meal snack
los informales: the informals (informal workers)
madrina: godmother
mandar: to lead
mano: small round crushing stone
más decente: more respectable
más pensadoras: brighter (smarter)
más seguro: more secure
más tranquilo: more peaceful
mayorista[s]: wholesaler[s]
mazamorra: cornstarch pudding

mercadillo: little market
mercado: market
mercado modelo: model market
mercado popular: popular market
mercería: housewares
mestizos: ethnic majority of the bilingual townspeople in Huaraz
metate[s]: curved grinding stone[s]
minifundios: small plots of land
minorista[s]: retailer[s]
mote: hominy-like product made from grains
movimiento: business traffic
nieta: granddaughter
no alcanza: does not reach (to meet a family's needs)
novio: suitor
obrera[s]: female worker[s]
obrero[s]: male worker[s] or worker[s]
oca: a tuber
olluco: a tuber
otro negocio: another business
padrino: godfather
padrinos: godparents
para comer no más: only to eat (not to sell)
partera: midwife
peones: farm laborers
poco a poco: little by little
pollera[s]: colorful wool skirt[s]
por producto: by the product
por vicio: as a vice
pueblos jovenes: squatter settlements (literally, young towns)
puesto: stall
qué diablo: what the devil
raspadillas: flavored ice snack
salchichas: sausages
salida: fee on goods taken out of a region
se entienden: understand and get along with one another
selva: jungle
serranos[as]: highlanders
seviche: marinated fish
shaqsha dancers (Quechua): young male fiesta participants
sindicatos: unions
sol: Peruvian monetary unit (equals one hundred *centavos*)
superarse: to get ahead
tallerín: noodle dish
tamales: prepared corn product wrapped in leaves
tocush (Quechua): corn or potato dish
triciclos: bicycle carts
zapallo: calabash

Bibliography

Books and Articles

Agüero León, Manuel R.
n.d.   *Tierra sobre tierra o Huaraz y el siniestro terremoto del 31 de mayo de 1970.* Huaraz, Peru: El Estado de la Educación Primaria en Huaraz.

Alberti, Giorgio, and Enrique Mayer, eds.
1974   *Reciprocidad e intercambio en los Andes peruanos.* Lima: Instituto de Estudios Peruanos.

Alvarez-Brun, Felix
1970   *Ancash, una historia regional peruana.* Lima: Ediciones P.L.V.

Amin, Samir
1976   *Unequal Development: An Essay on the Social Formations of Peripheral Capitalism.* New York: Monthly Review Press.

Anderson, Jeanine
1978   "The Middle Class Woman in the Family and the Community: Lima, Peru." Ph.D. dissertation, Cornell University.

Andradi, Esther, and Ana María Portugal
1978   *Ser mujer en el Perú.* Lima: Ediciones Mujer y Autonomía.

Andreas, Carol
1985   *When Women Rebel: The Rise of Popular Feminism in Peru.* Westport, Conn.: Lawrence Hill and Co.

Appleby, Gordon
1976a "Export Monoculture and Regional Social Structure in Puno, Peru." In *Regional Analysis,* vol. 2, *Social Systems,* edited by Carol A. Smith. New York: Academic Press.

1976b "The Role of Urban Food Needs in Regional Development, Puno, Peru." In *Regional Analysis,* vol. 1, *Economic Systems,* edited by Carol A. Smith. New York: Academic Press.

Arizpe, Lourdes
1975   *Indígenas en la ciudad de México: El caso de las "Marías."* Mexico City: Sep/Setentas.

1977   "Women in the Informal Labor Sector: The Case of Mexico City." *Signs* 3(1): 25–37.

Arnold, Katherine

    1977   "The Introduction of Poses to a Peruvian Brothel and Changing Images of Male and Female." In *The Anthropology of the Body*, edited by John Blacking. New York: Academic Press.

    1978   "The Whore in Peru." In *Tearing the Veil: Essays on Femininity*, edited by Susan Lipshitz. London: Routledge and Kegan Paul.

Babb, Florence E.

    1976   *The Development of Sexual Inequality in Vicos, Peru*. Council on International Studies Special Studies no. 83. Buffalo: State University of New York at Buffalo.

    1985   "Women and Men in Vicos: A Peruvian Case of Unequal Development." In *Peruvian Contexts of Change*, edited by William W. Stein. New Brunswick, N.J.: Transaction Books.

Barker, Jonathan, and Gavin Smith, eds.

    1986   *Rethinking Petty Commodity Production*. Special issue of *Labour, Capital and Society* 19(1).

Barkin, David

    1961   "Commercial Activity in a Peruvian Community." Columbia-Cornell-Harvard Summer Field Studies. Columbia University. Typescript.

Barrig, Maruja

    1979   *Cinturón de castidad: La mujer de clase media en el Perú*. Lima: Mosca Azul Editores.

    1982   *Convivir: La pareja en la pobreza*. Lima: Mosca Azul Editores.

    1986   *Las obreras*. Lima: Mosca Azul Editores.

Barrig, Maruja, ed.

    1985   *Mujer, trabajo y empleo*. Lima: Asociación de Defensa y Capacitación Legal (ADEC).

Barrig, Maruja, Marcela Chueca, and Ana María Yañez

    1985   *Anzuelo sin carnada: Obreras en la industria de conserva de pescado*. Lima: Mosca Azul Editores.

Baxandall, Rosalyn, Elizabeth Ewen, and Linda Gordon

    1976   "The Working Class Has Two Sexes." *Monthly Review* 28(3): 1–9.

Beals, Ralph L.

    1975   *The Peasant Marketing System of Oaxaca, Mexico*. Berkeley: University of California Press.

Beechey, Veronica

    1978   "Women and Production: A Critical Analysis of Some Sociological Theories of Women's Work." In *Feminism and Materialism*, edited by Annette Kuhn and AnnMarie Wolpe. London: Routledge and Kegan Paul.

Belshaw, Cyril S.

    1965   *Traditional Exchange and Modern Markets*. Englewood Cliffs, N.J.: Prentice-Hall.

Benería, Lourdes, and Gita Sen

    1981   "Accumulation, Reproduction, and Women's Role in Economic Development: Boserup Revisited." *Signs* 7(2): 279–298.

Bode, Barbara
  1974   "Explanation in the 1970 Earthquake in the Peruvian Andes."
          Ph.D. dissertation, Tulane University.
  1977   "Disaster, Social Structure, and Myth in the Peruvian Andes:
          The Genesis of an Explanation." *Annals of the New York Acad-
          emy of Sciences* 293:246–274.
Bohannan, Paul J., and George Dalton, eds.
  1962   *Markets in Africa.* Evanston, Ill.: Northwestern University Press.
Bollinger, William
  1978   "Peru: The Left Gathers Force." *North American Congress on
          Latin America Report* 12(5): 44–46.
  1980   "Peru Today—The Roots of Labor Militancy." *North American
          Congress on Latin America Report* 14(6): 2–35.
Boserup, Ester
  1970   *Woman's Role in Economic Development.* New York: St. Mar-
          tin's Press.
Bourque, Susan C., and Kay B. Warren
  1976   "Campesinas and Comuneras: Subordination in the Sierra."
          Journal of Marriage and the Family 38(4): 781–788.
  1980   "Multiple Arenas for State Expansion: Class, Ethnicity, and Sex
          in Rural Peru." *Ethnic and Racial Studies* 3(3): 264–280.
  1981a   "Rural Women and Development Planning in Peru." In *Women
          and World Change,* edited by Naomi Black and Ann Baker
          Cottrell. Beverly Hills, Calif.: Sage.
  1981b   *Women of the Andes: Partriarchy and Social Change in Two
          Peruvian Towns.* Ann Arbor: University of Michigan Press.
Braverman, Harry
  1974   *Labor and Monopoly Capital: The Degradation of Work in the
          Twentieth Century.* New York: Monthly Review Press.
Bromley, Raymond J.
  1974   "Marketplace Trade in Latin America." *Latin American Re-
          search Review* 9(3): 3–38.
  1975   "Periodic and Daily Markets in Highland Ecuador." Ph.D. disser-
          tation, Cambridge University.
  1978a   "Introduction—The Urban Informal Sector: Why Is It Worth
          Discussing?" *World Development* 6(9–10): 1033–1039.
  1978b   "Organization, Regulation and Exploitation in the So-called 'Ur-
          ban Informal Sector': The Street Traders of Cali, Colombia."
          World Development 6(9–10): 1161–1171.
  1981   "From Calvary to White Elephant: A Colombian Case of Urban
          Renewal and Marketing Reform." *Development and Change*
          12(1): 77–120.
Bucklin, Louis P.
  1972   *Competition and Evolution in the Distributive Trades.* Engle-
          wood Cliffs, N.J.: Prentice-Hall.
Buechler, Hans C., and Judith-Maria Buechler
  1977   "Conduct and Code: An Analysis of Market Syndicates and

Social Revolution in La Paz, Bolivia." In *Ideology and Social Change in Latin America*, edited by June Nash, Juan Corradi, and Hobart Spalding, Jr. New York: Gordon and Breach.

Buechler, Judith-Maria

1972 "Peasant Marketing and Social Revolution in the Province of La Paz, Bolivia." Ph.D. dissertation, McGill University.

1976a "Las negociantes-contratistas en los mercados bolivianos." *Estudios Andinos* 12 : 57 – 76. Special issue, *La mujer en los Andes*, edited by June Nash.

1976b "Something Funny Happened on the Way to the Agora: A Comparison of Bolivian and Spanish Galician Female Migrants." *Anthropological Quarterly* 49(1): 62 – 68.

1978 "The Dynamics of the Market in La Paz, Bolivia." *Urban Anthropology* 7(4): 343 – 359.

Bujra, Janet M.

1982 "Introductory: Female Solidarity and the Sexual Division of Labour." In *Women United, Women Divided*, edited by Patricia Caplan and Janet M. Bujra. Bloomington: Indiana University Press.

Bunster, Ximena

1983 "Market Sellers in Lima, Peru: Talking about Work." In *Women and Poverty in the Third World*, edited by Mayra Buvinic and Margaret A. Lycette. Baltimore: Johns Hopkins University Press.

Bunster, Ximena, and Elsa M. Chaney

1985 *Sellers and Servants: Working Women in Lima, Peru.* New York: Praeger.

Burkett, Elinor

1977 "In Dubious Sisterhood: The Case of Spanish Colonial South America." *Latin American Perspectives* 12 – 13 : 18 – 26.

Buse, H.

1957 *Huarás, Chavín.* Lima: Juan Mejia Baca & P. L. Villanueva.

CELATS (Centro Latinoamericano de Trabajo Social)

1983 *Manual de organización y funciones de los comedores populares de el Augustino.* Lima: CELATS.

CONAMUP (Comisión Nacional de la Mujer Peruana)

1976 *Analisis de la legislación vigente, relacionada con la situación laboral de la mujer.* Lima: CONAMUP.

Carpio, Lourdes

1975 "The Rural Woman in Peru: An Alarming Contradiction." In *Women in the Struggle for Liberation.* Dayton, Ohio: Women's Project, World Student Christian Federation.

Casaverde R., Juvenal

1977 "El trueque en la economía pastoril." In *Pastores de puna, uywamichiq punarunakuna*, edited by Jorge A. Floras Ochoa. Lima: Instituto de Estudios Peruanos.

Centro de Información, Estudios y Documentación (CIED)
    1981   *Presencia de la mujer en las barriadas.* Lima: CIED Publicaciones.
Chaney, Elsa M.
    1976   "Women at the 'Marginal Pole' of the Economy in Lima, Peru." Paper presented at the Conference on Women and Development, Wellesley College, June 4, 1976.
Chávez, Eliana
    1985   "Mujer y trabajo informal." In *Mujer, trabajo y empleo,* edited by Maruja Barrig. Lima: ADEC.
Chiñas, Beverly L.
    1973   *The Isthmus Zapotecs: Women's Roles in Cultural Context.* New York: Holt, Rinehart and Winston.
    1975   *Mujeres de San Juan: La mujer zapoteca del Istmo en la economía.* Mexico City: Sep/Setentas.
    1976   "Zapotec *Viajeras.*" In *Markets in Oaxaca,* edited by Scott Cook and Martin Diskin. Austin: University of Texas Press.
Chinchilla, Norma S.
    1977   "Industrialization, Monopoly Capitalism, and Women's Work in Guatemala." *Signs* 3(1): 38–56.
Clark, Gracia, ed.
    1988   *Traders vs. the State.* Boulder: Westview Press.
Collier, David
    1976   *Squatters and Oligarchs: Authoritarian Rule and Policy Change in Peru.* Baltimore: Johns Hopkins University Press.
Concha Contreras, Juan de Dios
    1975   "Relación entre pastores y agricultores." *Allpanchis Phuturinga: Revista del Instituto de Pastoral Andina* 8: 67–101.
Cook, Scott
    1976a   "The 'Market' as Location and Transaction: Dimensions of Marketing in a Zapotec Stoneworking Industry." In *Markets in Oaxaca,* edited by Scott Cook and Martin Diskin. Austin: University of Texas Press.
    1976b   "Value, Price, and Simple Commodity Production: The Case of the Zapotec Stoneworkers." *Journal of Peasant Studies* 3: 395–427.
Cook, Scott, and Martin Diskin
    1976a   "A Concluding Critical Look at Issues of Theory and Method in Oaxaca Market Studies." In *Markets in Oaxaca,* edited by Scott Cook and Martin Diskin. Austin: University of Texas Press.
    1976b   *Markets in Oaxaca.* Austin: University of Texas Press.
Cotler, Julio
    1970   "The Mechanics of Internal Domination and Social Change in Peru." In *Masses in Latin America,* edited by Irving Louis Horowitz. New York: Oxford University Press.
    1975   "The New Mode of Political Domination in Peru." In *The Peru-*

vian Experiment, edited by Abraham F. Lowenthal. Princeton: Princeton University Press.

Davies, Rob

1979 "Informal Sector or Subordinate Mode of Production? A Model." In *Casual Work and Poverty in Third World Cities,* edited by Ray Bromley and Chris Gerry. New York: John Wiley and Sons.

Davis, William G.

1973 *Social Relations in a Philippine Market.* Berkeley: University of California Press.

Deere, Carmen Diana

1976 "Rural Women's Subsistence Production in the Capitalist Periphery." *Review of Radical Political Economics* 8(1): 9–17.

1977 "Changing Social Relations of Production and Peruvian Peasant Women's Work." *Latin American Perspectives* 12–13:48–69.

Deere, Carmen Diana, and Alain de Janvry

1979 "A Conceptual Framework for the Empirical Analysis of Peasants." *American Journal of Agricultural Economics* 61(4): 601–611.

Deere, Carmen Diana, and Magdalena León de Leal

1981 "Peasant Production, Proletarianization, and the Sexual Division of Labor in the Andes." *Signs* 7(2): 338–360.

de Soto, Hernando

1986 *El otro sendero: La revolución informal.* Lima: Instituto Libertad y Democracia.

Dewey, Alice

1962 *Peasant Marketing in Java.* New York: Free Press.

Dore, Elizabeth, John Weeks, and William Bollinger, eds.

1977 "Peru: Bourgeois Revolution and Class Struggle." *Latin American Perspectives* 14.

Doughty, Paul L.

1970 "Behind the Back of the City: 'Provincial' Life in Lima, Peru." In *Peasants in Cities,* edited by William Mangin. Boston: Houghton Mifflin.

1976 "Social Policy and Urban Growth in Lima." In *Peruvian Nationalism, a Corporatist Revolution,* edited by David Chaplin. New Brunswick, N.J.: Transaction Books.

Dupré, Georges, and Pierre-Philippe Rey

1973 "Reflections on the Pertinence of a Theory of the History of Exchange." *Economy and Society* 2(2): 131–163.

Durant-Gonzalez, Victoria

1985 "Higglering: Rural Women and the Internal Market System in Jamaica." In *Rural Development in the Caribbean,* edited by P. I. Gomes. New York: St. Martin's Press.

Edholm, Felicity, Olivia Harris, and Kate Young

1977 "Conceptualizing Women." *Critique of Anthropology* 3(9–10): 101–130.

Ennew, Judith, Paul Hirst, and Keith Tribe
1977 "'Peasantry' as an Economic Category." *Journal of Peasant Studies* 4(4): 295–322.

Esculies Larrabure, Oscar, Marcial Rubio Correa, and Verónica Gonzales del Castillo
1977 *Comercialización de alimentos: Quiénes ganan, quiénes pagan, quiénes pierden.* Lima: Centro de Estudios y Promoción del Desarrollo (DESCO).

Esteva Fabregat, Claudio
1970 "Un mercado en Chinchero, Cuzco." *Anuario Indigenista* 30: 213–254.

Fee, Terry
1976 "Domestic Labor: An Analysis of Housework and Its Relation to the Production Process." *Review of Radical Political Economics* 8(1): 1–8.

Fernandez, Justo
1962 *Ancash: Personaje.* Lima: Ediciones Nueva Era.

Figueroa, Adolfo
1984 *Capitalist Development and the Peasant Economy in Peru.* New York: Cambridge University Press.

Figueroa, Blanca
n.d. "Women's Community Participation: An Experience in Peru." Typescript, in author's possession.

Figueroa, Blanca, and Jeanine Anderson
1981 *Women in Peru.* International Reports: Women and Society, no. 5. London: Change International Reports.

Fitzgerald, E. V. K.
1976 *The State and Economic Development: Peru since 1968.* Cambridge: Cambridge University Press.
1979 *The Political Economy of Peru 1956–78: Economic Development and the Restructuring of Capital.* New York: Cambridge University Press.

Flores Ochoa, Jorge A., ed.
1977 "Pastoreo, tejido e intercambio." In *Pastores de puna, uywamichiq punarunakuna,* edited by Jorge A. Flores Ochoa. Lima: Instituto de Estudios Peruanos.

Forman, Shepard, and Joyce F. Riegelhaupt
1970 "Market Place and Marketing System: Toward a Theory of Peasant Economic Integration." *Comparative Studies in Society and History* 12:188–212.

Foster-Carter, Aidan
1978 "Can We Articulate 'Articulation'?" In *The New Economic Anthropology,* edited by John Clammer. New York: St. Martin's Press.

Frank, Andre Gunder
1969 *Latin America: Underdevelopment or Revolution?* New York: Monthly Review Press.

Freedman, Dan, and Clifford Krauss
1977   "Left-wing Junta vs. the Bankers." *The Nation,* November 5, 1977, 466–468.
Galer, Nora, Virginia Guzmán, and María Gabriela Vega, eds.
1985   *Mujer y desarrollo.* Lima: Flora Tristan and Centro de Estudios y Promoción del Desarrollo (DESCO).
Gerry, Chris
1978   "Petty Production and Capitalist Production in Dakar: The Crisis of the Self-Employed." *World Development* 6(9–10): 1147–1160.
1979   "Small-scale Manufacturing and Repairs in Dakar: A Survey of Market Relations within the Urban Economy." In *Casual Work and Poverty in Third World Cities,* edited by Ray Bromley and Chris Gerry. New York: John Wiley and Sons.
Gridilla, P. Alberto
1933   *Huaraz, o apuntes y documentos para la historia de la ciudad.* Huaraz, Peru: Tip. "La Epoca."
1937   *Ancahs* [*sic*] *y sus antiguos corregimientos.* Vol. 1 of *La Conquista.* Arequipa, Peru: Editorial La Colmena.
Grollig, F. X.
1964   "Indian Markets in the Altiplano of Peru." *Proceedings of the XXXVI Congreso Internacional de Americanistas,* vol. 3:403–406.
Grompone, Romeo
1981   "Comercio ambulante: Razones de una terca presencia." *Quehacer* 13:95–109.
1985   *Talleristas y vendedores ambulantes en Lima.* Lima: Centro de Estudios y Promoción del Desarrollo (DESCO).
Halperin, Rhoda, and James Dow, eds.
1977   *Peasant Livelihood.* New York: St. Martin's Press.
Hansen, Karen Tranberg
1980   "The Urban Informal Sector as a Development Issue: Poor Women and Work in Lusaka, Zambia." *Urban Anthropology* 9(2): 199–225.
Harding, Timothy F., and Marjorie Bray, eds.
1976   "Dependency Theory and Dimensions of Imperialism." *Latin American Perspectives* 3.
Harrison, Kelly, Donald Henley, Harold Riley, and James Shaffer
1974   *Improving Food Marketing Systems in Developing Countries: Experiences from Latin America.* Latin American Studies Center Research Report no. 6. East Lansing: Michigan State University.
Hart, Keith
1973   "Informal Income Opportunities and Urban Employment in Ghana." *Journal of Modern African Studies* 2(1): 61–89.
Hartmann, Roswith
1971   "Algunas observaciones respecto al trueque y otras prácticas en

las ferias de la sierra ecuatoriana." *Archiv für Volkerkunde* 25:43–53.

Hill, Polly
    1969   "Hidden Trade in Hausaland." *Man* 4(3): 392–409.

Hobsbawm, E. J.
    1971   "Peru: The Peculiar 'Revolution.'" *New York Review of Books* 17(10): 29–36.

Huamán Poma de Ayala, Felipe
    1978   *Letter to a King: A Picture-History of the Inca Civilization.* Edited by Christopher Dilke. London: George Allen and Unwin.

ILMA (Instituto Latinoamericano de Mercadeo Agrícola)
    1965   *Estudio del sistema de mercados públicos propiedad de EMCALI.* Cali, Colombia: EMCALI (Establecimiento Público Empresas Municipales de Cali).

Jelin, Elizabeth
    1977   "Migration and Labor Force Participation of Latin American Women: The Domestic Servants in the Cities." *Signs* 3(1): 129–141.
    1980   "The Bahiana in the Labor Force in Salvador, Brazil." In *Sex and Class in Latin America*, edited by June Nash and Helen Icken Safa. New York: J. F. Bergin.

Jellinek, Lea
    1977   "The Life of a Jakarta Street Trader." In *Third World Urbanization*, edited by Richard Hay, Jr., and Janet Abu-Lughod. Chicago: Maaroufa Press.

Katzin, Margaret F.
    1959   "The Jamaican Country Higgler." *Social and Economic Studies* 8:421–435.
    1960   "The Business of Higglering in Jamaica." *Social and Economic Studies* 9:297–331.

Latin American Working Group (LAWG)
    1980   "Peru: Economic Crisis and Daily Bread." *LAWG Letter* 6(6).

Lehmann, David, ed.
    1982   *Ecology and Exchange in the Andes.* New York: Cambridge University Press.

Lele, Uma
    1971   *Food Grain Marketing in India.* Ithaca, N.Y.: Cornell University Press.
    1975   *The Design of Rural Development: Lessons from Africa.* Baltimore: Johns Hopkins University Press.

Lessinger, Johanna
    1986   "Work and Modesty: The Dilemma of Women Traders in South India." *Feminist Studies* 12(3): 581–600.

Lewis, Barbara
    1976   "The Limitations of Group Action among Entrepreneurs: The Market Women of Abidjan, Ivory Coast." In *Women in Africa,*

edited by Nancy J. Hafkin and Edna G. Bay. Stanford: Stanford University Press.

Littlefield, Alice
1979   "The Expansion of Capitalist Relations of Production in Mexican Crafts." *Journal of Peasant Studies* 6(4): 471–488.

Lloyd, Peter
1980   *The "Young Towns" of Lima: Aspects of Urbanization in Peru.* New York: Cambridge University Press.

Lobo, Susan
1982   *A House of My Own: Social Organization in the Squatter Settlements of Lima, Peru.* Tucson: University of Arizona Press.

Long, Norman, and Paul Richardson
1978   "Informal Sector, Petty Commodity Production, and the Social Relations of Small-scale Enterprise." In *The New Economic Anthropology,* edited by John Clammer. New York: St. Martin's Press.

Long, Norman, and Bryan R. Roberts, eds.
1978   *Peasant Cooperation and Capitalist Expansion in Central Peru.* Austin: University of Texas Press.
1984   *Miners, Peasants, and Entrepreneurs.* New York: Cambridge University Press.

Lowenthal, Abraham F.
1975   "Peru's Ambiguous Revolution." In *The Peruvian Experiment,* edited by Abraham F. Lowenthal. Princeton: Princeton University Press.

Mackintosh, Maureen
1981   "Gender and Economics: The Sexual Division of Labour and the Subordination of Women." In *Of Marriage and the Market,* edited by Kate Young, Carol Wolkowitz, and Roslyn McMullagh. London: CSE Books.

Mallon, Florencia E.
1987   "Patriarchy in the Transition to Capitalism: Central Peru, 1830–1950." *Feminist Studies* 13(2): 379–407.

Mandel, Ernest
1970   *Marxist Economic Theory.* Translated by Brian Pearce. 2 vols. New York: Monthly Review Press.

Mangin, William
1970a   "Similarities and Differences between Two Types of Peruvian Communities." In *Peasants in Cities,* edited by William Mangin. Boston: Houghton Mifflin.
1970b   "Tales from the Barriadas." In *Peasants in Cities,* edited by William Mangin. Boston: Houghton Mifflin.
1970c   "Urbanization Case History in Peru." In *Peasants in Cities,* edited by William Mangin. Boston: Houghton Mifflin.

Martín, Luis
1983   *Daughters of the Conquistadores: Women of the Viceroyalty of Peru.* Albuquerque: University of New Mexico Press.

Marx, Karl
1967   *Capital: A Critique of Political Economy.* 3 vols. Translated from the 3d German edition by Samuel Moore and Edward Aveling. Edited by Frederick Engels. New York: International Publishers. [Originally published in 1859.]
1970   *A Contribution to the Critique of Political Economy.* Translated from the German by S. W. Ryazanskaya. Edited by Maurice Dobb. New York: International Publishers. [Originally published in 1859.]
Matos Mar, José
1984   *Desborde popular y crisis del estado.* Lima: Instituto de Estudios Peruanos.
Mayer, Enrique
1974a   "El trueque y los mercados en el imperio incaico." In *Los campesinos y el mercado,* edited by Enrique Mayer, Sidney W. Mintz, and G. William Skinner. Lima: Pontificia Universidad Católica del Perú.
1974b   "Reciprocity, Self-Sufficiency and Market Relations in a Contemporary Community in the Central Andes of Peru." Ph.D. dissertation, Cornell University.
Mercado, Hilda
1978   La madre trabajadora: El caso de las comerciantes ambulantes. Serie C, no. 2. Lima: Centro de Estudios de Población y Desarrollo.
Ministerio de Educación
1976a   Diagnóstico situacional de la zona de educación, no. 84, Huaraz. Huaraz, Peru: Ministerio de Educación.
1976b   Diagnóstico situacional, núcleo educativo comunal, no. 06–84, Huaraz. Huaraz, Peru: Ministerio de Educación.
1977   Diagnóstico situacional, núcleo educativo comunal, no. 01–84, Huaraz. Huaraz, Peru: Ministerio de Educación.
Mintz, Sidney
1955   "The Jamaican Internal Marketing Pattern: Some Notes and Hypotheses." *Social and Economic Studies* 4:95–103.
1956   "The Role of the Middleman in the Internal Distribution System of a Caribbean Peasant Economy." *Human Organization* 15:18–23.
1959   "Internal Market Systems as Mechanisms of Social Articulation." In *Intermediate Societies, Social Mobility and Communication,* edited by V. F. Ray, 20–30. Proceedings of the 1959 Annual Spring Meeting of the American Ethnological Society. Seattle: University of Washington Press.
1964   "The Employment of Capital by Market Women in Haiti." In *Capital, Saving, and Credit in Peasant Societies,* edited by Raymond Firth and B. S. Yamey. Chicago: Aldine.

1971   "Men, Women, and Trade." *Comparative Studies in Society and History* 13:247–269.

1974   *Caribbean Transformations.* Chicago: Aldine.

Mintz, Sidney W., and Eric R. Wolf

1950   "An Analysis of Ritual Co-Parenthood (Compadrazgo)." *Southwestern Journal of Anthropology* 6:341–368.

Moser, Caroline

1977   "The Dual Economy and Marginality Debate and the Contribution of Micro Analysis: Market Sellers in Bogotá." *Development and Change* 8:465–489.

1978   "Informal Sector or Petty Commodity Production: Dualism or Dependence in Urban Development?" *World Development* 6(9–10): 1041–1064.

1980   "Why the Poor Remain Poor: The Experience of Bogotá Market Traders in the 1970s." *Journal of Interamerican Studies and World Affairs* 22(3): 365–387.

Mott, Luis, Robert H. Silin, and Sidney W. Mintz

1975   *A Supplementary Bibliography on Marketing and Marketplaces.* Exchange Bibliography no. 792. Monticello, Ill.: Council of Planning Librarians.

Murra, John V.

1975   "El control vertical de un máximo de pisos ecológicos en la economía de las sociedades andinas." In *Formaciones económicas y políticas del mundo andino,* edited by John V. Murra. Lima: Instituto de Estudios Peruanos.

Nash, June

1980   "A Critique of Social Science Roles in Latin America." In *Sex and Class in Latin America,* edited by June Nash and Helen Icken Safa. New York: J. F. Bergin.

Nash, June, and Helen Icken Safa, eds.

1980   *Sex and Class in Latin America.* New York: J. F. Bergin.

Nelson, Nici

1979   "How Women and Men Get By: The Sexual Division of Labour in the Informal Sector of a Nairobi Squatter Settlement." In *Casual Work and Poverty in Third World Cities,* edited by Ray Bromley and Chris Gerry. New York: John Wiley and Sons.

Núñez del Prado Béjar, Daisy Irene

1975*a*   "El poder de decisión de la mujer quechua andina." *América Indígena* 35(3): 623–630.

1975*b*   "El rol de la mujer campesina quechua." *América Indígena* 35(2): 391–401.

Oliver-Smith, Anthony R.

1974   "Yungay Norte: Disaster and Social Change in the Peruvian Highlands." Ph.D. dissertation, Indiana University.

1986   *The Martyred City: Death and Rebirth in the Andes.* Albuquerque: University of New Mexico Press.

Orlove, Benjamin S.
1977   *Alpacas, Sheep, and Men: The Wool Export Economy and Regional Society in Southern Peru.* New York: Academic Press.
Ortiz, Sutti
1967   "Colombian Rural Market Organization: An Exploratory Model." *Man*, n.s., 2:393–413.
Osterling, Jorge P.
1981   "La pobreza urbana a la luz del sector económico informal urbano: Una perspectiva transcultural." *Socialismo y Participación* 16:71–84.
n.d.   "La reubicación de los vendedores ambulantes de Lima: ¿Un ejemplo de articulación política?" Typescript, in author's possession.
Osterling, Jorge P., Jaime de Althaus, and Jorge Morelli S.
1979   "Los vendedores ambulantes de ropa en el cercado: Un ejemplo del sector económico informal en Lima metropolitana." *Debates en Antropología* 4:23–41.
Osterling, Jorge P., and Dennis Chávez de Paz
1979   "La organización de los vendedores ambulantes: El caso de Lima metropolitana." *Revista de la Universidad Católica* 6:185–202.
Oxaal, Ivar, Tony Barnett, and David Booth
1975   *Beyond the Sociology of Development.* London: Routledge and Kegan Paul.
Pásara, Luis
1979   "Peru: From Reformism to the Orthodoxy of 1977." *Contemporary Crises* 3(1): 41–51.
Patch, Richard
1967   *La Parada, Lima's Market.* American Universities Field Staff Reports, West Coast of South America Series, vol. 14, nos. 1–3. Hanover, N.H.
Peattie, Lisa R.
1975   "'Tertiarization' and Urban Poverty in Latin America." In *Latin American Urban Research*, vol. 5, edited by Wayne A. Cornelius and Felicity M. Trueblood. Beverly Hills, Calif.: Sage.
Perlman, Janice
1976   *The Myth of Marginality: Urban Poverty and Politics in Rio de Janeiro.* Berkeley: University of California Press.
Perú Mujer
1983   *Informe final—Congreso de investigación acerca de la mujer en la región andina.* Lima: Editorial Colmena.
Petras, James, and A. Eugene Havens
1979   "Peru: Economic Crises and Class Confrontation." *Monthly Review* 30(9): 25–41.
Plattner, Stuart, ed.
1985   *Markets and Marketing.* Monographs in Economic Anthropology, no. 4. Lanham, Md.: University Press of America.

Polanyi, Karl E.
1957   "The Economy As an Instituted Process." In *Trade and Markets in the Early Empires*, edited by Karl Polanyi, Conrad Arensberg, and Harry Pearson. Glencoe, Ill.: Free Press.
Portes, Alejandro, and John Walton
1981   *Labor, Class, and the International System.* New York: Academic Press.
Prieto de Zegarra, Judith
1980   *Mujer, poder y desarrollo en el Perú.* 2 vols. Callao, Peru: Editorial DORHCA Representaciones S.A.
Primov, George P.
n.d.   "Brothel Prostitution in Latin America: A Comparison of Four Case Studies." University of Missouri, Columbia. Typescript.
Quijano Obregón, Aníbal
1968   "Tendencies in Peruvian Development and in the Class Structure." In *Latin America, Reform or Revolution?* Edited by James Petras and Maurice Zeitlin. Greenwich, Conn.: Fawcett Publications.
1971   *Nationalism and Capitalism in Peru: A Study in Neo-Imperialism.* New York: Monthly Review Press.
1974   "The Marginal Pole of the Economy and the Marginalized Labour Force." *Economy and Society* 3(4): 393–428.
1977   "Las nuevas condiciones de la lucha de clases en el Perú." *Sociedad y Política* 7:2–15.
Raimondi, Antonio
1879   *El departamento de Ancash y sus riquezas minerales.* Lima: Imp. de "El Nacional."
Rakowski, Cathy
1987   "Desventaja multiplicada: La mujer del sector informal." *Nueva Sociedad* 90:134–146.
Remy, Dorothy
1975   "Underdevelopment and the Experience of Women: A Nigerian Case Study." In *Toward an Anthropology of Women,* edited by Rayna R. Reiter. New York: Monthly Review Press.
Roberts, Bryan R.
1975   "Center and Periphery in the Development Process: The Case of Peru." In *Latin American Urban Research,* vol. 5, edited by Wayne A. Cornelius and Felicity M. Trueblood. Beverly Hills, Calif.: Sage.
n.d.   "The Social History of a Provincial Town: Huancayo, 1890–1972." In *Social and Economic Change in Modern Peru,* edited by Rory Miller, Clifford T. Smith, and John Fisher. Centre for Latin American Studies Monograph Series, no. 6. Liverpool.
Robertson, Claire C.
1984   *Sharing the Same Bowl: A Socioeconomic History of Women and Class in Accra, Ghana.* Bloomington: Indiana University Press.

Rostworowski de Diez Canseco, María
1977 "Coastal Fishermen, Merchants, and Artisans in Pre-Hispanic Peru." In *The Sea in the Pre-Columbian World: A Conference at Dumbarton Oaks, October 26th and 27th, 1974,* edited by Elizabeth P. Benson. Washington, D.C.: Dumbarton Oaks Research Library and Collections.

Rubbo, Anna, and Michael Taussig
1983 "Up Off Their Knees: Servanthood in Southwest Colombia." *Latin American Perspectives* 39:5–23.

Rusque-Alcaino, Juan, and Ray Bromley
1979 "The Bottle Buyer: An Occupational Autobiography." In *Casual Work and Poverty in Third World Cities,* edited by Ray Bromley and Chris Gerry. New York: John Wiley and Sons.

Rutte García, Alberto
1976 Simplemente explotadas: El mundo de las empleadas domésticas de Lima. Lima: Centro de Estudios y Promoción del Desarrollo (DESCO).

Safa, Helen Icken
1977 "The Changing Class Composition of the Female Labor Force in Latin America." *Latin American Perspectives* 15:126–136.

Safa, Helen Icken, ed.
1982 *Towards a Political Economy of Urbanization in Third World Countries.* Delhi, India: Oxford University Press.

Sara-Lafosse, Violeta
1983 *Campesinas y costureras.* Lima: Pontificia Universidad Católica del Perú.
1986 "Communal Kitchens in the Low-income Neighborhoods of Lima." In *Learning about Women and Urban Services in Latin America and the Caribbean,* edited by Judith Bruce and Marilyn Kohn. New York: The Population Council.

Schmink, Marianne
1977 "Dependent Development and the Division of Labor by Sex: Venezuela." *Latin American Perspectives* 12–13:153–179.

Schmitz, Hubert
1982 "Growth Constraints on Small-scale Manufacturing in Developing Countries: A Critical Review." *World Development* 10(6): 429–450.

Scott, Alison MacEwen
1979 "Who Are the Self-employed?" In *Casual Work and Poverty in Third World Cities,* edited by Ray Bromley and Chris Gerry. New York: John Wiley and Sons.

Scott, Gregory J.
1985 *Markets, Myths, and Middlemen: A Study of Potato Marketing in Central Peru.* Lima: International Potato Center.

Shoemaker, Robin
1981 *The Peasants of El Dorado: Conflict and Contradiction in a Peruvian Frontier Settlement.* Ithaca, N.Y.: Cornell University Press.

Silverblatt, Irene
    1978   "Andean Women in the Inca Empire." *Feminist Studies* 4(3): 37–61.
    1980   "'The universe has turned us inside out . . . there is no justice for us here': Andean Women under Spanish Rule." In *Women and Colonization: Anthropological Perspectives,* edited by Mona Etienne and Eleanor Leacock. New York: Praeger.
    1987   *Moon, Sun, and Witches: Gender Ideologies and Class in Inca and Colonial Peru.* Princeton: Princeton University Press.
Sindicato de Trabajadoras del Hogar
    1982   *Basta: Testimonios.* Cuzco, Peru: Centro de Estudios Rurales Andinos "Bartolomé de Las Casas."
Smith, Carol A.
    1977   "How Marketing Systems Affect Economic Opportunity in Agrarian Societies." In *Peasant Livelihood,* edited by Rhoda Halperin and James Dow. New York: St. Martin's Press.
Smith, Margo L.
    1971   "Institutionalized Servitude: The Female Domestic Servant in Lima, Peru." Ph.D. dissertation, Indiana University.
    1973   "Domestic Service as a Channel of Upward Mobility for the Lower-class Woman: The Lima Case." In *Female and Male in Latin America,* edited by Ann Pescatello. Pittsburgh: University of Pittsburgh Press.
Stallings, Barbara
    1978   "Privatization and the Public Debt: U.S. Banks in Peru." *North American Congress on Latin America Report* 12(4): 2–19.
Stein, William W.
    1961   *Hualcan: Life in the Highlands of Peru.* Ithaca, N.Y.: Cornell University Press.
    1975   *Modernization and Inequality in Vicos, Peru: An Examination of the "Ignorance of Women."* Council on International Studies Special Studies no. 73. Buffalo: State University of New York at Buffalo.
    1978   "A Radical Perspective on Underdevelopment." In *Explorations in Philosophy and Society,* edited by Charles Cunneen, David H. Degrood, Dale Riepe, and William W. Stein. Amsterdam: B. R. Grüner.
    1980   "Rebellion in Huaraz: The Newspaper Account of an 'Obscure' Revolt in Peru." *Dialectical Anthropology* 5 : 127–154.
    1986   "The Practice of Economic Anthropology in the Peruvian Andes: Community, Household, and Relations of Production." *Revista Andina* 8 : 549–606.
Stolmaker, Charlotte
    1979   "The Sunday Fair at Huancayo: A Market's Contribution to the Regional Economy." *Journal of Anthropological Research* 35 : 456–476.

Strasma, John
　1976　"Agrarian Reform." In *Peruvian Nationalism: A Corporatist Revolution,* edited by David Chaplin. New Brunswick, N.J.: Transaction Books.
Sudarkasa, Niara
　1973　*Where Women Work: A Study of Yoruba Women in the Marketplace and in the Home.* Museum of Anthropology Anthropological Paper no. 53. Ann Arbor: University of Michigan Press.
Swetnam, John J.
　1978　"Interaction between Urban and Rural Residents in a Guatemalan Marketplace." *Urban Anthropology* 7(2): 137–153.
Tax, Sol
　1953　*Penny Capitalism: A Guatemalan Indian Economy.* Institute of Social Anthropology Publication no. 16. Washington, D.C.: Smithsonian Institution.
Thorp, Rosemary, and Geoffrey Bertram
　1978　*Peru 1890–1977: Growth and Policy in an Open Economy.* New York: Columbia University Press.
Tokman, Victor
　1978　"Competition between the Informal and Formal Sectors in Retailing: The Case of Santiago." *World Development* 6(9–10): 1187–1198.
Universidad Nacional de Ancash
　1980　*Boletín Informativo* no. 3. Huaraz, Peru: Universidad Nacional de Ancash.
Valcárcel, Luis E.
　1947　"Indian Markets and Fairs in Peru." In *Handbook of South American Indians,* vol. 2, edited by Julian H. Steward. Washington, D.C.: Smithsonian Institution.
Van Allen, Judith
　1976　"'Aba Riots' or Igbo 'Women's War'? Ideology, Stratification, and the Invisibility of Women." In *Women in Africa,* edited by Nancy J. Hafkin and Edna G. Bay. Stanford: Stanford University Press.
van den Berghe, Pierre L., and George P. Primov
　1977　*Inequality in the Peruvian Andes: Class and Ethnicity in Cuzco.* Columbia: University of Missouri Press.
Vandendries, René
　1973　"An Appraisal of the Reformist Development Strategy of Peru." In *Latin American Modernization Problems: Case Studies in the Crises of Change,* edited by Robert E. Scott. Urbana: University of Illinois Press.
Varon Gabai, Rafael
　1980　*Curacas y encomenderos: Acomodamiento nativo en Huaraz, siglos XVI y XVII.* Lima: P. L. Villanueva, Editor.

Vasques de Miranda, Glaura
    1977   "Women's Labor Force Participation in a Developing Society: The Case of Brazil." *Signs* 3(1): 261–274.

Villalobos de Urrutia, Gabriela
    1975   *Diagnóstico de la situación social y económica de la mujer peruana.* Lima: Centro de Estudios de Población y Desarrollo.

Villanueva, Victor, and William Bollinger
    1979   "Peru Workers Combat Austerity." *The Guardian*, January 17, p. 15.

Webb, Richard
    1975*a*   "Government Policy and the Distribution of Income in Peru, 1963–1973." In *The Peruvian Experiment*, edited by Abraham F. Lowenthal. Princeton: Princeton University Press.
    1975*b*   "Public Policy and Regional Incomes in Peru." In *Latin American Urban Research*, vol. 5, edited by Wayne A. Cornelius and Felicity M. Trueblood. Beverly Hills, Calif.: Sage.

Weldon, Peter, and Mary Vanisky Morse
    1970   "Market Structure in a Highland Peruvian Community." *Human Organization* 29(1): 43–48.

Wendorff M., Carlos
    1983   "El sector informal urbano en el Perú: Interpretación y perspectivas." In *El problema del empleo en el Perú*, edited by Narda Henriquez and Javier Iguíñiz. Lima: Pontificia Universidad Católica del Peru.

West, Jackie
    1978   "Women, Sex, and Class." In *Feminism and Materialism*, edited by Annette Kuhn and AnnMarie Wolpe. London: Routledge and Kegan Paul.

White, Langdon C.
    1951   "Huancayo and Its Famous Indian Market in the Peruvian Andes." *Journal of Geography* 50(1): 1–10.

Wrigley, G. M.
    1919   "Fairs of the Central Andes." *Geographical Review* 7(2): 65–80.

Yauri Montero, Marcos
    1972   *El problema de la universidad ancashina, in Ancash, o la biografía de la inmortalidad.* Lima: Talleres Gráficos P. L. Villanueva S.A.

Zamalloa, Edgar
    1981   "Comercio ambulatorio: Mito y realidad." *Debate* 8: 39–42.

Newspapers and Periodicals

Caretas, Lima
El Comercio, Lima
Daily Gleaner, Kingston, Jamaica
El Departamento, Huaraz
El Diario de Marka, Lima

Expreso, Lima
El Huascarán, Huaraz
Latin America Regional Reports: Andean Group, London
Marka, Lima
New York Times
Peru Update, New York
La Prensa, Lima

Index